DIRECTORY OF LITERARY MAGAZINES 1996–97

DIRECTORY OF LITERARY MAGAZINES 1996–97

Prepared in Cooperation with the
Council of Literary Magazines and Presses

ASPHODEL PRESS

Moyer Bell : Wakefield, Rhode Island & London

Published by Asphodel Press

**LIBRARY OF CONGRESS
CATALOGING-IN-PUBLICATION DATA**

Directory of literary magazines / prepared with the Council of Literary Magazines and Presses—1984—New York: The Council c1984–

v.;22cm

Annual.
Continues: CLMP literary magazine directory
ISSN 0884-6006 = Directory of literary magazines

1. Literature—Periodicals—Bibliography. 2. American periodicals—Directories. 3. Little magazines—United States—Directories. I. Council of Literary Magazines and Presses (U.S.)

Z6513.C37 85-648720
PN2 AACR 2 MARC-S

ISBN 1-55921-165-2 Pb

Printed in the United States of America
Distributed in North America by Publishers Group West, P.O. Box 8843, Emeryville, CA 94662, 800-788-3123 (in California 510-658-3453), and in Europe by Gazelle Book Services Ltd., Falcon House, Queen Square, Lancaster LA1 1RN England.

> The little magazine is something I have always fostered, for without it, I myself would have been early silenced. To me it is one magazine, not several. . . . When it is in any way successful it is because it fills a need in someone's mind to keep going. When it dies, someone else takes it up in some other part of the country—quite by accident—out of a desire to get the writing down on paper.
>
> —William Carlos Williams*

The *Directory of Literary Magazines* is compiled as a guide to the changing world of literary magazines of which Williams speaks. The literary magazine is a particularly American tradition that has provided early publishing opportunities for many of our important writers—including T.S. Eliot, E.L. Doctorow, Elizabeth Bishop, Ernest Hemingway, Ralph Ellison, Robert Lowell, Katherine Anne Porter, Raymond Carver, Richard Wright, Ezra Pound, Maxine Hong Kingston and Amiri Baraka. Through the medium of literary magazines, writers see their art in print and are given a permanent place in our culture. At the same time, readers are given an opportunity to discover new voices and talents and to experience a wide range of serious literature which is excluded from or underrepresented in the commercial marketplace.

This year's *Directory* includes nearly 600 magazines from the United States, Canada and Europe. Entries are designed to include information asked for by **readers, writers, librarians, publishers**, and others.

Entries include:

- descriptions of each magazine in the editor's own words in order to clarify for prospective **writers** the magazine's editorial directions and interests. Writers are strongly urged to research magazines before submitting work by using these entries, and most importantly, by purchasing and supporting the magazines that interest them;

---

* *The Autobiography of William Carlos Williams*, © 1951 William Carlos Williams. Reprinted by permission of New Directions Publishing Corporation.

- listings of types of material published by each magazine, subscription rates, ISSN numbers for use by **librarians** in selecting additions to their collections, and distributors for use by **bookstores** interested in increasing their magazine sections;

- advertising information for **publishers'** use, including ad rates and sizes as a complement to the activities of CLMP's Ad Program which offers advertising space in specially designed packages of literary magazines to interested publishers. For more information on ad rates and CLMP's advertising services to publishers, please contact CLMP.

The Council of Literary Magazines and Presses (CLMP) is dedicated to serving and supporting alternative publishing in the United States. As a membership service and advocacy organization, it works on behalf of literary magazines and small presses to strengthen the field from within, promote its many and varied accomplishments to the public, and provide an ongoing forum for the discussion of issues relevant to the greater literary community.

CLMP provides an array of programs and services to its member magazines and presses. The organization has also taken a leading role in field development, activities which benefit the entire field of literature (writers, readers, publishers, librarians, booksellers, literary centers), of which its members are a vital part. This work involves creating and implementing mechanisms for emerging publishers to learn from established ones; for literary publishers to collaborate with literary presenters; for the media, funders and other groups to be better informed about literary publishing and its role in America's cultural life; for research and data collection about the field to be undertaken and the results made public; for ensuring that literature has a place at the table where the politics of cultural policy are debated and decided; and ultimately for facilitating the flow of literature from the hands of writers into the hands of readers in America.

If you would like to receive further information about CLMP or becoming a member, please write us at 154 Christopher Street, Suite 3C, New York, NY 10014-2839.

DIRECTORY OF LITERARY MAGAZINES

We hope you are well-served by this edition of the *Directory of Literary Magazines*. CLMP would like to thank the staff at Moyer Bell for their dedication to this project. CLMP would also like to thank the National Endowment for the Arts and the New York State Council on the Arts for their general support, and the Andrew W. Mellon Foundation and the Lila Wallace-Reader's Digest Fund for their generous program support.

KEY

NAME OF MAGAZINE
Editor(s)
Address
Telephone number

Material published
Magazine description
Recent contributors
Unsolicited Manuscripts Received/Published per Year
Reading Period
Payment to contributors
Reporting time
Copyright
First year of publication; frequency; circulation
Subscription rate; single copy price; discount for resale
Number of pages; size of magazine
Advertising rates and sizes
International Standard Serial Number
Distributors

Abbreviations

ea—each
ind—individual
inst—institutional
irreg—irregular
pp—pages
var—varies
v—volume
yr—year

All entries contain the fullest information available at date of *Directory* publication.

Index by State (see p. 286)

A

ABACUS

Peter Ganick
181 Edgemont Ave.
Elmwood, CT 06110
(203) 233-2023

Poetry.

A 12 to 20 page, newsletter format, single-author-per-issue periodical devoted to experimental and language poetry.

Clark Coolidge, Jackson Mac Low, Carla Harryman, Laura Moriarty, Joan Retallack, Leslie Scalapino.

Unsolicited Manuscripts Received/Published per Year: 100/8.

Payment: 10 copies.

Reporting Time: variable.

Copyright held by author.

No ads

ISSN: 0886-4047

SPD, Small Press Traffic

ABIKO QUARTERLY, with James Joyce Studies

Laurel Sicks, Managing Editor & Publisher; Dr. Hamada, Director; Jesse Glass, Poetry Editor; D.C. Palter, Fiction Editor
8-1-8 Namiki
Abiko, Chiba 270-11 JAPAN
0471-84-7904

James Joyce Finnegans Wake papers, poetry, fiction.

AQ is primarily a James Joyce Finnegans Wake study journal, with poetry and fiction. Presently we allot ⅓ of the magazine to each category.

Burton Raffel, Skip Fox, Leo Connellan, Cid Corman, Peter Stambler.

Unsolicited Manuscripts Received/Published per Year: varies—most mss. from contests/600 pages.

Reading Period: Sept.–Dec. 31.

Payment: 1 copy/poets, 1 /fiction; $1,000 prize money each category.
Reporting Time: 2 weeks.
1988; 2/year; 600
$50/4 issues; $15/ea
600 pp; B-5
Ad Rates: $200/page; $100/½ page/; $50/¼; $500/back cover
Japan Publications Trading Co. Ltd.

ABRAXAS

Ingrid Swanberg, Warren Woessner
2518 Gregory St.
Madison, WI 53711
(608) 238-0175
Poetry, criticism, essays, reviews, translations, photographs, graphics/artwork, "found" cultural artifacts. No unsolicited manuscripts, except as announced.
Contemporary poetry: (non-academic). Emphasis on the lyric and experimental. Unusual graphics and "found" poems. Interested in poetry in translation and Native American poetry. Criticism and essays on the contemporary scene.
César Vallejo, Ivan Argüelles, Próspero Saíz, Andrei Codrescu, Andrea Moorhead.
Unsolicited Manuscripts Received/ Published per Year: 3,000/20.
Payment: in copies.
Reporting Time: varies per project.
Copyright held by Abraxas Press, Inc.; reverts to author upon publication.
1968; irregular; 500
$16/4 issues; $4/ea; 40%
80 pp; 6 x 9
Ad Rates: $60/page (5 x 8); $35/½ page (5 x 3½)
ISSN: 0361-1663

ACM (Another Chicago Magazine)

Barry Silesky
3709 N. Kenmore
Chicago, IL 60613
Poetry, fiction, reviews, essays, interviews.
Literary, contemporary, non-regional, socio-political outlook.
Pablo Antonio Cuadra, Maxine Chernoff, Lore Segal, Sterling Plumpp, Evelyn Lou, Albert Goldbarth.
Reading Period: year–round.
Unsolicited Manuscripts Received/ Published per Year: 7,500/65.
Payment: $5–$25.
Reporting Time: 8-12 weeks.
Copyright held by magazine; reverts to author upon publication.
1977; 2/yr; 750
$15/ind, $15/inst; $8/ea; 40%
220 pp; 5½ x 8½

Ad Rates: $150/page (5 x 8); $75/½ page (5 x 3⅞)
ISSN: 0272-4359
Ingram

AEGEAN REVIEW

Dino Siotis
220 West 19th St., 2A
New York, NY 10011

Modern Greek literature in translation. Works by American authors inspired by Greece.

Fiction, essays, interviews, poetry, art and photography.

Jorge Luis Borges, Lawrence Durrell, Truman Capote, Yannis Ritsos, Alice Bloom.

Payment: $25–$50.

Reporting Time: 6 weeks.

1985; 2/yr; 4,000

$10/yr ind, $18/yr inst; $5/ea; 40%

80 pp; 7½ x 10

Ad Rates: $265/page

ISSN: 0891-7213

DeBoer

AERIAL

Rod Smith
P.O. Box 25642
Washington, D.C. 20007
(202) 244-6258, 965-5200

Poetry, fiction, criticism, essays, reviews, translations, photos, graphics.

AERIAL 6/7 is devoted to John Cage & others. **AERIAL** #8 is a special issue on Barrett Watten. **AERIAL** #9 will be a special issue on Bruce Andrews.

Jessica Grim, Rachel Blau DuPlessis, Lyn Hejinian, Bob Perelman, Ron Silliman.

Unsolicited Manuscripts Received/Published per Year: 3,000/25–35.

Payment: copies.

Copyright held by magazine; we reserve the right to reprint accepted materials in anthology or other form. All other rights revert to author.

1985; irregular; 1,000

$20/2 issues; $35/2 issues inst; $7.50/ea; 6/7 $15; 40%

approx. 200 pp; 6 x 9; 6/7, 8½ x 10

Ad Rates: Contact CLMP for information.

Ubiquity, SPD, Desert Moon

AFRICAN AMERICAN REVIEW

Joe Weixlmann
Department of English
Stalker Hall
Indiana State University
Terre Haute, IN 47809
(812) 237-2968

Poetry, fiction, criticism, reviews, interviews, photographs, graphics/artwork.

Essays on African American literature, theater, film, art, music, dance, and culture; interviews; poems; fiction; book reviews; and graphics on black themes.
Amiri Baraka, Gwendolyn Brooks, Ishmael Reed, Houston A. Baker, Jr., Rita Dove, Henry Louis Gates, Jr.
Unsolicited Manuscripts Received/Published per Year: 450/50.
Payment: depends on grants.
Reporting Time: 3 months.
Copyright held by author.
1967; 4/yr; 3,768
$24/yr ind, $48/yr inst; $10/ea; 40%
176 pp; 7 x 10
$200/page (5 x 8½); $120/½ page (5 x 4¼)
ISSN: 1062-4783

THE AFRO-HISPANIC REVIEW

Marvin Lewis & Edward Mullen
Department of Romance Languages
U Missouri: 143 Arts & Science Building
Columbia, MO 65211
(314) 882-5041
Scholarly articles, translations of Afro-Hispanic texts.
A bilingual journal of Afro-Hispanic literature and culture, publishing literary criticism, book reviews, translations, creative writing, and relevant developments in the field. Published by the Department of Romance Languages of the University of Missouri-Columbia.
Rosemary Geisdorfer-Feal, Richard Jackson, Lorna V. Williams, William Luis, Miriam DeCosta-Willis.
Unsolicited Manuscripts Received/Published per Year: 44/15.
Payment: none.
Reporting Time: 3 months.
Copyright held by University of Missouri.
1982; 2/yr; 500
$20/yr inst; $7.50/ea; $1 off inst. rate
8½ x 11
No ads
ISSN: 0278-8969
Faxon, Ebsco, Readmore, Dawson

AGADA

Reuven Goldfarb
2020 Essex St.
Berkeley, CA 94703
(510) 848-0965
Poetry, fiction, midrash, memoir, essay, translation, and graphic.
AGADA has a specifically Jewish orientation and emphasis along with a universalist perspective and publishes work touching on traditional Jewish themes and

contemporary concerns. It seeks to share the insights, memories, and vision of creative Jewish people with people everywhere.

Thomas Friedmann, Yael Mesinai, Robert Stern, Shulamith Surhamer, Roger White.

Unsolicited Manuscripts Received/Published per Year: 160/20.

Payment: in copies.

Reporting Time: 2–3 months.

Copyright reverts to author.

1981; 1yr; 1,000

$12/2 issues; $6.50/ea; 40%

64 pp; 7 x 10

ISSN: 0740-2392

AGNI

Boston University Creative Writing Program

Askold Melnyczuk, Editor

236 Bay State Rd

Boston, MA 02215

Poetry, fiction, artwork, essays.

AGNI publishes poetry and fiction, translations, commissioned essays and reviews. Our special interests are new and underappreciated writers.

Thom Gunn, Ai, Patricia Traxler, Donald Hall, John Updike, Ha Jin, Joe Osterhaus, Robert Pinsky, Seamus Heaney, Tom Sleigh, Derek Walcott.

Reading Period: Oct. 1–April 30th.

Unsolicited Manuscripts Received/Published per Year: 2,000/50.

Payment: $10/page up to $150.

Reporting Time: 4 months.

Copyright held by AGNI; reverts to author upon publication.

1972; 2/yr; 2,000

$18/yr; $36/yr inst; $7/ea; 40%

250–320 pp; 5½ x 8½

Ad Rates: $200/page (4¾ x 7⅞); $125/½ page (4½ x 3½)

ISSN: 0191-3352

DeBoer

ALABAMA LITERARY REVIEW

Theron Montgomery and Jim Davis

253 Smith Hall

Troy State University

Troy, AL 36082

(334) 670-3307

Fax (334) 670-3519

Fiction, poetry, essays, photography, and short drama.

A state literary medium for local as well as national artists; supported by National Endowment for the Arts.

Eve Shelnutt, Paul Grant, Joe Colicchio, Elizabeth Dodd, F.R. Lewis, Paul Ruffin, A. Nanette Mansey, W.D. Gilardetti, Susan M. Gilbert.

Unsolicited Manuscripts Received/Published per Year: 3,000/36.

Payment: In copies.
Reporting Time: 2 months (except August).
1987; 2/yr; 850+
$10/yr; $4.50/ea; 40%
100 pp; 9 x 6
Ad Rates: swap equal ad or $25/8 x 5 page
ISSN: 0890-1554

ALASKA QUARTERLY REVIEW

Ronald Spatz, Executive Editor
University of Alaska Anchorage
College of Arts & Sciences
3211 Providence Drive
Anchorage, AK 99508
(907) 786-4775 (Phone/Fax)
Fiction, poetry, short plays, creative nonfiction.
A journal devoted to contemporary literature.
Stuart Dybek, Jerome Charyn, Tracy Kidder, Arthur Danto, Patricia Hampl, Susan Minot, Alison Baker, Steve Stern, Raymond Federman, Grace Paley, Amy Hempel, Rosellen Brown, Tobias Wolff, Jane Smiley.
Unsolicited Manuscripts Received/Published per Year: 2,300 fiction, 600 poetry, 100 other/30 fiction, 20 poetry.
Reading Period: Sept.–May 10.
Payment: in copies; other payment depends on grants.
Reporting Time: 3–20 weeks.
General copyright held by University of Alaska Anchorage; copyright to individual pieces reverts back to the author.
1981; 2/yr; 1,600
$8/yr ind, $10/yr inst; $5.95/ea; 50%
200 pp; 6 x 9
ISSN: 0737-268X
DeBoer, Fine Print

ALBATROSS

Richard Smyth, Richard Brobst
Box 7787
North Port, FL 34287-0787
Poetry, interviews, graphics/artwork.
Since we see the albatross as a metaphor for an environment that must survive, we are primarily interested in ecological/environmental/nature themes, written in a narrative style; however, this is not to say that we do not consider other themes and forms.
Walter Griffin, Daniel Comiskey, Stephen Meats, Duane Locke, Peter Meinke.
Unsolicited Manuscripts Received /Published per Year: 300-400/15-20.
Payment: in contributor's copies.
1986; 2/yr; 500
$5/yr ind/inst; $3/ea; 40%
32–44 pp; 5½ x 8
ISSN: 0887-4239

ALDEBARAN LITERARY MAGAZINE

Quantella Owens
Roger Williams University
1 Old Ferry Rd.
Bristol, RI 02809
(401) 253-1040

Fiction and poetry in all styles and genres.

We are an eclectic magazine that publishes both fiction and poetry in all forms, styles and topics. We accept submissions from amateurs and established writers.

Unsolicited Manuscripts Received/Published per Year: varies per year/50-100.

Payment: 2 free copies of issue.

Reporting Time: 6–12 weeks normally.

Copyright reverts to authors upon publication.

1971; A or S-A; 250–300

$5/ea; $4/past issues

50–100 pp; 6 x 9 or 5½ x 8½.

Ad Rates: write to us for information.

THE ALEMBIC

Rotating editors
Dept. of English
Providence College
Providence, RI 02918-0001
(401) 865-2057

Book reviews, poetry, fiction, plays, cross-genre art in b&w.

Nationally distributed annual of literature and reviews emphasizing exploratory forms and translation.

Mark Rudman, William Matthews, Ray Jordan, James Morrill, Jane Lurin Perel

Unsolicited Manuscripts Received/Published per year: 350/75.

Reading Period: September–December 12. Payment: 2 copies.

Reporting Time: 3–5 weeks.

Copyright reverts to author upon publication.

1977; 1/yr; 5,000

$12/2 yrs; $7/ea; 40%

120 pp; 7 x 11

Ad Rates: $100/page

AMELIA

Frederick A. Raborg, Jr.
329 "E" St.
Bakersfield, CA 93304
(805) 323-4064

Fiction, poetry, plays, graphics/artwork, criticism, reviews, essays, photographs, translation.

AMELIA is a reader's magazine, intended to be enjoyed over a period of time, offering a unique blend of the traditional with the contemporary in virtually every printed art form by both "name" and unknown writers and artists of superior talents. Contributors from its pages have been included in Pushcart Prizes, The Artist Market and other prestigious reprint anthologies.

Pattiann Rogers, David Ray, Lawrence P. Spingarn, Larry Rubin, Stuart Friebert, Merrill Joan Gerber, Maxine Kumin, Matt Mulhern, Thomas F. Wilson.

Unsolicited Manuscripts Received/Published per Year: 30,000/800+.

Payment: poetry/$2–$25; fiction/$10–$35; nonfiction/$10/1,000 words; artwork/$5–$50.

Reporting Time: 2 weeks–3 months.

Copyright held by magazine; reverts to author upon publication.

1984; 4/yr; 1,750

$25/yr ind, $25/yr inst; $8.95/ea; 40%

156 pp; 5½ x 8½

Ad Rates: $250/page (4½ x 7½); $140/½ page (4½ x 3¾); $80/¼ page (4½ x 1¾)

Rates for recognized literary magazines only. Others request rate card.

ISSN: 0743-2755

AMERICAN BOOK REVIEW

Charles B. Harris, Ronald Sukenick, Rochelle Ratner, John Tytell, Editors; Romayne C. Rubinas, Managing Editor

The Unit for Contemporary Literature

Illinois State Univ.

Campus Box 4241

Normal, IL 61790-4241

(309) 438-3026

Criticism, essays, reviews.

AMERICAN BOOK REVIEW is offered as a guide to current books of literary interest published by the small, large, university, regional, third world, women's and other presses. It is edited and produced by writers for writers and the general public.

Hayden Carruth, Robert Creeley, Diane Wakoski, Marge Piercy, Joe McElroy, Kirkpatrick Sale, Ihab Hassan, Ishmael Reed.

Unsolicited Manuscripts Received/Published per Year: 100/15–25.

Payment: $50 per review.

Reporting Time: 2 weeks to 2 months.

Copyright held by **ABR**; reverts to author upon publication.

1977; 6/yr; 5,000

$24/yr ind, $30/yr inst; $4/ea; 40%

32 pp; 10 x 14

Ad Rates: $425/page (10 x 14);

$260/½ page (5 x 14); $150/¼ page (5 x 7); $100/½ col (2¼ x 6¾); $60/¼ col (2¼ x 3¾); discounts available.

Ingram, Interstate, Armadillo, LS, Ubiquity

THE AMERICAN POETRY REVIEW

Stephen Berg, David Bonanno, Arthur Vogelsang
1721 Walnut St.
Philadelphia, PA 19103
(215) 496-0439

Poetry, translation, criticism, reviews, interviews, essays.

John Ashbery, Lucille Clifton, Louise Gluck, Gerald Stern, C. K. Williams.

Unsolicited Manuscripts Received/ Published per Year: 12,000/60.

Payment: $2.00/line for poetry; $120/page for prose.

Reporting Time: 10 weeks.

Copyright held by World Poetry, Inc.; reverts to author upon publication.

1972; 6/yr; 18,000

$16/yr ind, $16/yr inst; $3.50/ea; 50%

52 pp; 9¾ x 13¾

Ad Rates: $855/page (9¾ x 13¾); $520/½ page (9¾ x 6¾); $280/¼ page (4¾ x 6¾)

ISSN: 0360-3709

Eastern News

THE AMERICAN VOICE

Frederick Smock
332 W. Broadway, Suite 1215
Louisville, KY 40202
(502) 562-0045

Fiction, poetry, essays.

THE AMERICAN VOICE publishes daring new writers and the more radical work of established writers. Feminist, multicultural, pan-American.

Isabel Allende, Maya Angelou, Chaim Potok, Djuna Barnes, Jorge Luis Borges, Suzanne Gardinier.

Unsolicited Manuscripts Received/ Published per Year: 5,000/60.

Payment: varies.

Reporting Time: 4–5 weeks.

Copyright: first rights held by magazine; reverts to author upon publication.

1985; 3/yr; 1,500

$15/yr ind; $5/ea; 40%

130 pp

Ad Rates: swaps/$100 per page.

ISSN: 0884-4536

DeBoer.

THE AMERICAS REVIEW (formerly **REVISTA CHICANO-RIQUEÑA**)

Lauro Flores, Evangelina Vigil-Piñon
Arte Publico Press
University of Houston

Houston, TX 77204-2090
(713) 743-2841
(800) 633-ARTE (Orders only)

Poetry, fiction, criticism, review, interviews, photographs, graphics/artwork.

THE AMERICAS REVIEW, A Review of Hispanic Literature and Art of the USA, is the oldest (20 years) and most prestigious U.S. Hispanic literary magazine. It publishes works by outstanding Hispanic writers and artists of the USA, as well as works by new and emerging writers and artists. Analysis, interviews, commentary and reviews of U.S. Hispanic works and writers.

Alba Ambert, Roberto Fernández, Virgil Suárez, Floyd Salas, Tato Laviera.

Unsolicited Manuscripts Received/ Published per Year: 200/30-35.

Payment: varies.

Reporting Time: 3–4 months.

Copyright held by Arte Publico Press.

1972; 3/yr (2 + double issue); 3,000

$15/yr ind, $20/yr inst; $5/ea ($10/double issue); 40%

128 pp; 224 pp double issue; 5½ x 8½

Ad Rates: $200/page (5 x 8); $125/½ page (4 x 5); $75/¼ page (2½ x 4)

ISSN: 0360-7860

Ebsco, Ubiquity, Homing Pigeon, Armadillo

ANEMONE

Nanette Morin, Editor; Bill Griffin, Art Editor

Box 369
Chester, VT 05143

Poetry, reviews, interviews, translations, photographs, graphics/ artwork, paintings.

ANEMONE is a quarterly literary arts journal publishing the expressive voice of the people. Our purpose is to help bring the spirit of man closer to his true self through art. We look for work that is different, always looking for the new voice. **ANEMONE** encourages "political" and "social" poetry.

Robert Chute, Arthur Winfield Knight, Teresa Volta, Sesshu Foster, John Oliver Simon.

Unsolicited Manuscripts Received/ Published per Year: 1,600/240.

Payment: 1 year's subscription and 5 gifts.

Reporting Time: variable.

Copyright held by Anemone Press Inc.; permission given to publish with mention.

1984; 4/yr; 3,000

$10/yr ind, $10/yr inst; $2.50/ea; 40%

32 pp; 10 x 15

Ad Rates: $200/page (10 x 15); $100/½ page (10 x 7 or 5 x 15); $50/¼ page (5 x 7)
ISSN: 8756-7709

ANTERIOR FICTION QUARTERLY

Tom Bergeron
993 Allspice Ave.
Fenton, MO 63026-4901
(314) 343-1761
Short stories.
Fiction quarterly.
Lois Hayn, Rob Staggenborg, Thomas Lynn, Salvatore Amico Buttaci, Marian Ford Park.
Unsolicited Manuscripts Received/ Published per Year: 75/25
Reading Period: year round.
Payment: 1st place each issue $25.00.
Reporting Time: within 2 weeks.
Copyright held by author.
1993; 4/yr; 50
$15.00/yr
20 pp; 8½ x 11
No ads
ISSN 1074-2042
Anterior Bitewing

ANTERIOR POETRY MONTHLY

Tom Bergeron
993 Allspice Ave.
Fenton, MO 63026-4901
(314) 343-1761
Poetry.
Poetry monthly.
Katherine Brooks, Marian Ford Park, C. David Hay, Ruth McDaniel.
Unsolicited Manuscripts Received/ Published per Year: 500/250
Reading Period: year round.
Payment: 1st, 2nd, 3rd, 4th, $25, $15, $10, $5.
Reporting Time: within 2 weeks.
Copyright held by author.
1993; 12/yr; 200
$20.00/yr
20 pp
No ads
ISSN 1074-2026
Anterior Bitewing Ltd.

ANTIETAM REVIEW

Ann B. Knox, Crystal Brown, & Susanne Kass
7 W. Franklin St.
Hagerstown, MD 21740
(301) 791-3132
Poetry, fiction, photographs.
The **ANTIETAM REVIEW** is a literary magazine for fiction writers, poets and photographers who are natives or residents of Delaware, Maryland, Pennsylvania, Virginia, West Virginia, and the District of Columbia. We look for strong literary and artistic quality rather than local

interest. Guidelines available with SASE.

Pinckney Benedict, Maxine Clair, Amy Clampitt, Diane Wolkstein, Dick Scanlan, Ellyn Bache.

Unsolicited Manuscripts Received/ Published per Year: 450–500 fiction, 1,500 poems/8-10 fiction, 18-22 poems.

Reading Period: Sept—Feb. 1.

Payment: $100 for fiction; $25 for poems.

Reporting Time: 6 weeks–4 months depending on pub. date.

Copyright held by Washington County Arts Council; reverts to author upon publication.

1984; 1 or 2/yr; 1,600

$5.25/yr; $5.25/ea; 20%

60 pp; 8½ x 11

No ads

ANTIGONISH REVIEW

George Sanderson

P.O. Box 5000

St. Francis Xavier University

Antigonish, Nova Scotia B2G 2W5

CANADA

(902) 867-3962

E-mail: TAR@stfx.ca

Poetry, fiction, reviews, articles.

Literary quarterly; new and established writers; short fiction; reviews and light critical articles.

Michael Hulse, Sr. Bernetta Quinn, Achy Obejas, Louis Dudek, Omar Pound.

Reading Period: year–round.

Unsolicited Manuscripts Received/ Published per Year: 1,300-1,500/200.

Payment: copies.

Reporting Time: poetry, 2 months; fiction, 4 months.

Copyright retained by author.

1970; 4/yr; 900

$20/yr; $6/ea; 20%

150 pp; 6 x 9

ISSN: 0003-5661

Canadian Magazine Publishers Association

ANTIOCH REVIEW

Robert S. Fogarty

P.O. Box 148

Yellow Springs, OH 45387

Poetry, fiction, criticism, essays, reviews.

ANTIOCH REVIEW is an independent quarterly of critical and creative thought which prints articles of interest to both the liberal scholar and the educated layman. Authors of articles on the arts, politics, social and cultural problems as well as short fiction and poetry find a friendly reception regardless of formal reputation.

Emile Capouya, Raymond Carver,

Perri Klass, Gordon Lish, Joyce Carol Oates.
Unsolicited Manuscripts Received/ Published per Year: 3,200/25–30.
Reading Period: year–round, except poetry; (Sept.–May 14.)
Payment: $10/published page.
Reporting Time: 3–6 weeks.
Copyright reverts to author upon publication.
1941; 4/yr; 4,500
$35/yr ind; $48/yr inst; $6/sample
160 pp; 6 x 9
Ad Rates: $250/page (4½ x 7⅞); $150/½ page; $100/¼ page
ISSN: 0003-5769
Eastern News

ANTIPODES

Marian Arkin, Robert Ross
190 Sixth Ave.
Brooklyn, NY 11217
(718) 789-5826 or (718) 482-5680
Fiction, reviews, criticism, essays, poetry, interviews, photographs, graphics/artwork.
Focus is on Australian literature.
Thomas Keneally, A.D. Hope, Judith Wright, Thea Astley, Olga Masters.
Unsolicited Manuscripts Received/ Published per Year: 300/50.
Payment: a small honorarium and copies for fiction & poetry; copies for all others.
1987; 2/yr; 600
$20/yr ind, $35/yr inst; overseas $27/yr ind, $42/yr inst;
60–75 pp; 8½ x 11
Ad Rates: $300/page (7½ x 10); $175/½ page (7½ x 5 or 3½ x 10); $100/¼ page (7½ x 2½ or 3½ x 5)

APALACHEE QUARTERLY

Barbara Hamby, Lara Moody, Kim MacQueen, Mary Jane Ryals, Monifa Love
P.O. Box 10469
Tallahassee, FL 32302
Poetry, fiction, reviews, translation, photographs, essays, graphics/artwork.
We are interested in well-crafted, modern fiction and poetry. Stylistic innovation is encouraged.
Peter Meinke, Alfred Corn, Janet Burroway, Steven Barthelme, David Kirby.
Unsolicited Manuscripts Received/ Published per Year: 1,000/70–100.
Reading Period: Sept.–May.
Payment: in copies and money when grants permit.
Reporting Time: 12 weeks.
Copyright reverts to author upon publication.
1971; 3/yr; 500
$15/yr; $5 ea
100–200 pp; 6 x 9
Ad Rates: $50/page

APPEARANCES

Robert Witz, Ron Kolm, Joe Lewis, Bill Mutter
165 West 26th St.
New York, NY 10001
(212) 675-3026

Poetry, fiction, interviews, photographs, graphics/artwork.

APPEARANCES. Literature, art, civilization. New talent. The works. Why wait.

Jill Rapaport, Alfred Vitale, J.D. Rage, Joe Maynard, John Yau, Anne McDonald

Unsolicited Manuscripts Received/Published per Year: 150/3 or 4 to 10.

Payment: occasional.

Copyright held by magazine; reverts to author upon publication.

1976; 2/yr; 900

$15/3 issues; $5/ea; 40%

76 pp; 8½ x 11

Ad Rates: $180/page (7½ x 10); $110/½ page (7 x 5½); $80/¼ page (3½ x 5)

ARACHNE

Susan L. Leach
2363 Page Road
Kennedy, New York 14747
(716) 267-5307

Poetry, fiction.

ARACHNE is a small press dedicated to publishing well written poetry with a largely, but not exclusively, rural theme. We are interested in new poets and in poets who have been writing but have not been largely published. We publish 4 contributors' issues yearly.

Gary Fincke, Penny Kemp, Norbert Krapf, Walt Franklin, Wallace Whatley.

Unsolicited Manuscripts Received/Published per Year: 1,000/85.

Payment: in copies.

Reporting Time: 1 week–2 months.

1980; 2/yr; 250

$18/yr ind, $20/yr inst; $5/ea; 40%

28 pp; 5¼ x 8¼

ARARAT

Leo Hamalian
31 E. 52nd St.
NYC 10019
(212) 831-6857

Fiction, poetry, expository prose.

Publishes material relevant to Armenian culture or history; quality fiction and poetry.

Laura Kalpakian, Edward Alexander, James Hatch, David Kherdian, David Ignatius, Diana Der Hovanessian, Peter Balakian.

Unsolicited Manuscripts Received/Published per Year: 70/10-15.

Payment: $50-$200

Reporting Time: 6 weeks.

Copyright reverts to author.
1960; 4/yr; 1200
$24/yr; $7/ea
72 pp; 9 x 11
Ad Rates: back inside cover
ISSN: 003-7583

ARSHILE: A Magazine of the Arts

Mark Salerno
P.O. Box 3749
Los Angeles, CA 90078

Poetry, fiction, essay, art.

The bulk goes to (1) poetry; (2) fiction; (3) essays on the arts; (4) color covers. Inside black & white reproductions. Mix of established artists with up-and-coming.

Notley, Corbett, Sorrentino, Bronk, Creeley, Ashton.

Reading Period: year-round.
Payment: copies.
Reporting Time: 3 months.
Copyright reverts to author upon publication.
1993; 2/yr; 1,000
$18/yr; $10/ea
172 pp; 5½ x 11½
Ad Rates: $250/page (4 x 7)
ISSN: 1066-8721
DeBoer, Fine Print, Armadillo, BookPeople, Ubiquity, Small Press Distribution.

ARTFUL DODGE

Daniel Bourne
Department of English
The College of Wooster
Wooster, OH 44691
(216) 262-8353

Poetry, fiction, translation, graphics, reviews.

ARTFUL DODGE is open not just to American work combining the human and the aesthetic, but also to translation, from all over the world. We also have an ongoing section on American poets who translate, featuring the poet's own work and his or her adaptations of work going on in landscapes other than English.

Stuart Dybek, Naomi Shihab Nye, Jorge Luis Borges, Julia Kasdorf, Charles Simic, Jim Daniels, William Stafford, Zbigniew Herbert.

Unsolicited Manuscripts Received/Published per Year: 2,500/60
Reading Period: year–round.
Payment: in copies, plus $5 honorarium, as funding allows.
Reporting Time: 1–6 months.
Copyright reverts to author.
1979; 2/yr; 1,000
$10/yr; $5/ea
150-200 pp; 6 x 9
ISSN: 0196-691X
DeBoer, Fine Print, Ubiquity

ARTS INDIANA MAGAZINE

Lou Harry, Editor in Chief; Elizabeth Weiner, Editor
47 South Pennsylvania, Suite 701
The Majestic Building
Indianapolis, IN 46204
(317) 632-7894
Fax (317) 632-7966

Profiles, previews, reviews, service essay, fiction, poetry.

ARTS INDIANA MAGAZINE is the only publication in the country providing statewide coverage of the literary performing and visual arts—art issues, people & organizations.

Scott Russell Sanders, Peter Jacobi

Unsolicited Manuscripts Received/Published per year: 50/10.

Reading Period: All

Payment: Varies ($30–$400)

Reporting Time: 8 weeks.

Copyright held by magazine.

1979; 10/yr; 12,000

$25 (40 pp; 12 x 14); $4.95/ea

Ad Rates: vary with size and frequency.

ISSN 0897-859X

Ingram

ASCENT

Audrey Curley
P.O. Box 967
Urbanna, IL 61801

Fiction, poetry.

Eclectic.

Stuart Friebert, G.E. Murray, Thomas Reiter, Marjorie Stelmach, Kathleen Wakefield.

Unsolicited Manuscripts Received/Published per Year: 1,050/40.

Reading Period: year–round.

Payment: 3 copies.

Reporting Time: 1 week–2 months.

Copyright held by magazine; reverts to author upon publication.

1975; 3/yr; 750

$3/yr; $3/ea; 40%

64 pp; 6 x 9

ISSN: 0098-9363

ASIAN PACIFIC AMERICAN JOURNAL

Asian American Writers' Workshop; Curtis Chin, Managing Editor; Julie Koo, Soo Mee Kwon, Co-Editors
37 St. Mark's Place
New York, NY 10003
(212) 228-6718

Poetry, fiction, essays.

The **APA JOURNAL** publishes prose and poetry that show the richness and variousness of Asian American and Pacific Islander Literature and experience. As a branch of the Asian American Writers Workshop, we seek to create a vibrant network that connects writers and readers of Asian American literature. We encourage both emerging and established writers.

Koon Woon, Justin Chin, Zamora Linmark, Susan Ito, Cathy Song, Russell Leong, Kimiko Hahn, Zamora Linmark, Yoji Yamaguchi, Katherine Min.

Payment: 2 complimentary issues upon publication, discounts on other copies.

Reporting Time: 2–3 months.

Copyright reverts to author upon publication.

1992; 2/yr; 1,500

$20/yr, $30/2yrs; $12/ea; 40%

150 pp; 5⅜ x 8⅜

Ad Rates: $150/page (4¼ x 7¼); $80/½ page (4¼ x 3⅜); $50/¼ page (2 x 3½)

Inland, Fine Print, SPD, Armadillo, DeBoer

ATLANTA REVIEW

DANIEL VEACH

P.O. Box 8248

Atlanta, GA 30306

(404) 636-0052

Fax (404) 577-5158

Poetry, fiction, nonfiction, interviews.

Quality poetry of genuine human appeal, plus short fiction and nonfiction, interviews with leading writers. Each Spring issue features a different country.

Charles Simic, Linda Pastan, Mark Jarman, Charles Wright, Josephine Jacobsen

Unsolicited Manuscripts Received/ Published per Year: 12,000/100.

Reading Period: Not in December or August.

Payment: 2 copies, year's subscription, discounts.

Reporting Time: 2 months

Copyright held by Author.

1994; 2/yr; 3,000

$10/yr; $6/ea; 33%

112 pp; 6 x 9

ISSN: 1073-9696

Ingram, Bernhard DeBoer

ATOM MIND (Mother Road Publications)

Gregory Smith

P.O. Box 22068

Albuquerque, NM 87154

Poetry, short fiction, essays, artwork, photographs.

ATOM MIND, originally published in 1968–70, is a throwback to Jack Kerouac and the Beats, Steinbeck, Faulkner and Hemingway, a reflection of the original voices in American literature.

Charles Plymell, Charles Bukowski, Lawrence Ferlinghetti.

Unsolicited Manuscripts Received/ Published per Year: 1,000+/120

Reading Period: year–round.

Payment: copies, occasional small cash payments.
Reporting Time: 2–4 weeks.
Copyright held by Mother Road Publications, with all rights reverting to authors.
1993; 4/yr; 1000+
$20/yr; $6/ea; 40%
120 pp; 8½ x 11
Ad Rates: $80/page; $50/½ page; $30/¼ page
ISSN: 0004-704X

AURA LITERARY/ARTS REVIEW

Steve Mullen
P.O. Box 76
University Center, UAB
Birmingham, AL 35294–1150
(205) 934-3354
Poetry, fiction, interviews, essay
Contemporary poetry and prose. Experimental, traditional or genre. Looking for work that distinguishes itself from the crowd yet remains successful. Interested in artwork and documentary photography.
Payment: 2 copies.
Reporting Time: 3 months.
Copyright reverts to author.
1974; 2/yr; 500
$6/yr; $3/ea
120 pp; 6 x 9
ISSN: 0889-7433

A/B: AUTO/BIOGRAPHY STUDIES

Rebecca Hogan
English Department
University of Wisconsin
Whitewater, WI 53190
and/or
Timothy Dow Adams
English Department
University of West Virginia
Morgantown, WV 26506
Criticism, reviews, bibliographical and newsletter information.
Purpose of magazine is to publish essays—literary and critical—about autobiography and biography. Emphasis of recent issues has been on special topics: women's autobiography, Mexican, therapeutic (forthcoming), European, etc. The journal serves also as a clearinghouse for information about convention panels, members' interests, etc.
Lynn Bloom, Janet Verner Gunn, Richard D. Woods, G. Thomas Couser, Silonie Smith.
Payment: none.
Copyright held by author.
1985; 4/yr; 200
$15/yr ind, $45/yr inst
70 pp; 7 x 8½
Ad Rates: $150/page (7 x 8½); $75/½ page (7 x 4¼); $40/¼ page (3½ x 4¼)

AVEC

Cydney Chadwick
P.O. Box 1059
Penngrove, CA 94951
(707) 769-0880

Contemporary poetry, prose, & translations.

Innovative, challenging work from established and emerging writers. **AVEC** is particularly interested in translations of recent French writing and the Russian avant–garde.

Norma Cole, Peter Gizzi, Laura Moriarty, Keith Waldrop, Michael Palmer, Claude Royet-Journoud, Leslie Scalapino, Aleksei Parshchikov, Elizabeth Willis.

Unsolicited Manuscripts are only read in June & December: 1,000+/2 or 3.

Reporting Time: 8 weeks.

Copyright reverts to author upon publication.

1988; 2/yr

$12/yr; $8.50/ea; 40%

192 pp

Ad Rates: $200/page (7½ x 10); $100/½ page (7½ x 4¾) $75/¼ page (3¼ x 4¾)

ISSN: 0899-3750

BookPeople, SPD, Spectacular Diseases (UK)

AZOREAN EXPRESS

Art Coelho
P.O. Box 249
Timber, MT 59011

Southern Appalachian Mountains, Okie, American West, Hobo, Rural, Working Class, American Indian and Central California.

There's a focus on themes where people work with their hands; there's a celebration of life like in the poems of Sandburg and the stories of London and Gerald Haslam.

Badger Stone, C.L. Rawlins, Ann Fox Chandonnet.

Unsolicited Manuscripts Received/ Published per Year: 500/35.

Payment: in copies.

Reporting Time: 6 weeks.

1985; 1/yr; 500

$6.75 (post paid); 30%

80 pp; 5½ x 8½

B

B CITY

Connie Deanovich
517 North Fourth St.
DeKalb, IL 60115
(815) 758-4633

Poetry: 10th Anniversary issue, celebrating the 100th anniversary of the movies; Edward Field, Hilda Morley, others.
Special issues: 8–sestinas.
Unsolicited Manuscripts Received/ Published per Year: 700/2%.
Reading Period: Query.
Payment: copies.
$5/yr ind, $6/yr inst; $5/ea; 40%

THE BAFFLER

Thomas Frank
P.O. Box 378293
Chicago, IL 60637
(312) 493-0413

Essays, stories, poetry, art.
THE BAFFLER publishes essays, criticism, and literature that derive from its unique interpretation of 20th century culture. The American Mercury of the '90s.
Thomas Frank, Steve Albini, Janice Edius, Owen Hatteras.
Unsolicited Manuscripts Received/ Published per Year: 200/5.
Reading Period: year–round.
Reporting Time: 5 months.
Copyright retained by magazine.
1988; 4/yr; 15,000
$16/4 issues, $5/ea; 40%
128 pp, 6 x 9
Ad Rates: $500/page (6 x 8½); $300/½ page (6 x 4)
ISSN: 1059-9789
Ubiquity, Fine Print, Desert Moon, Small Changes, Dormouse

BAKUNIN

Jordan Jones
P.O. Box 1853

Simi Valley, CA 93062-1853

Poetry, fiction, essays, reviews, artwork, drama.

BAKUNIN, a magazine for the dead Russian anarchist in all of us, seeks well-crafted and challenging writing and artwork, especially of sexual and social critique.

William Stafford, Sandra McPherson, Benjamin Saltman, Dorianne Laux, Stephen Dixon.

Unsolicited Manuscripts Received/Published per Year: 1,000/60.

Payment: 2 copies.

Reporting Time: 2 weeks–12 weeks.

Copyright reverts to author on publication.

1990; 1/yr; 1000

$10/yr, $12/yr foreign, $20/yr inst.; $10/ea; 40%

200 pp, 6 x 9

Ad Rates: $100/page; $50/½ page

ISSN: 1052-3154

Ubiquity, Fine Print, Armadillo

BALL MAGAZINE

Douglas M. Kimball, Editor; Jen Jarrell, Poetry Editor; Collin Coggins, Music Editor

Box 775

Northampton, MA 01061-0775

(413) 634-5687

Reviews (music, art, lit, sci-fi), fiction, nonfiction.

BALL MAGAZINE publishes all work of quality received biannually. Our format and content evolve according to what is received.

Des Lewis, Byron Coley, Matt Ernst, Lenora Rogers.

Unsolicited Manuscripts Received/Published per Year: 500/50+.

Reading Period: year–round.

Payment: copies.

Reporting Time: 2 weeks–2 months.

Copyright: magazine holds first rights.

1993; 2/yr; 2,000

$8/yr, $4.95/ea; 40%

80 pp, 8½ x 11

Ad Rates: $100/page; $60/½ page; $35/¼ page; $20/⅛ page; $12/classifieds

Fine Print

BAMBOO RIDGE: The Hawaii Writers' Quarterly

Eric Chock and Darrell Lum

P.O. Box 61781

Honolulu, HI 96839-1781

Poetry, fiction.

BAMBOO RIDGE has special interest in literature reflecting the multi-ethnic cultures and peoples of the Hawaiian Islands.

Juliet Kono, Wing Tek Lum, Gary Pak, Marie Hara, Frederick B. Wichman, Sylvia Watanabe,

Rodney Morales, Cathy Song, Lois-Ann Yamanaka.

Unsolicited Manuscripts Received/ Published per Year: 500-700/60-80

Payment: $25/poem; $50/short story; plus 2 copies and 1 year subscription.

Reporting Time: 3–6 months.

Copyright held by Bamboo Ridge Press; reverts to author upon publication.

1978; 2/yr; 1,000

$16/yr; $5/sample copy; 40%

120 pp; 6 x 9

Ad Rates: $120/page (5¼ x 8¼)

ISSN: 0733-0308

SPD

THE BEACON

Varies from year to year

The Beacon, SWOCC

1988 Newmark

Coos Bay, OR 97420-2956

888-2525 ext. 335

Short stories, poetry, plays, essays, line drawings and black and white photograph.

Magazine varies each year.

Public and students, local submissions only.

Unsolicited Manuscripts Received/ Published per year: varies/varies.

$4/ea

Page number and size of magazine varies with editor.

BEAT SCENE

Kevin Ring

27 Court Leet

Binley Woods

Coventry, England CV32JQ

(020) 354-3604

Beat influenced interviews, reviews, features.

SOS America onwards. Heavy emphasis on Beat generation writers such as Jack Kerouac, William Burroughs, Charles Bukowski. Interviews, features, and information magazine. Full colour covers/glossy pages.

Charles Bukowski, Allen Ginsberg, William Burroughs, Gary Snyder.

Copyright with contributors

1988; 4/yr; 8,000

$35 for 5 issues; $8/ea; all payments must be in actual US dollars—no checks please.

44 pp.

Ad Rates: $150/page; $75/½ page; $40/¼ page

Caroline International, Beat Scene

BELLES LETTRES: A Review of Books by Women

Janet Mullaney

11151 Captain's Walk Ct.

North Potomac, MD 20878

(301) 294-0278

Fax (301) 294-0023

Reviews, criticism, essays, interviews, personal essays, photographs, graphics/artwork.

BELLES LETTRES reviews literature by women in all genres. Our purpose is to promote and celebrate writing by women and to inform and entertain. Interviews, rediscoveries, retrospectives, theme reviews, and publishing news are regularly featured. Queries from writers are welcome.

Jewelle Gomez, Cheryl Clarke, Lynne Sharon Schwartz, Carole Maso, Deirdre Bair, Faye Moskowitz.

Unsolicited Manuscripts Received/Published per Year: 300/10.

Payment: in copies & honorarium, depending on grant funding.

Copyright held by magazine; reverts to author upon publication.

1985; 3/yr; 8,000

$21/yr ind, $40/yr inst; $7/ea; 40%

96 pp; 8½ x 11

Ad Rates: $500/page (7½ x 10); $500/back page (7¼ x 8½ or 8½ 7¼);
$400/⅔ page (4¾ x 10 or 7½ x 6½); $300/½ page (3½ x 10 or 7½ x 5); $200/¼ page (3½ x 5 or 7½ x 2½); $100/⅛ page (2.25 x 3.25 or 3.25 x 2.25)

ISSN: 0084-2957

Ubiquity, Small Changes, Inland, IPD, Fine Print

THE BELLINGHAM REVIEW

Robin Hemley, Editor
The Signpost Press
MS 9053
Western Washington University
Bellingham, Wa 98225

Poetry, fiction, creative nonfiction, reviews, plays, photographs, graphics/artwork.

David shields, Charles Wright, Jane Hirshfield, Gary Soto, R.T. Smith, Rebecca McClanahan, Bret Lott.

Reading Period: Sept.–May.

Payment: 1 year subscription and extra copy.

Reporting Time: 2–3 months.

Copyright reverts to author upon publication.

1977; 2/yr; 800

$10/yr, $12 if agencied; $5/ea; 40% on 5 or more

120 pp; 6 x 9

ISSN: 0734-2934

BELLOWING ARK

Robert R. Ward
P.O. Box 45637
Seattle, WA 98145
(206) 545-8302

Poetry, fiction, essays, graphics/artwork, novel serializations, short autobiography, plays.

We feature work in the American Romantic tradition, i.e. editorial content is concerned with universal truths and the idea of transcending individual limitation. Content of a work is the primary consideration; form is a distant second, leading to a wryly eclectic mix; we are currently serializing our fifth novel.

Peter Russell, Susan McCaslin, Irene Culver, Muriel Karr, Harold Witt, Natalie Reciputi, Ray Mizer, Paula Milligan.

Unsolicited Manuscripts Received/ Published per Year: 4,000+/200+.

Reading Period: year–round.

Payment: 2 copies upon publication.

Copyright held by **BELLOWING ARK**; reverts to author upon request.

1984; 6/yr; 800

$15/yr ind, $15/yr inst; $3/ea; 40%; comp to libraries on request

32 pp; 11 x 16

Ad Rates: only in special circumstances.

ISSN: 0887-4115

Ubiquity, Faxon, Popular Subscription Service

THE BELOIT POETRY JOURNAL

Marion K. Stocking
Box 154, RFD 2
Ellsworth, ME 04605
(207) 667-5598

Poetry, reviews.

We publish the best poems we receive without bias as to length, form, subject, or tradition. We especially hope to discover new voices. Occasional chapbooks; recently Afro-American, American Indian, and new Chinese poetry.

A.E. Stallings, Sherman Alexie, Alice Jones, Brooks Haxton, Lola Haskins.

Unsolicited Manuscripts Received/ Published per Year: 11,000 poems (3,000 envelopes)/80 poems.

Reading Period: year–round.

Payment: 3 copies.

Reporting Time: immediately—four months.

Copyright held by magazine; reverts to author upon publication.

1950; 4/yr; 1,500

$12/yr ind, $18/yr inst; $4/ea; 20%

48 pp; 5½ x 8½

No ads

ISSN: 0005-8661

DeBoer, Maine Writer's and Publisher's Alliance, Ubiquity

THE BERKELEY POETRY REVIEW

Rotating Editors
200 MLK Student Union Bldg.
University of California at Berkeley
Berkeley, CA 94720

Poetry, translation, interviews, photographs, graphics/artwork.

THE BERKELEY POETRY REVIEW is a long-standing literary journal that publishes primarily poetry. Poets should submit 4 poems maximum; we are always on the lookout for emerging writers.

Victor Hernandez Cruz, Thom Gunn, Heather McHugh, Robert Hass, Lyn Hejinian, Ishmael Reed.

Unsolicited Manuscripts Received/Published per Year: 4,000/100.

Reading Period: not in summer.

Payment: 1 copy upon publication.

Copyright held by author.

1973; 1–2/yr; 500–1,000

$10/yr ind, $12/yr inst; $10/ea; 40%

100 pp; 5 x 8

Ad Rates: $55/page (4 x 7); $30/½ page (2½ x 3½)

THE BILINGUAL REVIEW/LA REVISTA BILINGÜE

Gary D. Keller
Hispanic Research Center
Arizona State University
P.O. Box 872702
Tempe, AZ 85287-2702
(602) 965-3867

Poetry, fiction, criticism, reviews, scholarly articles.

Devoted to the linguistics and literature of bilingualism, primarily Spanish/English, in the United States. We publish creative literature by and/or about United States Hispanics, literary criticism and reviews of United States Hispanic literature. We do not publish translations.

David Rice, Judith Ortiz Cofer, Nash Candelaria, Martin Espada.

Unsolicited Manuscripts Received/Published per Year: 400/35.

Payment: in copies.

Reporting Time: 30 days.

Copyright held by magazine.

1974; 3/yr; 2,000

$19/yr ind; $32/yr inst; sample copies: $7 ind, $11 inst

96 pp; 7 x 10

Ad Rates: $200/page (5½ x 8½); $125/½ page (5½ x 4)

ISSN: 0094-5366

BLACK BEAR REVIEW

Ave Jeanne & Ron Zettlemoyer
1916 Lincoln St.
Croydon, PA 19021

Poetry, reviews, graphics, market listings, ads.

BLACK BEAR REVIEW is an international literary/fine arts magazine published twice a year. We welcome poetry that shows: knowledge of the craft, depth, and potency. Submissions should reflect a social awareness and concern. First Rights. Chapbooks considered.

A.D. Winans, Elliot Richman, Andrew Gettler, John Grey, R.M. Host.

Unsolicited Manuscripts Received/ Published per Year: 3,500/100.

Reading Period: year–round.

Payment: in copy.

Copyright held by magazine; reverts to author upon publication.

1984; 2/yr; 600

$10/yr ind, $12/yr inst; $5/ea; 40%

64 pp; 5½ x 8

ISSN: 8756-0666

BLACK ICE

Ronald Sukenick, Publisher, and Mark Amerika, Editor

English Dept. Publications Center

Campus Box 494

Boulder, CO 80309-0494

(303) 492-8947

Fiction.

BLACK ICE publishes only fiction, with emphasis on nontraditional fiction. We intend to take risks with the fiction we publish and encourage writers to do the same.

Steve Katz, Erik Belgum, Thomas Glynn, Harold Jaffe, Cris Mazza.

Unsolicited Manuscripts Received/ Published per Year: 350/15–20.

Payment: 2 contributors copies.

Copyright held by magazine; reverts to author upon publication.

1984; 1–2/yr; 800

$7/ea; 40%

100 pp; 5½ x 8½

Ad Rates: $150/page (5 x 8)

ISSN: 1047-515X

BLACK JACK/VALLEY GRAPEVINE

Art Coelho

P.O. Box 249

Big Timber, MT 59011

Poetry, fiction, photographs, graphics/artwork; mostly poetry and short stories.

BLACK JACK's focus is on rural America, regional writing; interests are on the the Dustbowl; Okie migration; southern Appalachia; Hoboes; American Indians; the West; American farmer and rancher. **VALLEY GRAPEVINE** focuses on anything in the San Joaquin and Sacramento Valley in Central California.

Bill Rintoul, Gerry Haslam, Wilma McDaniel, Dorothy Rose, Frank Cross.

Payment: in copies.

Reporting Time: 6 weeks.

Copyright held by Seven Buffaloes Press; reverts to author upon publication.

1973; 1/yr; 750
$10/yr; $6.75/ea (post paid); 20%–40%
85 pp; 5¼ x 8¼

BLACK RIVER REVIEW

Deborah Glaefke Gilbert, Kaye Coller, Editors
855 Mildred Ave.
Lorain, OH 44052-1213
(216) 244-9654 aa 1250 @ freenet.lorain.oberlin.edv.

Poetry, fiction, critical essay, book review, b & w Art.

BRR presents contemporary writing of diverse styles and genres aimed toward a broad audience. We print work that exhibits originality, craftsmanship, vivid style, by writers both well-known and as-yet-to-be-discovered. More detailed guidelines are available for SASE. Please, no children's, young adult, or women's magazine fiction.

B. Z Niditch, Sandra Nelson, Ioanna-Veronika Warwick, L. E. McCullogh, Paul Weinman, David Mouat, Alysice K. Harpootean.

Unsolicited Manuscripts Received/Published per Year: 1,000+/65+.
Reading Period: Jan.–May. Those received any other time are returned unread. No response without SASE.
Payment: in copies.
Reporting Time: 2 weeks–6 months.
Copyright reverts to author upon publication.
1985; 1/yr; 400
$4/ea + 1.50 ph
60 pp; 8½ x 11
Ad Rates: query

THE BLACK SCHOLAR

Robert Chrisman, Editor-in-Chief: Robert L. Allen, Senior Editor
P.O. Box 2869
Oakland, CA 94609
(510) 547-6633

Poetry, fiction, sociology, politics, economy, education, book reviews.

A journal of black studies and research, addressing such issues as black culture, black politics, black education, economics, Southern Africa, etc. . . . A journal on the cutting edge of contemporary black thought.

Jesse Jackson, Jayne Cortez, Johnnotta B. Cole, Gwendolyn Brooks, Haki R. Madhubuti, P.P. Sarduy

Unsolicited Manuscripts Received/Published per Year: 100–150/8–10.

Payment: subscription plus 10 copies.
Reporting Time: 2 months.
Copyright held by Black World Foundation.
1969; 4/yr; 10,000
$30/ind, $50/inst; $6/ea; 20%–40%
64 pp; 7 x 10
$1,000/page; $600/½ page; query
ISSN: 0006-4246
L-S Dist., DeBoer

BLACK WARRIOR REVIEW

Mindy Wilson
P.O. Box 2936
Tuscaloosa, AL 35486-2936
(205) 348-4518

Poetry, fiction, essays, reviews, translations, interviews.
The **BLACK WARRIOR REVIEW** publishes the best of contemporary writing by the best of contemporary writers.
David Wojahn, Dana Wier, Rodney Jones Gerald Stern, Andre Dubus, Janet Peery.
Unsolicited Manuscripts Received/Published per Year: 20,000/100.
Reading Period: year–round.
Payment: varies, avg $75 per story/$33 per poem.
Reporting Time: 1–3 months.
Copyright held by magazine; reverts to author upon publication.
1974; 2/yr; 3,000
$11/yr ind, $17/yr inst; $6/ea
180 pp; 6 x 9
Ad Rates: $150/page (5 x 8); $85/½ page (5 x 3½)
ISSN: 0193-6301

THE BLOOMSBURY REVIEW

Tom Auer, Publisher & Editor in Chief
Marilyn Auer, Assoc. Publisher & Editor
1762 Emerson St.
Denver, CO 80218-1012
(303) 863-0406
Fax (303) 863-0408

Reviews, graphics/artwork, poetry, interviews, photographs, essays.
THE BLOOMSBURY REVIEW is a "Book Magazine" that includes reviews, interviews, essays, poetry, profiles, and previews of new titles, with an emphasis on new titles from small, medium-sized, and university presses.
Harlan Ellison, Gregory McNamee, John Nichols, Linda Hogan, Peter Wild.
Unsolicited Manuscripts Received/Published per Year: 1,000/100.
Reading Period: year–round.
Payment: $15/review; $10/poetry; $20/interviews.
Reporting Time: 2 months.
Copyright reverts to author.
1980; 6/yr; 50,000

$16/yr; $3/ea; 40%; less discount through distributors.
32 pp; 11¼ x 16
Ad Rates: $3,150/page (9⅞ x 15¼); $1,680/½ page (9⅞ x 7½); $890/¼ page (4⅞ x 7½ or 2⁵⁄₁₆ x 15¼ or 9⅞ x 3⅝)
ISSN: 0276-1564

BLUE MESA REVIEW

David Johnson, Editor; Patricia Spaott, Managing Editor
Dept. of English
University of New Mexico
Albuquerque, NM 87131
(505) 277-6347
Fax (505) 277-5573
Original fiction, poetry, essays, photography, art.
Generous but discriminating venue for new, emerging and experimental writers, not necessarily regional.
David Axelrod, Bobby Byrd, Harvena Richter, Luci Tapahanso, Virgil Suarez.
Unsolicited Manuscripts Received/Published per Year: 400/60
Reading Period: May–Nov.
Payment: 2 copies
Reporting Time: 6 months (max.)
Copyright held by magazine; 1st time rights, then copyright reverts to writer.
1989; 1/yr; 1,500
$10/yr; $10/ea; 40%
230 pp; 6 x 9
Ad Rates: Does Not Apply
ISSN: 1042-2951
UNM Press, DeBoer Inc.

BLUE UNICORN

Ruth G. Iodice, Martha Bosworth, Fred Ostrander, Editors; Robert L. Bradley, Art Editor; Harlan Bosworth, Contest Chairperson
22 Avon Rd.
Kensington, CA 94707
(510) 526-8439
Poetry, translation, artwork.
We are looking for excellence of the individual poetic voice, whether that voice comes through in form or free verse, rhyme or not. We want originality of image, thought and music, poems which are memorable and communicative. We publish both well-known poets and unknowns who deserve to be known better.
John Ciardi, Charles Edward Eaton, Emilie Glen, Diana O'Hehir, William Stafford.
Unsolicited Manuscripts Received/Published per Year: 35,000/100.
Payment: in copies.
Reporting Time: 3–4 months.
Copyright held by magazine; reverts to author upon publication.
1977; 3/yr; 500
$14/yr, $18/yr foreign; $5/ea
56 pp; 5½ x 8½
ISSN: 0197-7016

BLUELINE

Anthony Tyler
English Dept.
SUNY
Potsdam, NY 13676

Poetry, fiction, essays, reviews, graphics/artwork, oral history, journals.

BLUELINE is dedicated to prose and poetry about the Adirondacks and other regions similar in geography and spirit. We are interested in historic and contemporary writing, from new and established writers, that interprets the region as well as describes it.

Eric Ormsby, Robert Morgan, Annie David, Joan Conner.

Unsolicited Manuscripts Received/Published per Year: 130/31. Previously unpublished mss. Need SASE for response.

Reading Period: Sept.–Nov.

Payment: in copies.

Reporting Time: 2–10 weeks.

Copyright held by magazine; reverts to author upon publication.

1993; 300

$6/yr; $6/ea; $4

100 pp; 6 x 9

ISSN: 0198-9901

BOGG

John Elsberg, George Cairncross
422 North Cleveland
Arlington, VA 22201

Poetry, prose poems, visual/concrete poems, criticism, essays, reviews, interviews, graphics/artwork.

Editing is a subjective affair, and we print what takes our fancy. **BOGG** is an Anglo-American literary journal, with contributions from the U.S., Canada, England, Australia/New Zealand and India.

Ann Menebroker, Ron Androla, Harold Witt, Robert Peters, John Millett, Tina Fulker, Richard Peabody, Jon Silkin, Laurel Speer, Charles Plymell, A.D. Winans, Charles Bukowski.

Unsolicited Manuscripts Received/Published per Year: 10,000 poems/100-150 US poems; 3-6 prose pieces; 2-3 interviews; 3-6 essays.

Payment: in copies.

Reporting Time: immediately.

Copyright held by author.

1968; 2–3/yr; 850

$12/3 issues; $4.50/ea; $3.50/sample; 40%

68 pp; 6 x 9

ISSN: 0882-648X

BOHEMIAN CHRONICLE

Emily W. Skinner, Ellen M. Williams
P.O. Box 387
Largo, Fl 34649-0387

Fiction, nonfiction, essays, poetry, humor.

An international newsletter/ magazine promoting sensitivity in the arts, **BOHEMIAN CHRONICLE**'s primary focus is to extend an arm to communities worldwide whose voices have been quelled.

Reading Period: Dec.–Sept.

Payment: $5.00 per article; $3.00 per art used.

Reporting Time: 2 months.

Copyright: each issue is copyrighted as a whole (magazine buys first rights; SASE for guidelines).

1991; 12/yr; 500+

$12/U.S. yr; $15/outside U.S. yr; $1/ea

12 pp; 8½ x 5½

Noncommercial. We depend on subscriptions and the sale of sample issues for our revenues.

BOMB MAGAZINE

Betsy Sussler
594 Broadway
Suite 905
New York, NY 10012
(212) 431-3943

Interviews, poetry, fiction, photographs, art.

BOMB MAGAZINE is a spokespiece for new art, fiction, theater and film in New York. Named after Wyndham Lewis's "Blast," it promotes and encourages intergenerational and intercultural dialogue artists, writer, directors, musicians..

Thulani Davis, Jessica Hagedorn, Gary Indiana, Roland Legiareli-Laura, Patrick McGrath, Caryl Phillips, Lynne Tillman.

Unsolicited Manuscripts Received/ Published per Year: 2,000/4.

Payment: $100.

Copyright reverts to author.

1981; 4/yr; 15,000

$18/yr; $4/ea; 40%

100 pp; 10 x 14½

Ad Rates: available on request

BONE & FLESH

Publisher: Lester Hirsh

Editors: Lester Hirsh, Frederick Moe, Amy Shea

Chapbook Editor: Susan Bartlett

Managing Editor: Monica Nagle

P.O. Box 728
Concord, NH 03302-0728

Prose, poetry, art, essays, chapbooks, short stories, haiku.

We publish well-seasoned work on most any subject with a literary slant that links with our life and times or other lives and times.

Lyn Lifshin, Bayla Winters, Mara

Attina, Tim Hoppey, David Brooks

Unsolicited Manuscripts Received/Published per year: 400/30–40

Reading Period: February–May.

Payment: In copy.

Reporting Time: 6–10 weeks.

Copyright held by magazine; reverts to author upon publication.

1988; 2/yr; 200–300

$14/yr, $7/ea

60–75 pp; 8 x 10, chapbooks are 5 x 7 or 6 x 8

Ad Rates: $35/¼ page, $50/½ page, $75/full page.

ISSN: 9130-1940

Ebsco, Bone & Flesh, working on others

BOOKENDS

Chet Hagan, Editor
P.O. Box 227
Wernersville, PA 19565
(610) 678-6480

Book Review Editor:
Harry L. Eshleman
323 S. Whiteoak St.
Kutztown, PA 19530
(610) 683-5508

Library news (locally & statewide); book reviews aimed at the local market—Reading & Berks County. Literary columns.

Published six times a year, **BOOKENDS** is totally financed by the Friends of the Reading-Berks (PA) Public Libraries. All writing is volunteered.

John Updike, James L. Holton, Christopher Hinz, Lloyd Arthur Eshbach, Chet Hagan, others.

Payment: none; all volunteer contributions.

Copyright: authors, if they wish, copyright own material. the magazine is not copyrighted per se.

1981; 6/yr; 2,000

16+ pp; 8½ x 11

ISSN: 0893-6471.

THE BOOKPRESS

Jack Goldman
DeWitt Building
215 N. Cayuga St.
Ithaca, NY 14850
(607) 277-2254
Fax (607) 275-9221

Articles, interviews, reviews, fiction, poetry, art, photographs.

THE BOOKPRESS is a monthly cultural newspaper dedicated to promoting the discussion and exchange of ideas and opinions concerning the literary and visual arts.

Ann Druyan, Gunilla Feigenbaum, Michael Serino, Mark Schechner, Paul West.

Unsolicited Manuscripts Received/Published per Year: 20/3.

Reading Period: Aug.–May.

Payment: varies.
Reporting Time: 1 month.
Copyright: Bookpress, Inc.
1991; 8/yr; 7,500
$12/yr
20 pp; 11 x 17
Ad Rates: $720/full page (11 x 17), $600/¾ pg, $440/½ pg, $330/⅜ pg, $240/¼ pg, $180/3/16 pg, $130/⅛ pg, $70/1/16 pg.

BORDERLANDS: Texas Poetry Review
Editors rotate from among our permanent board members
P.O. Box 49818
Austin, TX 78765
(512) 444-7320
Original poetry, short reviews, essays on contemporary poetry.
BORDERLANDS publishes outward-looking, accessible poems on society, environment, history, other cultures, landscape, or spiritual life; and essays setting contemporary poetry in some large context, often social or political.
Stephen Dobyns, Ted Kooser, David Romtvedt, Elizabeth Socolow, Naomi Nye, William Stafford, Laurel Speer, Walt McDonald, Patianne Rogers.
Unsolicited Manuscripts Received/ Published per Year: 2,000/200.
Payment: 1 copy.
Reporting Time: 3–4 months.
Copyright: 1st North American Rights only.
1992; 2/yr; 500
14/yr ind, $16/yr inst; $8.50/ea; 50%
100 pp; 5½ x 8½
Ad Rates: will trade ads with other literary journals.
ISSN: 1065-0342
Fine Print, Ebsco

BOSTON LITERARY REVIEW (BLUR)
Gloria Mindock
Box 357
W. Somerville, MA 02144
(617) 625-6087
Poetry, short fiction (under 3,000 words).
We seek work that pushes form or content, and that has a unique, even idiosyncratic voice. 5–10 poems are welcome, as we prefer to publish several poems by each author.
Eric Pankey, David Ray, Stuart Freibert, Richard Kostelanetz.
Unsolicited Manuscripts Received/ Published per Year: 2,500/35.
Payment: 2 copies.
Reporting Time: 2–4 weeks.
Copyright reverts to author upon publication.
1984; 2/yr; 500
$9/yr; $5/ea
24 pp; 5½ x 13

THE BOSTON REVIEW

Josh Cohen, Editor
Building E-53, Room 407
M.I.T
Cambridge, MA 02139
(617) 253-3642

THE BOSTON REVIEW is an award-winning national magazine with unconventional coverage of politics, culture, and all the arts. Meet the next generation of gifted young writers alongside established authors saying what's really on their minds. People like Ralph Nader, Henry Louis Gates, Jr., Sharon Olds, Sven Birkerts, bell hooks, Michael Dorris, Robert Pinsky.

Unsolicited Manuscripts Received/Published per Year: 1,000/40.

Payment: $40–$250/depending on length and author.

Copyright held by Boston Critic, Inc.; reverts to author upon publication.

1975; 6/yr; 20,000

$15/yr ind, $18/yr inst

40–48 pp; 11⅜ x 14½

Ad Rates: $800/page (10 x 14); $550/½ page (10 x 6¾); $250/¼ page (4¾ x 6¾)

ISSN: 0734-2306

Interstate, Ingram, Total

BOTTOMFISH

David Denny
DeAnza College
21250 Stevens Creek Blvd.
Cupertino, CA 95014
(408) 864-8786 or (408) 864-8623

Poetry, fiction, creative nonfiction, interviews, essays.

BOTTOMFISH is interested only in carefully crafted work.

Lyn Lifshin, Robert Cooperman, Edward Kleinschmidt.

Unsolicited Manuscripts Received/Published per Year: 500-1,000/30 poems, 6 stories.

Reading Period: September-February.

We read mss. from September-February, make final decisions in March, print in April.

Payment: 2 copies.

Copyright held by magazine; reverts to author upon publication.

1976; 1/yr; 500

$5/ea; 40%

80–100 pp; 17.5 x 21 cm.

Full page ad $100; half page $50

BOULEVARD

Richard Burgin, Editor
P.O. Box 30386
Philadelphia, PA 19103
(215) 568-7062

Poetry, fiction, criticism, essays, translations, interviews, photos, graphics.

BOULEVARD publishes exceptional fiction and poetry and essays by impressive new talent as well as established literary voices. The editors believe a critical dimension is essential to an outstanding literary publication; thus, each issue publishes essays on literature and the other arts. **BOULEVARD** believes in the school of talent.

John Ashbery, John Barth, Joyce Carol Oates, Alice Adams, John Updike.

Unsolicited Manuscripts Received/ Published per Year: 6,000+/75.

Reading Period: Oct.–May.

Payment: $25–250+/poetry; $50–250+/fiction & other prose.

Copyright held by Opojaz Inc. for First North American Serial Rights; reverts to author upon publication.

1986; 3/yr; 3,000

$12/yr ind, $20/2yrs, $25/3 yrs; $6/yr inst; $7/ea. 40%

200+ pp

Ad Rates: $150/pg, $100/½ pg

ISSN: 0885-9337

DeBoer, Ingram, Ubiquity

BOUNDARY 2

William V. Spanos
SUNY/Binghamton
Binghamton, NY 13901
(607) 798-2743

Poetry, fiction, criticism, essays, plays, translation, interviews, photographs, graphics/artwork.

BOUNDARY 2 publishes poetry, fiction and literary criticism that try to break out of the impasse that traditional, including modernist, literature and literary criticism have become stalled in. We are especially interested in providing a forum for experiments in open forms that ultimately interrogate the literary tradition and the dominant culture this tradition supports.

Armand Schwerner, Jerome Rothenberg, John Taggart, Charles Bernstein and the l=a=n=g=u=a=g=e poets.

Payment: none.

Reporting Time: 4–6 months.

1972; 3/yr; 1,000

$15/yr ind, $13/yr students; $25/yr inst; $8/ea; 40%

300 pp; 9 x 5¾

Ad Rates: $100/page; $50/½ page; $25/¼ page

THE BRIDGE: a journal of fiction & poetry.

Jack Zucker; Helen Zucker, Fiction Editors; Mitzi Alvin, Poetry Editor; Marion Meilgaard, Kathleen Devereaux, Associate Fiction Editors; Lorene Erickson, Managing Editor.

14050 Vernon St.
Oak Park, MI 48237
(313) 547-6823

Fiction, poetry, reviews (1–2).

Eclectic collection of 48% fiction, 48% poetry, 4% reviews, etc.

Our writers run from national to new. We devote about 10% of each issue to Michigan writers.
Grace Bauer, X. J. Kennedy, Ruth Whitman, Daniel Hughes, Barbara Greenberg.
Unsolicited Manuscripts Received/Published per Year: 1,000+/80.
Reading Period: year–round.
Payment: none.
Reporting Time: 3–4 months.
Copyright: first rights only.
1990; 2/yr; 700
$10/yr; $5/ea; $15/2yr; 40%
192 pp; 5½ x 8
Ad Rates: $45/page
ISSN: 1052-1569

BRIDGES: A JOURNAL FOR JEWISH FEMINISTS AND OUR FRIENDS

Clare Kinberg, Ruth Atkin, Deb Crespin, Toby Finkelstein, Sarah Jacobus
P.O. Box 24839
Eugene, OR 97402
(503) 935-5720
Essays, poetry, fiction, reviews, letters
Showcase for Jewish women's creativity emphasizing Jewish identity and activism for social and political transformation.
Judith Arcana, Ruth Behar, Irena Klepfisz, Margorie Agosin, Elana Pykewomon
Unsolicited Manuscripts Received/Published per year: 200/20
Reading Period: All the time.
Payment: $50 per manuscript.
Reporting Time: 6--9 months.
Copyright held by author.
1990; 2/yr; 1,500
$15/yr.; $7.50/ea; 40%
128 pp; 7 x 10
ISSN: 1046-8358
Inland, Buokpeople, Small Changers, Ubiquity

BRIEF

Jim Hydock
P.O. Box 33
Canyon, CA 94516
(415) 376-5509
Poetry, fiction, post-modern fiction/poetry.
Subscription only. Sold in select bookstores.
Larry Eigner, Fielding Dawson, August Kleinzahler, Anselm Hollo, Martha King.
Payment: none.
Reporting Time: 2–4 weeks.
Copyright held by magazine; reverts to author upon publication.
1988; 3/yr; 250
$10/yr ind, $12/yr inst; $2.50/ea; 40%
25 pp; 5½ x 8½
No ads

THE BROOKLYN REVIEW

2308 Boylan Hall, Brooklyn College
Brooklyn, NY 11210
(718) 951-5195

Short fiction, poetry.

An annual magazine featuring established writers, while also publishing dynamic emerging voices in both fiction and poetry.

Allen Ginsberg, John Ashbery, Amy Gerstler.

Unsolicited Manuscripts Received/Published per Year: about 5%.

Reading Period: Sept.–Nov. 15.

Payment: 2 copies.

Reporting Time: 6–10 weeks.

1974; 1/yr; 500

$5/ea

120 pp; digest-sized

No ads.

BRÚJULA/COMPASS

Isaac Goldemberg
Latin American Writers Institute
Hostos Community College
500 Grand Concourse,
Bronx, NY 10451
(718) 518-4195

Devoted to Latino Literature in the U.S. Bilingual (Spanish & English). Publishes fiction, poetry, reviews, personal essays, literary criticism, interviews & information on grants, calls for manuscripts, residencies, other magazines, opportunities for publication, literary contests for Latino writers.

Julia Alvarez, Luis Rafael Sánchez, Iván Silén, Ilán Stavans, Magali Alabau, Julio Ortega, Judith Ortiz Coffer.

Unsolicited Manuscripts Received/Published per Year: 300/120.

Reading Period: year–round.

Payment: in-kind.

1987; 4/yr; 5,000

$20/yr; $4/ea

32 to 40 pp; tabloid

Ad Rates: $400/page; $250/½ page; $150/¼ page; $100/⅛ page; $75/1/16 page

BUTTON

Sally Cragin
Box 876
Lunenburg, MA 01462

Poetry, fiction, sheet music, recipes, interviews, celebrity facts.

New England's tiniest quarterly of real poetry, convincing fiction and gracious living, with a readership aged 9 to 93 spanning the continent.

David Barber, William Corbett, Gary Leib, Romayne Dawnay, Stephen McCauley, Wayne Wilson.

Unsolicited Manuscripts Received/Published per Year: 250/10–12.

Reading Period: year–round.

Payment: 2 one-year subscriptions; everlasting gratitude.
Reporting Time: 6–8 weeks.
Copyright reverts to author after publication.
1993; 3/yr; 1200
$5/$10/yr ($10 deluxe subscription includes objets d'art); $1.00/ea; 40%.
27 pp; 4 x 5
Thimble

C

CAFE SOLO

Glenna Luschei
Box 2814
Atascadero, CA 93422
(805) 243-1058

Poetry, criticism, essays, reviews, translation, photographs, graphics/artwork and letters to the editor.

We seek excellence and the avant-garde: Subconscious navigation in strange waters and Columbus sighting land. We print new writers next to known ones. We emphasize poetry, but encourage imaginative essays and new literary art forms.

Robert Bly, Denise Levertov, Ai, Gene Frumkin, Gary Snyder, Lawrence Ferlinghetti, Thomas McGrath, Brenda Hillman, David Oliveria, and Ioanna Carlson.

Unsolicited Manuscripts Received/Published per year: 3000/50.

Reading Period: Oct.–Feb.

Payment: in copies.

Reporting Time: 8 weeks.

Please do not submit until you have ordered a sample copy.

Copyright held by Solo Press.

1969; 3/yr; 500

$20/yr; $5/ea; 40%

44 pp; 8½ x 11

ISSN: 0773-1796

CALIBAN

Lawrence R. Smith
P. O. Box 561
Laguna Beach, CA 92652
(714) 497-7437

Poetry, fiction, translation, interviews, graphics/artwork.

CALIBAN has redefined the literary and artistic avant-garde by cutting across partisan lines, making different writers and

artists in serious pursuit of the new aware of each other. **CALIBAN** also insists that the avant-garde is not the exclusive domain of white, middle-class males, bohemian or otherwise.
Berssenbrugge, Vizenor, Komunyakaa, Kingston, Wakoski.
Unsolicited Manuscripts Received/Published per Year: 2,000/20.
Payment: $15–$20, plus 2 copies.
Reporting Time: 1–2 months.
Copyright held by magazine; reverts to author upon publication.
1986; 2/yr; 1,700
$14/yr; $26/2 yr ind; $24/yr inst; $8/ea; 40%, 25% textbook orders
192 pp; 6 x 9
Ad Rates: $100/page (5 x 8)
ISSN: 0890-7269
DeBoer, BookPeople, SPD

CALLALOO

Charles H. Rowell
Department of English
Bryan Hall
University of Virginia
Charlottesville, VA 22903
(804) 924-6616
Poetry, fiction, criticism, essays, reviews, plays, translation, photographs, graphics/artwork.
CALLALOO is a quarterly journal which features the arts and literature of Africans, and Africans in the Diaspora, (the United States, the Caribbean, Latin America, Europe, Canada, and Southeast Asia & Australia). **CALLALOO** now also features a special section, "Cultural Criticism," which presents challenging essays by critics and theorists on all topics and areas of cultural interest.
Rita Dove, John Edgar Wideman, Maryse Condé, Judith Ortiz Cofer, Derek Walcott, K. Anthony Appiah, Caryl Phillips, Audre Lorde, Yusef Komunyakaa. Recent issues focused on Haitian arts and literature, Puerto-Rican women writers, Post Colonial discourse, and native American writers, Guyanese-British writer Wilson Harris, and the playwright George C. Wolfe.
Payment: (When grants are available from NEA.)
Copyright registered under Callaloo by Johns Hopkins University Press; transferable to author; previous copyrights with notification.
1976; 4/yr; 1400
$27/yr, $54/yr inst; $8.50/ea ind, Foreign subs. add $7 + 7% GST Canada; +$7 Mexico; $17 all other countries.
256 pp; 7 x 10
Ad Rates: $225/page (5½ x 8);

$155/½ page (5½ x 4); cover 3/$250
ISSN: 0161-2496

CALLIOPE

Martha Christina
Creative Writing Program
Roger Williams University
Bristol, RI 02809
(401) 254-3217
Poetry, fiction.
Interested in both established and emerging writers, but need not have published elsewhere. Prefer concrete to abstract images, work that appeals to the emotions through the senses.
Thomas Lux, Mark Doty, Mark Cox, Tim Seibles, Allison Joseph.
Unsolicited Manuscripts Received/Published per Year: about 2,000/about 50.
Reading Period: Aug. 15–Oct. 15; Jan. 15–Mar. 15.
Payment: 2 copies and subscription.
Copyright held by magazine; reverts to author upon publication.
1977; 2/yr; 500
$5/yr; $3/ea; 40%
5½ x 8½

CALYX: A Journal of Art and Literature by Women

Margarita Donnelly, Beverly McFarland, Micki Reaman, Co-Managing Editors; & collective members
P.O. Box B
Corvallis, OR 97339
(503) 753-9384; Fax (503) 753-0515
E-mail: CALYX@PEAK.ORG
Poetry, fiction, essays, translations, reviews, photographs, visual art, interviews.
Considered one of the finest literary magazines in the U.S., **CALYX** publishes work by women and presents a wide spectrum of women's experience. **CALYX** is committed to publishing work by women of color, working class women, lesbians, politically active women, and older women. Recipient of the 1993 & 1994 American Literary Magazines Awards. Recipient of the 1994 OSU Friends of the Library inaugural Achievement Award, & the U of O Oregon Women of Achievement Award.
Haunani-Kay Trask, Kathleen Crown, Jana Harris, Mallikā Sengupta, Shauna Singh Baldwin, & Sarah Sarai.
Unsolicited Manuscripts Received/Published per Year: 3,500–8,000/75–100.
Reading Period: Oct. 1–Nov. 15.
Payment: in copies & subscription.
Reporting Time: 3–9 months.
Copyright reverts to authors at publication.

1976; 3/volume (2/yr); 5,000
$18/vol ind, $22.50/vol inst, $30/yr Canadian, $36/vol foreign; $8/ea + postage; 30%–40%
128+pp.
Ad Rates: $550/page (5¾ x 7); $285/½ page (5¾ x 3⅜)
ISSN: 0147-1627
Small Changes, BookPeople, Fine Print, Ingram, SPD, Airlift, Armadillo

THE CAPE ROCK

Harvey Hecht
English Department
Southeast Missouri State University
Cape Girardeau, MO 63701
(314) 651-2636

Poetry, photographs.
We have no restrictions on subjects or forms. Our criterion for selection is the quality of the work rather than the bibliography of the authors. We prefer poems under 70 lines. We feature a single photographer each issue.
Laurel Speer, Laurie Taylor, Martin Robbins, Charles A. Waugaman.
Unsolicited Manuscripts Received/ Published per Year: 2,500/100.
Reading Period: Aug.–Apr.
Payment: each issue we award $200 for the best poem and $100 for the photography. All contributors are paid in copies.
Reporting Time: 1–4 months.
Copyright held by magazine; reprint rights granted upon request provided reprint credit is given to the magazine.
1964; 2/yr; 700
$7/yr; $5/ea; 40%
64 pp; 5½ x 8½
ISSN: 0146-2199

CAPRICE

James Mechem, Lynne Savitt
229 N. Fountain St.
Wichita, KS 67208-3833
(316) 683-8728

Fiction, poetry, movie reviews
Non-academic women writers, mostly.
Ai, Sibyl James, Marge Piercy, Ursule Molinaro, Toi Derricotte, Lola Haskins, Alma Luz Villanueva, Alicia Ostriker, Kelly Cherry, Nikki Giovanni, Jodi Braxton.
Unsolicited Manuscripts Received/ Published per Year: 30/8.
Reporting Time: 3 months.
1987; 12/yr
$50/yr; $5/ea
60 pp; 7 x 8 ½

THE CARIBBEAN WRITER

Erika J. Waters
University of the Virgin Islands

RR 02, Box 10,000 Kingshill
St. Croix, VI 00850
(809) 692-4152
Fax (809) 692-4152

Poetry, fiction, reviews, personal essays, graphics/ artwork.

THE CARIBBEAN WRITER is an international magazine with a Caribbean focus. The Caribbean should be central to the work, or the work should reflect a Caribbean heritage, experience, or perspective.

Opal Palmer Adisa, Julia Alvarez, Kamau Brathwaite, Olive Senior, Derek Walcott.

Unsolicited Manuscripts Received/ Published per Year: 600/50.

Annual deadline: Sept. 30.

Payment: 2 copies.

Copyright held by Research Publications Center; reverts to author upon publication.

1987; 1/yr; 1,500

$9/ea; 30%

150–200 pp; 6 x 9

Ad Rates: $250/page (6 x 9); $150/½ page; $100/¼ page

ISSN: 0893-1550

THE CAROLINA QUARTERLY

Amber Vogel
Greenlaw Hall CB #3520
University of North Carolina at Chapel Hill
Chapel Hill, NC 27599-3520
(919) 962-0244

Poetry, fiction, reviews, nonfiction.

A literary journal published three times yearly.

Barry Hannah, Denise Levertov, Mark Doty, Stephen Dunn.

Unsolicited Manuscripts Received/ Published per Year: 4,000/60-80.

Reading Period: year–round.

Reporting Time: 2–4 months.

First-publication rights (held by magazine).

1948; 3/yr; 1,500

$10/yr ind, $12/yr inst; $5/ea

80 pp; 6 x 9

Ad Rates: $80/page; $60/½ page; $40/¼ page

ISSN: 0008-6797

CAT'S EAR

Jim Roland, Founding Editor; Scott Ludtke, Assoc. Editor; Jack Holcomb, Asst. Editor
Galliard Group Publishers
P.O. Box 946
Kirksville, MO 63501
(816) 785-4185

Poetry, fiction.

CAT'S EAR publishes poetry and fiction with an emphasis on the lyrical and metaphorical, always with an eye on future directions of the tradition.

Diane Wakoski, Charles Edward Eaton, Robert Peters, Laurel Speer, Naomi Shihab Nye.

Payment: 2 copies.

Reporting Time: 9 weeks.

Copyright held by Galliard Group Publishers, but reverts to author upon publication.

1992; 3/yr; 250

$10/ind, $12/inst; $4/ea; 40%

48 pp; 5½ x 8½

Ad Rates: $50/page (4 x 7); $30/½ page (4 x 3¼ or 2 x 7); $20/¼ page (4 x 1 or 1 x 7)

ISSN: 1062-6379

CATALYST MAGAZINE

Pearl Cleage
236 Forsyth St., Suite 400
Atlanta, GA 30303
(404) 730-5785

Fiction, nonfiction, poetry, criticism, essays.

Focuses primarily on Southern writers, but welcomes all submissions in fiction, poetry, drama and criticism. The magazine presents writers in a format designed to stimulate discussion and encourage the exchange of ideas.

Willie Woods, Zaron Burnett, Mari Evans.

Unsolicited Manuscripts Received/Published per Year: 800/500.

Payment: $20–$200.

Reporting Time: 6–8 months.

SASE for return of submissions and immediate acknowledgement of work received.

Copyright authors.

1986; 2/yr; 5,000

$10/2 yrs; $2.50/ea

96 pp; 7½ x 14

ISSN: 0896-7423

THE CATHARTIC

Patrick M. Ellingham
P.O. Box 1391
Fort Lauderdale, FL 33302
(305) 967-9378

Poetry, reviews, photographs, artwork.

THE CATHARTIC is devoted to the unknown poet, with the understanding that most poets are unknown in America. All types of poetry except those that are racist or sexist. Avoid poems over 50 lines or rhyme for the sake of rhyme. Experiment with language and form. Poems that deal with or come from the dark side; intense poems that use words sparingly and forget the poet; poems that jar the reader's sensibilities; darkly erotic poems; poems that show social awareness.

Joy Walsh, Harry Knickerbocker, Paul Weinman.

Unsolicited Manuscripts Received/ Published per Year: 500+/50.
Payment: 1 copy.
Copyright reverts to author upon publication.
1974; 2/yr; 200
$5/yr; $3/ea
28 pp; 5½ x 8½
No ads
ISSN: 0145-8310

CENTRAL PARK

Stephen-Paul Martin; Richard Royal, Prose and Visuals; Eve Ensler, Poetry
P.O. Box 1446
New York, NY 10023
(212) 691-0890 or (212) 242-0302

Experimental fiction, narrative fiction, theory, graphics/ artwork, poetry, photographs, translation, interviews, reviews.

CENTRAL PARK is moving in three main directions: poetry and fiction of an either experimental or aggressively political nature, essays in social or esthetic theory, and visual work that moves the eye to think about how it sees. Prospective contributors are advised to order a sample copy ($5) before submitting.

Marc Kaminsky, Rosmarie Waldrop, Rae Armantrout, Ron Silliman, Jackson Mac Low.
Payment: 1 copy.
Reporting Time: 8 weeks.
Copyright held by magazine.
1981; 2/yr; 1,000
$8/yr; $5/ea; 40%
100 pp; 7½ x 10
Ad Rates: $100/page; $50/½ page; $25/¼ page
Ubiquity, Edge

CHAMINADE LITERARY REVIEW

Loretta Petrie
Chaminade University of Honolulu
3140 Waialae Ave.
Honolulu, HI 96816-1578
(808) 735-4723

Poetry, fiction, criticism, reviews.

CHAMINADE LITERARY REVIEW intends to bring together work from both artists and writers, talented new ones along with those nationally or internationally recognized. We want writing from Hawaii side by side with writing from the mainland to demonstrate how well our local writers compare. We want a magazine at once regional and cosmopolitan. We hope to reflect the diversity of Hawaii's people, their writers, their interests.

Cathy Song, John Unterecker, Phyllis Thompson, William

Stafford, Tony Quagliano.
Unsolicited Manuscripts Received/ Published per Year: 200/60+.
Payment: 1 year's subscription, upon publication.
Copyright held by Chaminade Press; reverts to author upon publication.
1987; 2/yr; 350
$10/yr; $18/2 yrs (ind & inst); $5/ea; 20%
175 pp; 6 x 9
Ad Rates: $50/page (4 x 7¼); $25/½ page (4 x 3⅞)
ISSN: 0894-6396

CHANTS

Terrell Hunter
R 1 Box 1738
Dexter, ME 04930
(207) 924-3673

Poetry, translations of poetry.
CHANTS publishes the best poetry we can find, regardless of style. We value intensity, originality, involvement—poems that grab you hard and won't let go.
Bill Shields, Jorie Graham, James Laughlin, Michael Kreps, Michael LaBruno.
Unsolicited Manuscripts Received/ Published per Year: 1,000/75–100.
Reading Period: year–round.
Payment: 2 copies
Reporting Time: 2–3 months, sometimes longer.
Copyright reverts to poet.
1989; 2/yr; 500
$12/3 issues; $4/ea; 30–40%
64 pp; 6 x 9
Ad Rates: $25/½ page

THE CHARIOTEER

Pella Publishing Company
337 West 36th St.
New York, NY 10018-6401
(212) 279-9586

Poetry, fiction, criticism, essays, reviews, plays, translation, graphics/artwork.
Purpose: to bring to English-speaking readers information on, appreciation of, and translations from modern Greek literature, with criticism and reproductions of modern Greek art and sculpture.
Unsolicited Manuscripts Received/ Published per Year: 6/none.
Payment: none.
Reporting Time: 3 months.
Copyright held by Pella Publishing Company; reverts to author upon request.
1960; 1/yr; 1,000
$15/yr; $28/2 yrs; $40/3 yrs
200 pp; 5½ x 8½
Ad Rates: $125/page (4⅛ x 7); $75/½ page (4⅛ x 3½)
ISSN: 0577-5574

THE CHARITON REVIEW

Jim Barnes
Truman State University
Kirksville, MO 63501
(816) 785-4499

Poetry, fiction, essays, reviews, translation.

Excellence in literature only. We like the old; we like the new.

Jack Cady, Phyllis Barber, Barry Targan, David Ray, Robert Canzoneri, Patricia Goedicke, Gordon Weaver, Steve Heller, Elizabeth Moore.

Unsolicited Manuscripts Received/Published per Year: 6-8,000/100.

Payment: $5/page.

Reporting Time: 1 week–1 month.

Copyright held by Truman State University; reverts to author upon publication.

1975; 2/yr; 700

$9/yr, $15/2yr, $5/ea; $5/sample copy

100 pp; 6 x 9

Ad Rates: $100/page (4 x 7); $50/½ page (4 x 3½)

ISSN: 0098-9452

THE CHARLOTTE POETRY REVIEW

A.A. Jillani, Lisa Kerley
P.O. Box 36701
Charlotte, NC 28236

Poetry, book reviews, short–short fiction, poet interviews.

Regardless of percentages, **CPR** as a rule regularly publishes first-time poets alongside some of the best in the country. Freshness is the key here.

Tony Moffeit, William Walsh, Chuck Sullivan, Harry Brody.

Published per Year: 3,000/100.

Payment: none.

Reporting Time: 2–3 months.

Copyright reverts to author upon publication.

1992; 4/yr; 1,500

$18/yr; $4.50/ea

48 pp; 8½ x 11

Ad Rates: $35/business card

THE CHATTAHOOCHEE REVIEW

Lamar York
DeKalb College
2101 Womack Road
Dunwoody, GA 30338-4497
(770) 551-3166

Poetry, fiction, criticism, essays, reviews, interviews.

THE CHATTAHOOCHEE REVIEW promotes fresh writing and encourages as yet unacknowledged writers by giving them space in print next to their acclaimed peers.

Leon Rooke, Fred Chappell,

George Garrett, Jim Wayne Miller, Peter Meinke.
Unsolicited Manuscripts Received/Published per Year: 3,000/100.
Reading Period: year–round.
Payment: 2 copies of **THE CHATTAHOOCHEE REVIEW**.
Reporting Time: 2 months.
Copyright held by DeKalb College; reverts to author upon publication.
1980; quarterly; 1,250
$16/yr; $30/2 yrs; $5/ea; 30%
100 pp; 6 x 9
Ad Rates: $125/page (4½ x 7); $75/½ page (4½ x 3½)
ISSN: 0741-9155

CHELSEA

Richard Foerster, Alfredo de Palchi, Andrea Lockett
Box 773
Cooper Station
New York, NY 10276-0773
Poetry, fiction, criticism, essays, translations, interviews, art.
Stress on style, variety, originality. No special biases or requirements. Flexible attitudes, eclectic material. Active interest, as always, in crosscultural exchanges, in superior translations. Leaning toward cosmopolitan avant-garde, interdisciplinary techniques, but no strictures against traditional modes. Annual competition (send SASE for guidelines).
Chim Nwabucze, Mei-mei Berssenbrugge, D.E. Steward, Ha Jin, Laura Kasischke, LuAnn Keener, Jean Monahan, Carl Phillips, Ruth L. Schwartz, Bob Hicock, Veralyn Behenna.
Unsolicited Manuscripts Received/Published per Year: 4,000/60.
Payment: $15/page.
Reporting Time: immediately–4 months.
Copyright held by magazine; reverts to author upon publication.
1958; 2/yr; 1,300
$13/2 issues or 1 double issue; $16/foreign; ($8 each); $17/yr inst.; $21/foreign inst. Back issue samples: $5.
128 pp; 6 x 9
$125/page (4½ x 7½); $75/½ page (4½ x 3½); exchange ads also available
ISSN: 0009-2185
DeBoer, Faxon, Ebsco

CHICAGO REVIEW

David Nicholls
The University of Chicago
5801 S. Kenwood
Chicago, IL 60637
(312) 702-0887
Poetry, fiction, criticism, essays, reviews, translation, interviews, photographs, graphics/artwork.

CHICAGO REVIEW is an international journal of writing and cultural exchange published at the University of Chicago.
Elizabeth Alexander, Alice Fulton, Albert Goldbarth, Barry Hannah, Yusef Komunyakaa, Gary Snyder, Gerald Vizenor.
Unsolicited Manuscripts Received/Published per Year: 2,000/70.
Payment: copies/subscription.
Reporting Time: 2 months.
Copyright held by magazine; transfers to author upon request.
1946; 4/yr; 2,600
$18/yr ind, $35/yr inst; $6/ea; 40%
128 pp; 6 x 9
Ad Rates: $150/page (4½ x 7½); $75/½ page (2½ x 7½)
ISSN: 0009-3696
Armadillo, Fine Print, Ingram, Olson, Ubiquity

CHIRON REVIEW
Michael Hathaway
522 E. South Ave.
St. John, KS 67576-2212
(316) 549-3933
Poetry, fiction, nonfiction, reviews, all press news.
Presents the widest possible range of contemporary creative writing, traditional and off-beat in an attractive, professional tabloid format, including artwork and photos of featured writers.
Charles Bukowski, Robert Peters, Lyn Lifshin, Lorri Jackson, Antler, Joan Jobe Smith.
Unsolicited Manuscripts Received/Published per Year: 1,825+/100.
Payment: copies.
Reporting Time: 2-6 weeks.
Copyright: author retains rights.
1982; 4/yr; 1,000
$12/ind; $3/ea; 40%
20-48 pp; 10 x 13
Ad Rates: send SASE
ISSN: 1046-8897

CIMARRON REVIEW
E.P. Walkiewicz, Editor; Peter Donahue, Jubl Tiner, Associate Editors; Thomas E. Kennedy, European Editor.
205 Morrill Hall
Oklahoma State University
Stillwater, OK 74078-0135
(405) 744-9476
Poetry, fiction, essays, reviews.
Seeks well-written material, which emphasizes attempts to find value and purpose in a dehumanized and dehumanizing world. Avoids "easy" answers of extremes and would not publish work which espouses any specific religious or political view or advocates simple escapism. It does not publish children's stories; but does publish

stories about children aimed at adult understanding.
Unsolicited Manuscripts Received/Published per Year: 2,275/12–16.
Payment: $50/prose; $15/poem.
Reporting Time: 8–12 weeks.
Copyright held by magazine.
1967; 4/yr; 450
$12/yr; $3/ea
112 pp; 6 x 9
ISSN: 0009-6849

CINCINNATI POETRY REVIEW

Jeffrey Hillard
Humanities Department
College of Mount St. Joseph
Cincinnati, OH 45233
(513) 244-4930

Poetry.

CINCINNATI POETRY REVIEW sets local writers in a national context. One fourth to one third of each issue is local; the rest is national. "Local" means about 150 from the city. All types of poetry considered. Poetry contest held once per year.

Alvin Greenberg, Pat Mora, David Citino, Enid Shomer, Walter McDonald.

Payment: none.
Reporting Time: 4–6 weeks.
Copyright held by magazine; reverts to author upon publication.
1985; 2/yr; 600
$9/yr; $2/ea (samples); 40%; 50% for direct purchase by dealers
72 pp; 5½ x 8½

CLOCKWATCH REVIEW

James Plath, Editor; Robert, C. Bray, Lynn DeVore, James McGowan, Pamela Muirhead, Associate Editors
Dept. of English
Illinois Wesleyan University
Bloomington, IL 61702-2900
(309) 556-3352

Fiction, poetry, interviews, essays, photographs, graphics/artwork.

CLOCKWATCH REVIEW seeks to present quality work in a format lively enough to attract a popular as well as literary/academic audience. Special feature: an ongoing interview series with contemporary artists and musicians.

Bob Shacochis, Koko Taylor, Jamaica Kincaid, Albert Goldbarth, Pat Hutchings, Charlotte Mandel.

Unsolicited Manuscripts Received/Published per Year: 3,500/40-50.
Payment: 3 copies and a small cash award.
Reporting Time: 3–4 months.
Copyrighted.

1983; 2/yr; or one double issue; 1,500
$8/yr; $4/ea
80 pp; 5½ x 8½
ISSN: 0740-9311
Ingram

Reporting time: one month
Copyright held by author.
1990; 4/yr; 600
$4/2yrs (8 issues)
Sample copy: $1
20 pp; digest 5½ x 8½
ISSN: 1061-5687

CLUES: A Journal of Detection

Pat Browne
Journals Department
Popular Press
Bowling Green State University
Bowling Green, OH 43403
(419) 372-2981

Articles, reviews.

A magazine focusing upon detective fiction.

Unsolicited Manuscripts Received/Published per Year: 50–60/25.

Reading Period: year–round.

1982; 2/yr; 700
$12.50/yr; $7.75/ea

COFFEEHOUSE

Ray Foreman
P.O. Box 77
Berthoud, CO 80513
(970) 532-3118

Poetry, short stories, commentaries.

A high quality narrative poetry and short story magazine.

Unsolicited Manuscripts Received/Published per Year: 600/100.

Reading Period: year–round.

COLLAGES & BRICOLAGES

Marie-José Fortis
P.O. Box 86
Clarion, PA 16214
(814) 226-5799

Poetry, fiction, criticism, essays, reviews, plays, translation, interviews, photographs, graphics/artwork (b & w).

COLLAGES & BRICOLAGES, which has published authors from the five continents, believes in innovative writers who have read the classics. We would like to receive less egocentric, more politically engaged, pieces. 1996 will focus on Beckett, and Ionesco, as well as on many important non-mainstream authors.

Unsolicited Manuscripts Received/Published per Year: 600/20-25.

Reading Period: Aug.–Nov.

Payment: 1 or 2 copies. Extras: ½ price.

1996; 1/yr; 800
$7.50/ea

120 pp; 8½ x 11

Ad Rates: $50/page (6½ x 9); $30/½ page (3 x 8); $15/¼ page (2 x 4)

C & B also exchanges ads with other lit. mags.

COLORADO REVIEW

David Milofsky, Editor; Robert Olen Butler, George Cuomo, James Galvin, Jorie Graham, Joanne Greenberg, Michael Martone, Dan O'Brien, Carol Oles, Toby Olson, Robert D. Richardson, Jr., Alberto Rios, Contributing Editors.

Department of English

Colorado State University

Fort Collins, CO 80523

Fiction, poetry, essays, and reviews.

Although published in Colorado, **COLORADO REVIEW** is more than a regional literary magazine. We seek to print the best fiction, poetry, translations, interviews, reviews, and articles on contemporary literary subjects that we receive from a contributorship that is national and international. We continue to be interested in Magical Realist writing, but any writing that is vital, highly imaginative and highly realized in artistic terms and that avoids mere mannerism to embody important human concerns will find support here.

Reg Saner, Patricia Goedicke, Bin Ranke, Carole Oles, T. Alan Broughton, Rita Ciresi, David Huddle; interviews with Carolyn Forche; Gwendolyn Brooks, Gretel Ehrlich.

Unsolicited Manuscripts Received/Published per Year: 7,000/varies.

Reading Period: Sept.–May.

Payment: when funding permits.

1977; 2/yr 1,000

$15/yr, $28/2 yr; $8/ea; 40%

112 pp; 6 x 9

Ad Rates: $100/page (7½ x 5); $50/½ page

COLUMBIA: A Magazine of Poetry and Prose

Rotating Editors

404 Dodge Hall

Columbia University

New York, NY 10027

(212) 854-4391

Poetry, fiction, essays.

Reading Period: Aug.-May.

Payment: in copies; Editors' awards also.

Reporting Time: 1–2 months.

Copyright reverts to author.

$18/3 issues; $13/2 issues; $7 ea

Approx. 220 pp; 5 x 8

Ad Rates: on request

COMMON JOURNEYS

Leslie Keyes, Bobbi Mlekuda, Claire Griffen
4136 43rd Ave. South
Mineapolis, MN 55406
(612) 729-7552

Only on the illness experience.

COMMON JOURNEYS provides a literary forum for writers who live with chronic pain or illness.

Margaret Robison, S. K. Duff, Cheri Register, Lee Varon, Kathleen Kramer

Unsolicited Manuscripts Received/ Published per year: 1,200/ varies.

Reading Period: Ongoing

Payment: One copy.

Reporting Time: 1–4 months.

Copyright held by magazine.

1994/2 yr; 500+

$12/yr, $6/ea.

117 pp; 5½ x 8½

ISSN: 1071-9814

Mail-Order only.

CONFRONTATION

Martin Tucker
L.I.U. Dept. of English
C.W. Post, Northern Blvd.
Brookville, NY 11548
(516) 299-2391

Poetry, fiction, criticism, essays, plays, translation, interviews.

We are eclectic in our tastes, preferring a mix of traditional and experimental, of the known and relatively unknown writers. We have no prohibition except that of poor literary quality.

Cynthia Ozick, William Styron, Stephen Dixon, Joyce Carol Oates, Thomas Fleming, Joseph Brodsky.

Unsolicited Manuscripts Received/ Published per Year: 5,000/250.

Reading Period: Sept.–May.

Payment: $10 to $100.

Reporting Time: 6 weeks.

Copyright held by Long Island University; reverts to author upon publication.

1968; 2/yr; 2,000

$10/yr ind, $10/yr inst; $6/ea

160–190 pp; 5½ x 8½

CONJUNCTIONS

Bradford Morrow
Bard College
Annandale-on-Hudson, NY 12504
(914) 758-1539

Poetry, fiction, translation, interviews, photographs, graphics/ artwork, essays.

CONJUNCTIONS publishes formally innovative writing, with equal emphasis on fiction and poetry; also essays on culture and the arts, special features.

Editorial staff: Walter Abish, Chinua Achebe, John Ashbery, Mei-Mei Berssenbrugge, Guy

Davenport, Elizabeth Frank, Robert Kelly, William Gass, Susan Howe, Ann Lauterbach, Patrick McGrath, Nathaniel Tarn, Quincy Troupe, John Edgar Wideman.

Unsolicited Manuscripts Received/ Published per Year: 5,000+/10.

Payment: in copies, and $175.

Reporting Time: 4–6 weeks.

Copyright reverts to author upon publication.

1981; 2/yr; 7,500

$18/yr; $32/2yr; $12/ea

360 pp; 6 x 9

Ad Rates: $350/page (4⅜ x 7½); $250/½ page

ISSN: 0278-2324

THE CONNECTICUT POETRY REVIEW

Harley More, J. Claire White
P.O. Box 818
Stonington, CT 06378

Poetry, criticism, reviews, translations, interviews, excerpts from verse plays.

Marge Piercy, John Updike, Margaret Randall, Allen Ginsberg, Eugenio de Andrade.

Unsolicited Manuscripts Received/ Published per Year: 1,500/18–20.

Payment: $5/poem; $10/review; $20/interview; $20/verse play.

Reporting Time: 3 months.

1981; 1/yr; 500

$3/ea

50 pp; 5¾ x 9¼

ISSN: 0277-7770

CONNECTICUT RIVER REVIEW

Norah Christianson
35 Lindsley Place
Stratford, CT 06497

Poetry.

The **CRR** uses highest quality poetry, in which logic and emotion, picture and sound cohere, making for authentic music. All forms welcome, except haiku. Prefer poems of 40 lines or under; submit no more than 5 poems at a time.

Unsolicited Manuscripts Received/ Published per Year: 800–1,000/ 90–100.

Reading Period: year–round.

Payment: 1 copy.

Reporting Time: 2–8 weeks.

Copyright held by Connecticut Poetry Society; reverts to author upon publication.

1978; 2/yr; 400

$20/2 yrs; $6/ea; 40%

40 pp; 6 x 9

CONTACT II

Maurice Kenny, J.G. Gosciak
P.O. Box 451, Bowling Green

New York, NY 10004
(212) OR4-0911

Poetry, reviews, criticism, translation, interviews, photographs, graphics/artwork.

Contemporary American poetry.

Janice Mirikitani, Charlotte de Clue, Carolyn Stoloff, Shalin Hai-Jew, Karoniaktatie.

Unsolicited Manuscripts Published per Year: 20%.

Payment: in copies; when payment is cash, $10/poem, $15/review.

Reporting Time: 6 months.

Copyright held by Contact II Publications; reverts to author upon publication with credit.

1976; 2/yr; 2,500

$10/ind, $16/inst; $7/ea; 40%; 50% prepaid on 10 or more.

92 pp; 7¾ x 10½

Ad Rates: $150/page; $80/½ page; $50/¼ page

ISSN: 0197-6796

CONTEXT SOUTH

David Breeden, Craig Taylor, Paul Hadella
Campus Box 4504
Schreiner College
2100 Memorial Blvd.
Kerrville TX 78028-5697

Poetry, fiction, criticism, graphics/artwork.

A magazine based in the South, but not confined to it, **CONTEXT SOUTH** endeavors to be a collection by artists interested in pushing boundaries.

Wayne Dodd, Andrea Hollander Budy, Diane Glancy, William Greenway.

Unsolicited Manuscripts Received/Published per Year: 1,000+/50.

Copyright held by author.

300

$12/yr; $5/ea; 40%

65 pp; 5½ x 8½

$100/page; $50/½ page; $25/¼ page

ISSN: 1045-2265

CORNFIELD REVIEW

Stuart Lishan, Editor; Ann Bower, Fiction Editor; Terry Hermson, Poetry Editor; Larry Sauselen, Art Editor
OSU at Marion
1465 Mt. Vernon Ave
Marion, OH 43302
(614) 389-2361

Poetry, short stories, nonfiction essays; original art (black & white) and photography.

All campus community publications.

No outside submissions accepted

Reporting Time: 2–4 months.

Copyright reverts to author.

1976; 1/yr; 1,500

$5/ea

64 pp

ISSN: 0363-4574

COTTONWOOD

George Wedge, Editor; Phil Wedge, Poetry Editor; Christy Prahl, Fiction Editor
University of Kansas
Box J, 400 Kansas Union
Lawrence, KS 66045
(913) 864-3777

Poetry, fiction, reviews, interviews, photographs, graphics/artwork.

COTTONWOOD uses fiction and poetry with clear images and interesting narratives and reviews of books by writers or from publishers in our area. The magazine welcomes submissions from all parts of the country.

Robert Day, Rita Dove, Patricia Traxler, Gerald Early, Gloria Vando, Thomas Averill.

Unsolicited Manuscripts Received/Published per Year: 3,000+/50.

Payment: 1 copy.

Reporting Time: 2–6 months.

Copyright held by magazine; reverts to author upon publication.

1965; 3/yr; 500

$15/yr; $6.50/ea; 30%

120 pp; 6 x 9

ISSN: 0147-149X

COUNTRY CONNECTIONS

Britt Leach, Catherine Leach
P.O. Box 6748
Pine Mountain, CA 93222
(805) 242-1047
Fax (805) 242-5704

Poetry, fiction, book reviews, personal essays.*

COUNTRY CONNECTIONS, the magazine of alternatives for those seeking change and a challenge to the status quo. From cultural commentary to urban/rural issues. Poetry, fiction, reviews, humor, essays.

Scott Lannberg, Kres Morsky, Wayne Hogan, Rebecca Bailey.

Unsolicited Manuscripts Received/Published per Year: 500/25.

Reading Period: All year

Payment: $15 poetry/columns, $25 book reviews/stories/features.

Reporting Time: 1 month or less.

Copyright held by magazine; reverts to author upon publication.

1995; 6/yr; 2,000+

$22/yr; $4.50/ea.

52 pp; 8¼ x 10¾

Ad Rates: Classified to full page display from .80 a word to $430/page (one-time rate).

ISSN: 1082-0558

IPD, Desert Moon, Tower Magazine, Ubiquity, Armadillo, Day Break

*We strongly recommend submitters read the magazine first.

CRAB CREEK REVIEW

Linda Clifton; Carol Orlock; Fiction
4462 Whitman Ave., N.
Seattle, WA 98103
(206) 633-1090

Poetry, fiction, translation, essays, graphics/artwork.

". . . well-crafted and perceptive works . . . technically proficient and sensitive poems . . . powerfully expressed images . . . tightly controlled narrative . . . diverse enough to appeal to a variety of literary tastes . . ." Literary Magazine Review. *Not accepting submissions until further notice.*

William Stafford, Rebecca Wells, Mary Kollar, Tim McNulty.

Unsolicited Manuscripts Received/Published per Year: 400/0 until 1994.

Payment: 2 copies.

Reporting Time: 4–8 weeks.

Copyright held by CCR; reverts to author upon publication. Current publication: *Crab Creek Review Anniversary Anthology* paperbound.

1983; Currently available: *10th Anniversary Anthology,* $10.00

Back issues: $3.00; 40%; 50% through distributor Small Changes, 316 Terry N. P. O. Box 19046 Seattle, WA 98109 (206) 382-1980

Anthology 160 pp; 5x8

$120/page (6 x 10); $65/½ page (6 x 5); $35/¼ page (6 x 2½); $20/⅛ page (3 x 2½)

ISSN: 07380-7008

CRAZYHORSE

Zabelle Stodola, Business Manager; Judy Troy, Fiction Editor; Ralph Burns, Poetry Editor; Dennis Vannatta, Criticism Editor.

English Department
University of Arkansas at Little Rock
2801 S. University
Little Rock, AR 72204
(501) 569-3161

Poetry, fiction, criticism, reviews, interviews.

A literary magazine which publishes quality work by established and promising new writers.

Andre Dubus, Bobbie Ann Mason, Raymond Carver, Jorie Graham, John Updike.

Unsolicited Manuscripts Received/Published per year: 20,000/60.

Reading Period: Sept.–Oct. for fiction.

Payment: 2 copies and $10/page.

Annual fiction and poetry awards: $500 each.

Reporting Time: 3 months.

Copyright reverts to author upon request.

1960; 2/yr; 1,000

$10/yr; $5/ea; 25%–40%
135 pp; 6 x 9
Ad Rates: $85/page; $50/½ page
ISSN: 0011-0841

CRAZYQUILT

Jim Kitchen
P.O. Box 632729
San Diego, CA 92163-2729
(619) 688-1023

Poetry, fiction, criticism, essays, plays, photographs, graphics/artwork.

All kinds of poetry; short stories with good character development; nonfiction about writers; literary criticism; one-act plays and black and white photography and art work. Accept translations of poetry. Publish new writers as well as established authors.

Mimi Albert, Ruth Good, Gordon Grice, Louis J. Phillips, Victoria Golden McMains.

Unsolicited Manuscripts Received/Published per Year: 500/70-80.

Payment: 2 copies.

Reporting Time: 10–12 weeks.

Copyright held by Crazyquilt Press; reverts to author upon publication.

1986; 4/yr; 180

$19/yr (ind & inst); $33/2 yrs; $6/ea; 40%

100 pp

ISSN: 0887-5308

CREAM CITY REVIEW

Mark Drechsler and Andrew Rivera, Editors-in-Chief; Brian Jung, Editor
P.O. Box 413
University of Wisconsin-Milwaukee
Milwaukee, WI 53201
(414) 229-4708

Poetry, fiction, reviews, essays, interviews, plays, photographs, graphics/artwork.

The **CREAM CITY REVIEW** is an eclectic literary magazine affiliated with the University of Wisconsin-Milwaukee; it strives to publish the best of traditional and non-traditional work by new and established writers.

Tess Gallagher, Stuart Dybek, Donald Hall, Cathy Song, David Ignatow, Marge Piercy, Maxine Kumin, Amy Clampitt, Derek Walcott, Amiri Baraka, Mary Oliver & William Stafford, Lawrence Ferlinghetti.

Unsolicited Manuscripts Received/Published per Year: 12,000/226+.

Reading Period: year–round, but response time is longer in the summer.

Reporting Time: 2–8 weeks.

Copyright held by the Board of Regents of the University of Wisconsin; reverts to author upon publication.

1975; 2/yr; 2,000
$12/yr, $21/2yr; sample $5.00; 40%
300 pp; 5½ x 8½
Ad Rates: inquire with SASE
ISSN: 1070-0714
DeBoer, Desert Moon, Ingram Marginal

CREATIVE NONFICTION

Lee Gutkind
P.O. Box 81536
Pittsburgh, PA 15217
(412) 422-8404
Fax (412) 422-8405

First journal to focus on emerging genre of creative nonfiction/literary journalism. Publishes essays, memoirs, profiles by new and established writers. Readership spans entire writing community.

Christopher Buckley, Adrienne Rich, Michael Stephens, Charles Simic, Lauren Slater, Louis Simpson.

Unsolicited Manuscripts Received/Published per Year: 300/30.

Reading Period: year–round.

Payment: $5–$10 per published page.

Copyright held by Creative Nonfiction Foundation.

1993; 3/yr; 2,500

$22.50/4 issues, $39/7 issues, $10/ea.

100 pp; 5½ x 8¼

$250/page; $175/½ page; discounts are available for cash, extended runs.

THE CRESCENT REVIEW

J. T. Holland
P.O. Box 15069
Chevy Chase, MD 20825
(301) 986-8788

Short stories.

Approximately 15 to 22 short stories are published per issue, no poems, essays, excerpts from novels, interviews.

Unsolicited Manuscripts Published 3 times per Year: 15–22.

Payment: Two copies & discount on authors' copies.

Reporting Time: 6–10 weeks.

$21/1yr; $39/2yrs; sample; $8 + shipping $1.40

CROSSCURRENTS

Linda Brown Michelson
2200 Glastonbury Rd.
Westlake Village, CA 91361
(818) 991-1694

Fiction, graphics.

CROSSCURRENTS features previously unpublished, literary short fiction. Select pieces are highlighted by photos and line drawings. Two special issues each year.

Alice Adams, Saul Bellow, Josephine Jacobsen, Joyce Carol Oates, John Updike.
Unsolicited Manuscripts Received/Published per Year: 5,000/60.
Reading Period: June–Nov. 30.
Payment: varies, $35 minimum/story.
Reporting Time: 6 weeks.
Copyright reverts to author.
1980; 4/yr; 3,000
$18/yr; $6/ea; 40%
176 pp; 6 x 9
ISSN: 0739-2354
Faxon, Ebsco, Boley, L-S Distributors, Ingram

CUMBERLAND POETRY REVIEW

Editorial Board
P.O. Box 120128 Acklen Station
Nashville, TN 37212
(615) 373-8948

Poetry, criticism, interviews.

CUMBERLAND POETRY REVIEW is devoted to poetry and poetry criticism and presents poets of diverse origins to a widespread audience. We place no restrictions on form, subject, or style. Manuscripts will be selected for publication on the basis of the writer's perspicuous and compelling means of expression. We welcome translations of high quality poetry. Our aim is to support the poet's efforts to keep up the language.

Seamus Heaney, Lewis Horne, Emily Grosholz, Francis Blessington, Mairi McInnes.
Payment: in contributor's copies.
Reporting Time: 6 months.
Copyright held by Poetics, Inc.; reverts to author upon publication.
1981; 2/yr; 500
$14/yr ind, $17/yr inst; $7/ea sample back issue
100 pp; 6 x 9
Ads Rates: Only on exchange basis
ISSN: 0731-7980
Faxon, Swets, Ebsco, McGregor

CUTBANK

Editors
Dept. of English
University of Montana
Missoula, MT 59812
(406) 243-5231

Poetry, fiction, essays, reviews, interviews, photographs, graphics/artwork.

CUTBANK is a literary magazine with a national scope and a regional bias, often featuring new writers alongside more well-known names.

Rick DeMarinis, Amiri Baraka, William Kittredge, Mark Levine, Patricia Goedicke.

Unsolicited Manuscripts Received/ Published per Year: 1,000/50.
Reading Period: Sept.–March
Reporting Time: 8-12 weeks.
1973; 2/yr; 400
$12/yr; $6.95/ea; 40%
128 pp; 5½ x 8½
Ad Rates: $90/page; $45/½ page
ISSN: 0734-9963

D

DAUGHTERS OF NYX: A MAGAZINE OF GODDESS STORIES, MYTHMAKING, AND FAIRY TALES.

Kim Antieau
P.O. Box 1100
Stevenson, WA 98648

Fiction

A woman-centered fiction magazine. Stories that retell myths, fairy tales, and legends from a matristic point of view.

Antiga, Jessica Amanda Salmonson, Patricia Monaghan, Z. Budapest, Susan S. Weed.

Unsolicited Manuscripts Received/Published per year: 200/15

Reading Period: all.

Payment: ½¢/word.

Reporting Time: 1–6 months.

Copyright held by author.

1993; 2/yr; 21,000

$14/4 issues; $4.50/ea.

Ad Rates: $225/full page; $120/½ page; $85/⅓ page; $40/⅙ page; $20/1/12 page, Classifieds 50¢/word.

Book People, Desert Moon, Book Tech, Armadillo, Fine Print.

DECEMBER MAGAZINE

Curt Johnson
Box 302
Highland Park, IL 60035
(708) 940-4122

Fiction, nonfiction, poetry.

A magazine of the arts and opinion.

Unsolicited Manuscripts Received/Published per Year: 150/10.

Payment: 2 copies.

Reporting Time: 4–8 weeks.

1958; irreg.; 1,200

$25/4 issues; $6/ea; 20%

6 x 9

ISSN: 0070-3141

DEFINED PROVIDENCE

Gary J. Whitehead
P.O. Box 16143
Rumford, RI 02916

Poetry, reviews of poetry books, interviews with poets, poetics.

DEFINED PROVIDENCE is a perfect-bound annual poetry magazine devoted to publishing new and unknown poets alongside those poets considered to be among the best in America.

Neal Bowers, David Citino, Peter Cooley, Mark Doty, Gary Fincke, X.J. Kennedy, Robert Morgan, Jack Myers, Vivian Shipley.

Unsolicited Manuscripts Received/Published per Year: 1,500/30-40.

Reading Period: year-round.

Payment: copies.

Reporting Time: 2–8 weeks.

Copyright reverts to author upon publication.

1992; 1/yr; 300

$4/yr, $7/2yrs; $4/ea; 40%

72 pp; digest size

Ad Rates: $100/page (5 x 8); $50/½ page (5 x 4); $10/business card; exchanges

ISSN: 1066-2197

DENVER QUARTERLY

Bin Ramke
University of Denver
Denver, CO 80208
(303) 871-2892

Poetry, fiction, reviews, criticism, essays, interviews.

For almost thirty years the **DENVER QUARTERLY** has been publishing work by distinguished as well as promising new writers. The magazine generally publishes material reflecting on modern culture as it has developed over the past century. It is recognized as one of the premiere literary publications of the Rocky Mountain region.

James Tate, Charles Baxter, Jorie Graham, Ann Lauterbach, Marjorie Perloff.

Unsolicited Manuscripts Received/Published per Year: 4,000/80.

Reading Period: Sept. 15–May 15.

Payment: $5/page for fiction, essays, reviews; $5/page for poetry.

Copyright held by magazine.

1966; 4/yr; 900

$15/yr ind, $18/yr inst; $5/ea; 20%

160 pp; 6 x 9

Ad Rates: $150/page (5 x 8½); $75/½ page (5 x 4½)

ISSN: 0011-8869

DESCANT

Karen Mulhallen
P.O. Box 314
Station P. Toronto, ON M55 258

CANADA
(416) 593-2557

Short fiction, poetry, essays, plays, visual essays.

Literary magazine interested in all the arts and their interrelationship. Aims to publish works of excellence from established and emerging writers and artists. Quality bound.

Leon Rooke, Isabel Allende, Joseph Skvorecky, Michael Ondaatje, Margaret Atwood.

Unsolicited Manuscripts Received/Published per Year: 700/10.

Reading Period: year–round.

Payment: varies.

Copyright: 1st Canadian Rights

1970; 4/yr; 1,200

$20/yr ind; & $31/yr inst.; $10–$13

130 pp; 5¾ x 8¾

$225/page 5¾ x 8¾-one issue; $400-two issues (B&W)

ISSN: 0382-909-X

Canadian Magazine Publishers Association

DJINNI

Kalo Clarke, Kim Alan Pederson
29 Front St. # 2
Marblehead, MA 01945
(617) 639-1889

Essays, poetry, fiction, drawings, B&W photographs.

Literary magazine looking for unique voices and original style.

Unsolicited Manuscripts Received/Published per Year: 350–400/50–60.

Reading Period: June – Dec.

Payment: 1 copy.

Reporting Time: 2–4 months.

Copyright: 1st North American Serieal Rights.

1990; 1/yr

60-100 pp; half sheet

ISSN: 1061-2378

DOG RIVER REVIEW

Laurence F. Hawkins
5976 Billings Road
Parkdale, OR 97041-9610
(503) 352-6494

Poetry, fiction, reviews, short plays, black and white art, essays.

Open to all poetic forms. Favorite poets/writers: Whitman, Jeffers, Thomas, Patchen, Cardenal, Bukowski, Celine, Bowles, Miller Burroughs, Whinkla.

David Chorlton, Richard Kostelanetz, Sheila Nickerson, Nathaniel Tarn.

Unsolicited Manuscripts Received/Published per Year: 400–450/50–60.

Payment: in copies.

Reporting Time: immediately to 4 months.

Copyright reverts to author of publication.

1981; 2/yr; 300

$8.00/yr; $4.00/ea; $3.00/sample; 40%
56-64 pp; 5½ x 8½
ISSN: 0749-260X

DOMINION REVIEW

John McCarey, Managing Editor
c/o English Dept.
BAL 220, Old Dominion Univ.
Norfolk, VA 23529
(804) 683-3991

Poetry, fiction, creative nonfiction, book reviews, interviews, artwork.

DOMINION REVIEW seeks work from both established and previously unpublished writers. Nominal cash prizes awarded to the best work in each genre.

Alberto Rios, Diane Ackerman, W.D. Snodgrass, Brighde Mullins.

Unsolicited Manuscripts Received/ Published per Year: 500-600/ 25-30.

Reading Period: Sept.–Jan.
Payment: 1 copy.
Reporting Time: 1 month.
Copyright held by: author.
1984; 1/yr; 500
$5/yr; $9.50/2yrs; $5/ea; ?%
150 pp; 8½ x 5½
ISSN: 1043-769X

DOUBLETAKE

Robert Coles, Alex Harris
1317 W. Pettigrew St.
Durham, NC 27705
(919) 660-3669
Fax (919) 681-7600

Photography, fiction, essays, poetry.

DOUBLETAKE is a general interest magazine that aims to treat writing and photography with equal weight and consequence.

Nadine Gordiner, James Alan McPherson, Susan Faludi, Thomas Roma, Wendy Ewald.

Unsolicited Manuscripts Received/ Published per Year: 5000/120.

Reading Period: all year
Payment: Good rates.
Reporting Time: 2 months.
Copyright held by magazine; reverts to author upon publication.
1995; 4/yr; 20,000
$24/yr; $10/ea.
144 pp; 9 x 11
Ad Rates: Call for current rates (919) 681-2596.
ISSN: 1080-7241
Eastern News

THE DRAMA REVIEW

Richard Schechner, Editor
MIT Press Journals
55 Hayward St.
Cambridge, MA 02142
(617) 253-2866
Editorial office:
721 Broadway #626
New York, NY 10003
Fax (212) 995-4060

TDR is a quarterly journal of performance with a strong intercultural, intergeneric, and interdisciplinary focus. We consider everything from wrestling to ritual, from Peter Brook's Mahabharata to what is going on at "Downtown Beirut." **TDR** borrows from the fields of anthropology, performance theory, popular culture, ethology, psychology, and politics. We combine scholarship and journalism in the form of essays, interviews, letters and editorials.

Payment: $50–250.

Copyright held by MIT Press.

1955; 4/yr; 6,000

$20/yr students, $36/yr ind, $95/yr inst; $9/ea
Outside USA add $16 p&h
Canada: add 7% GST

160 pp; 7 x 10

ISSN: 1054-2043

E

EARTH'S DAUGHTERS: A Feminist Arts Periodical

Kastle Brill, Joan Ford, Pat Colvard, Bonnie Johnson, Joyce Kessel, Ryki Zuckerman

Box 41

Central Park Stn

Buffalo, NY 14215

Poetry, fiction, plays, photographs, graphics/artwork.

EARTH'S DAUGHTERS is a feminist literary and art periodical published in Buffalo, New York. We believe ourselves to be the oldest feminist arts periodical extant, having published our first issue in February, 1971. Our focus is the experience and creative expression of women.

Jimmie Canfield, Lyn Lifshin, Marge Piercy, Kathryn Machan Aal, Susan Fantl Spivack.

Unsolicited Manuscripts Received/Published per Year: 1,000–1,500/200+.

Payment: 2 copies.

Reporting Time: 3 months.

Copyright held by magazine; reverts to author upon publication.

1971; 3/yr; 1,000

$14/yr ind, $22/yr inst; $5/ea; 30%

Sample copy: $5

60 pp; 6 x 9

No ads

ISSN: 0163-0989

Ebsco, Faxon, Burroughs

1812

Dan Schwartz, Richard Lywch, Joe Todaro

Box 1812

Amherst, NY 14226-7812

Fiction, poetry, art.

The war along the Niagara.

Unsolicited Manuscripts Received/

Published per Year: 400/25.
Payment: various/arranged.
Reporting Time: 2 months.
Copyright.
1995; 1/yr; 1,000+
100+ pp; 4½ x 11
Ad Rates: arranged

1991; 4/yr; 5,200
$16/yr; $5.50/ea
56–60 pp; 8½ x 11
Ad Rates: inquire for rate sheet.
ISSN: 1054-3376
Ingram, DeBoer

ELF: Eclectic Literary Forum
C. K. Erbes
P.O. Box 392
Tonawanda, NY 14150
(716) 693-7006
Poetry, short fiction, essays on literary themes, critical reviews, special features.
Professionally printed quarterly, publishing well-crafted contemporary works in an uncluttered, readable format; continuing Native American folklore. ". . . a good choice for any literatures collection,"—Library Journal.
Gwendolyn Brooks, William Stafford, Joyce Carol Oates, Nikki Giovanni, William Greenway, John Dickson, Daniel Berrigan, John Haines, Dana Gioia, Siv Cedering, David Ignatola.
Unsolicited Manuscripts Received/ Published per Year: 3,000+/ 100–125.
Reading Period: year–round.
Payment: 1 copy.
Reporting Time: 4–6 weeks.
Copyright: ELF Associates, Inc.

EMERGENCE
Michele Friske, Donna Maria Chappell
P.O. Box 1615
Bridgeview, IL 60455
(708) 423-6681
Short fiction and poetry.
EMERGENCE is a literary journal by, for, and about women. A strong, active voice is the most important quality we seek.
Cris Burks, Sally Elizabeth Colford, Zoe Keithley, Betty Shiflett, Lynda Rutledge Stephenson.
Unsolicited Manuscripts Received/ Published per Year: 1,000/25.
Reading Period: June–August.
Payment: 2 copies.
Reporting Time: 3 months.
Copyright reverts to author.
1993; 1/yr; 1,000
$6/yr; $8/ea; 40%
136 pp; 7 x 10
Ad rates: $100/full page
ISBN: 0-9635187-1-2
Fine Print Distributors

THE EMRYS JOURNAL

Jeanine Halva-Neubauer
P.O. Box 8813
Greenville, SC 29604
(803) 294-2066

Poetry, fiction, essays.

Our journal is interested in publishing the work of new writers, especially that of women and other minorities. We are interested in maintaining a high literary standard.

Maxine Kumin, Carole Oles, Linda Paston, Amy Clampitt, Pattiann Rogers.

Unsolicited Manuscripts Received/Published per Year: 1,000/18.

Payment: in copies.

Reporting Time: 6 weeks.

Copyright held by The Emrys Foundation.

1984; 1/yr; 400

$10/ea; 40%

No ads

EPOCH

Michael Koch
251 Goldwin Smith Hall
Cornell University
Ithaca, NY 14853
(607) 255-3385

Poetry, fiction.

EPOCH is primarily a journal of fiction, poetry and essays. Publishes work by a wide range of writers, some established, some just beginning their careers.

Harriet Doerr, Rick DeMarinis, Stuart Dybek, Thylias Moss, Lee K. Abbott, Alice Fulton.

Reading Period: Sept. 15–April 15.

Payment: $5/magazine page (prose); 50¢/line (poetry). These are minimum payments. We pay more when we have the funds.

Reporting Time: 1 month.

Copyright held by Cornell University; reverts to author upon publication.

1947; 3/yr; 1,000

$11/yr; $5/ea

128 pp; 6 x 9

Ad Rates: $180/page (5 x 8); $100/½ page (3 x 8)

ISSN: 0145-1391

DeBoer

EUROPE PLURILINGUE/PLURILINGUAL EUROPE

Françoise Wuilmart, Editor-in-chief; Nadine Dormoy, Director of Publication; Albert Russo, Assistant Editor.

Nadine Dormoy
44 rue Perronet
92200 Neuilly, FRANCE
(331) 46.24.12.76

Articles, essays, interviews, poetry and short prose, pluridisciplinary.

All material should involve any of the 15 nations of the European union, their culture and languages and must be written in any of its 12 official languages, i.e.: English, French, German, Spanish, Italian, Portuguese, Danish, Dutch, Greek, Gaelic, Swedish, Finnish—High specialization in every field required.

George Steiner, Umberto Eco, Hugo Claus, Jacques Darras, Renzo Titone, Paolo Fabbri, Eduardo Lourenco, Theodore Zeldin, Harald Weinrich, Hilde Domin.

Unsolicited Manuscripts Received/ Published per Year: dozens/20.

Payment: 2 copies of the issue.

Reporting Time: 2–3 months—send 3 IRC (international reply coupons) with mss.

Copyright is property of the review, but may be negotiated with author.

1991; 8 as of 1995; 1,000

$30/yr; $15/ea; published twice a year. 15%; postage included, checks to be made out and sent to: Liliane Lazar, 37 Hill Lane, Roslyn Heights, NY 11517, but mss *must* be sent to Nadine Dormoy—44 rue Perronet—92200 Neuilly, FRANCE.

150+ pp; 15cm x 20cm.

Ad Rates: upon request

ISSN: 1161-8884

THE EVERGREEN CHRONICLES

Jim Berg, Senior Editor; Susan Raffo, Managing Editor

P.O. Box 8939

Minneapolis, MN 55408

Essays, short fiction, plays, poetry, visual art.

A journal of gay and lesbian arts and cultures.

Lev Raphael, Ruthann Robson, Terri Jewell, Rane Arroyo.

Unsolicited Manuscripts Received/ Published per Year: 500/50.

Payment: $50 and copy.

Reporting Time: 3 months.

Copyright: First run rights only.

1985; 3/yr; 2,000

$20/yr; $7.95/ea

80–100 pp; 6¾ x 8¾

Ad Rates: Write for rates.

ISSN: 1043-3333

Fine Print, Inland

EXCURSUS LITERARY ARTS JOURNAL

Giancarlo Malchiodi and a revolving collective

P.O. Box 1056

Knickerbocker Station

New York, NY 10002

Poetry, fiction, creative nonfiction.

Eclectic. Quality work in varied styles.

First issue Fall 1995; contributors include Doug Dorph, Eve Packer, Hilary Tham, Vincent Young.

Unsolicited Manuscripts Received/Published per Year: est. 800/80.

Reading Period: Sept.–June.

Payment: in copies.

Copyright held: magazine has first time rights, then reverts.

1995; 1/yr; 1,000–1,200

$10.00/2 yrs; $7.50/ea

88-96 pp; 8½ x 11

EXHIBITION

Brett Alexander, Editor
261 Madison Ave. S.
Bainbridge Island, WA 98110
(206) 842-7901

Short fiction, essays, poetry, artwork.

Seek work which is innovative and challenging from Pacific Northwesterners.

Unsolicited Manuscripts Received/Published per Year: 600/45+.

Payment: 2 copies.

2/yr; 1,000

$5/ea

35 pp; 8½ x 11

Ad Rates: available on request.

EXQUISITE CORPSE

Andrei Codrescu
P.O. Box 25051
Baton Rouge, LA 70894

Poetry, criticism, essays, reviews, translation, photographs, graphics/artwork, polemics, letters, reports from many countries.

A review of books and ideas. We are a print cafe, hopeful that vigorous dialogue on general culture is still possible in Mandarin US. We encourage honesty, combativeness and openness. We have published wide-ranging polemics, as well as essays on various matters of literary interest. Our foreign bureaus report on goings-on in several European and Asian cities. We also publish translations, and reprint important but overlooked texts. Our contributors are both famous and unknown.

Lawrence Ferlinghetti, Hayden Carruth, Maggie Estep, James Laughlin, Laura Rosenthal.

Unsolicited Manuscripts Received/Published per Year: 10,000/500.

Payment: some payment to contributors.

Reporting Time: 1 month.

Copyright held by authors.

1983; 6/yr; 5,500

$20/yr; $5/ea

28 pp; 6 x 15½

ISSN: 0740-7815

Inland Fine Print

EYEBALL

Jabari Asim, Andrea M. Wren
P.O. Box 8135
St. Louis, MO 63108
(314) 947-6313

Poetry, fiction, essays, reviews, interviews, art.

EYEBALL exists to defend and extend the quest of literature to function as a unifying force in a world challenged by disorder and division.

Gwendolyn Brooks, Dennis Brutus, Paul Beatty, Kevin Powell.

Unsolicited Manuscripts Received/ Published per Year: 50-100/20+.

Payment: 2 copies.

Reporting Time: within 1 year.

Copyright reverts to author.

1992; 2/yr; 2,000

$7/yr; $3.50/ea

48 pp; 13 x 10¾

Ad Rates: negotiable

ISSN: 1063-9675

F

F MAGAZINE

John Schultz
1405 West Belle Plaine
Chicago, IL 60613
(312) 281-7642

Fiction, criticism, essays, reviews, translations, interviews.

F MAGAZINE has the contemporary purpose of being devoted to the publication of fiction that is part of a literary movement toward a synthesis of fiction techniques, emphasizing story—content, imagery, character, voice, style, a rich exploration of points of view, forms, dimensions of time, dramatic and self relationships. Award winning fiction.

Andrew Allegretti, Betty Shiflett, Beverlye Brown, Gary Johnson, Shawn Shiflett, John Schultz, Charles Johnson, Harry Mark Petrakis, Cyrus Colter, Paul Carter Harrison.

Reading Period: Sept. 1–May 15.
Payment: varies, from $5/page.
Reporting Time: 4 months.
Copyright held by magazine; reverts to author upon publication.
2/yr; 1,500
$6.95/ea; 40%
210 pp; 6 x 9
Ad Rates: Contact CLMP for information.
ISBN: 0-936959-00-2
Ingram, DeBoer

FARMER'S MARKET

Patrick Parks, Joanne Lowery, Rachael Tecza
ECC, 1700 Spartan Drive
Elgin, IL 60123-7193

Poetry, fiction, essays, translation, graphics.

A national, award-winning magazine, publishing quality literary work reflective of Midwestern literary traditions and consciousness.

Philip Dacey, Mark Jacobs, Elizabeth Klein, John Knoepfle, Elisabeth Stevens, Elaine Fowler Palencia.

Unsolicited Manuscripts Received/ Published per Year: 2,000/40.

Payment: 2 copies and author's discount.

Reporting Time: 8–12 weeks.

Copyright held by author.

1982; 2/yr; 500

$10/yr; $6/ea; 40%

100-200 pp; 5½ x 8½

No ads

ISSN: 0748-6022

FAULTLINE

Alyn Warren, Executive Editor; Alice Verbeck, Davi Loren, Managing Editors

(714) 824-6547

Poetry, fiction, creative nonfiction and art.

A literary journal based at UC Irvine featuring the work of established and emerging writers and artists.

James D. Houston, Stuart Dybek, Mitsuye Yamada, Peter Bacho, Heather McHugh.

Unsolicited Manuscripts Received/ Published per year: 1400/64.

Reading Period: Sept.-May.

Payment: Two copies.

Copyright held by author.

1992; 2/yr; 375

$15/yr; $7.50/ea.; 40%

104 pp; 8½ x 7

$160/page (6 x 7¼); $90/½ page (6 x 3¼); $60/¼ page (2⅞ x 3½), $40/business card (2⅞ x 1¾).

ISSN: 1076-0776

Avaialable by subscription only.

FELL SWOOP

X.J. Dailey

3003 Ponce De Leon St.

New Orleans, LA 70119

(504) 943-5198

Poetry, fiction, essay, drama, art, photographs.

The All Bohemian Revue, **FELL SWOOP** is a guerilla/gorilla venture exploring the edge of 'acceptability' in contemporary writing. We like a good laugh at anyone's expense, especially our own.

Richard Martin, Elizabeth Thomas, Andrei Codrescu, Ed Dorn, Clara Talley-Vincent, R. Speck.

Unsolicited Manuscripts Received/ Published per Year: 1,000/25.

Reading Period: year–round.

Payment: in copies.

Reporting Time: immediately.

Copyright reverts to author upon publication.
1983; 3/yr; 1,000
$8/yr; $3/ea
pp vary; 8½ x 11
ISSN: 1040-5607
200 pp; 9 x 6
Ad Rates: negotiable
ISSN: 74470 80497
Ingram, DeBoer

FICTION

Mark Mirsky, Editor; Caryn Stabinsky, Managing Editor
c/o Dept. of English
The City College
138th & Convent Ave.
New York, NY 10031
(212) 650-6319

Prose fiction, translations.

FICTION represents no particular school of fiction other than the inventive and the innovative. We publish the difficult, the experimental, the unusual, without excluding the well known.

Amdahl, Brodkey, Oates, Minot, Musil, Macauley, Mirsky, Cherry.

Unsolicited Manuscripts Received/ Published per Year: 2,000–3,000/20–30.
Reading Period: Oct.–May.
Payment: $25 and copies.
Reporting Time: 3–6 months.
Copyright: Fiction, Inc. Reverts to author on request.
1972; 2/yr; 3,000
$20/3 yrs; $6.95/ea; 50%

FICTION INTERNATIONAL

Harold Jaffe
Department of English
San Diego State University
San Diego, CA 92182
(619) 594-5469

Fiction, reviews, essays, visuals.

FICTION INTERNATIONAL has one thematic issue per year. Current theme is "pain." Favor innovative writing.
Note: Special issues advertised in *Poets & Writers* or *American Book Review*.

Robert Coover, Claribel Alegria, Gerald Vizenor, Michel Serres, Marianne Hauser, Pierre Guyotat, Margaret Randall, Roque Dalton.

Unsolicited Manuscripts Received/ Published per Year: 500-700/20-30.
Reading Period: Sept.–Dec. 15.
Payment: copies.
Reporting Time: 1–3 months.
$12/yr ind, $24/yr inst; $6/ea; 40%
Fine Print, Blackwell North American, Faxon, Baker & Taylor

THE FIDDLEHEAD

Don McKay
Campus House, UNB P.O. Box 4400
Fredericton, New Brunswick, E3B5A3
CANADA
(506) 453-3501

Short fiction, poetry, book reviews (Canadian books only).

Canada's oldest continuing literary magazine, with a world-wide circulation. Any good writing, from any place, will be welcome here.

Christine Barton, Jim Meirose, Ruth Warat.

Unsolicited Manuscripts Received/ Published per Year: 2,000/20–25. Include SASE with International coupons or *Canadian stamps*.

Payment: $10/page

Reporting Time: 4–6 months.

Copyright: First serial rights only—copyright remains with author.

1945; 4/yr; 800

$20/yr; $8/ea; 30%

120–128 pp; 6 x 9

Ad Rates: $100/page

ISBN: 015-0630

Canadian Magazine Publishers Association

FIELD

Stuart Friebert, David Young
Rice Hall
Oberlin College
Oberlin, OH 44074
(216) 775-8408

Poetry, criticism, essays, reviews, translation.

We look for the best in contemporary poetry, poetics and translations and emphasize essays by poets themselves on the craft.

Marianne Boruch, Margaret Atwood, Karl Krolow, Beckian Fritz Goldberg, Charles Simic, James Tate, Shirley Kaufman, Miroslav Holub.

Unsolicited Manuscripts Received/ Published per Year: 25,000/100.

Reading Period: year–round.

Payment: $20–30/page.

Reporting Time: 2 weeks.

Copyright held by Oberlin College; reverts to author upon publication.

1969; 2/yr; 2,500

$14/yr, $24/2 yrs; $6/ea; 20–30%

100 pp; 5½ x 8½

FINE MADNESS

Sean Bentley, Louis Bergsagel, Christine Deavel, John Malek, John Marshall
P.O. Box 31138
Seattle, WA 98103-1138

Poetry, fiction.

We look for poetry that shows wit, imagination, love of language, technical skill and individual style.

Pattiann Rogers, Peter Wild, Caroline Knox, Mark Svenvold, Tess Gallagher, Albert Goldbarth.

Unsolicited Manuscripts Received/ Published per Year: 1,500/50.

Payment: copies.

Reporting Time: 3 months.

Copyright held by magazine; reverts to author upon publication.

1980 3 every 2 years; 1,000

$9/yr; $5/ea

80 pp; 5½ x 8

ISSN: 0737-4704

Small Changes, Ubiquity, Armadillo, Fine Print

FIRST INTENSITY

Lee Chapman

P.O. Box 140713

Staten Island, NY 10314-0713

Poetry, short fiction.

Robert Kelly, Diane di Prima, Barry Gifford, Kenneth Irby, Lucia Berlin.

Unsolicited Manuscripts Received/ Published per Year: 200/60.

Reading Period: year-round.

Payment: 2 copies.

Reporting Time: 6–8 weeks.

Copyright held by First Intensity, reverts to authors upon publication.

1993; 2/yr; 250

$17/yr, $9/ea; 40%

130 pp; 6 x 9

Small Press Distribution

Bernard DeBoer

FISH STORIES

Amy G. Davis, Editor in Chief

5412 N. Clark, South Suite

Chicago, IL 60640

(312) 334-6990

Fax (312) 334-6673

Contemporary American, short stories, short-shorts, and poetry.

Diverse collection of approximately thirty-five pieces by well-known writers and poets side-by-side with exciting work by at least three writers never before published.

Robert Olen Butler, Charles Baxter, Susan Power, Lan Samantha Chang, Edward Falco

Unsolicited Manuscripts Received/Published per year: 500/30.

Reading Period: Oct. 1-Feb. 1.

Payment: 2 copies (Best Fiction Contest pays $50–$200)

Reporting Time: 2–6 months.

Copyright held by authors.

1995; 1/yr; 1,000

$10.95/ea.; 40%

224 pp; 5⅜ x 8½

$110/page; $65/½ page

ISSN: 1082-1465

B. DeBoer

FIVE FINGERS REVIEW

John High, Aleka Chase, Thoreau Lovell
P.O. Box 15426
San Francisco, CA 94115

Poetry, fiction, essays.

The **FIVE FINGERS REVIEW** seeks to publish fresh, innovative writing and artwork that is not necessarily defined by the currently "correct" aesthetic or ideology. **FIVE FINGERS REVIEW** welcomes work that crosses or falls between genres. In addition to new fiction and poetry, **FIVE FINGERS REVIEW** presents essays, interviews, and translations. Each issue explores a theme; recent issues have focused on spirituality and the avant–garde, the new lyric and shifting narrative, and new writing from Moscow to San Francisco.

Francisco Alarcon, C. D. Wright, Norman Fischer, Mikhail Epshtein, Leslie Scalapino, Lyn Hejinian, David Levi–Strauss, Thaisa Frank, Keith Waldrop, Rosmarie Waldrop, Peter Gizzi, Aleksei Parschikov.

Unsolicited Manuscripts Received/Published per Year: 1,000/75.

Payment: in copies.

Reporting Time: 3 months.

Copyright held by magazine; reverts to author upon publication.

1984; 2/yr; 1,000–1,500

$15/yr, $28/2yrs; $12 inst; $9/ea; 40%

150–250 pp; 6 x 9

Ad Rates: $150/page (4½ x 7½); $100/½ page (4½ x 3½ or 2 x 7½); $75/¼ page (2 x 3½)

BookPeople, Inland, SPD, L-S Distributors, Spectacular Diseases (UK)

THE FLINT HILLS REVIEW

Mary Jane Ryals, Editor-in-Chief
Michael Trammell, Associate Editor
Box 4019
Emporia State Univ.
Emporia, KS 66801
(316) 341-5545

A semi-annual literary magazine that publishes the best in poetry, fiction, and nonfiction.

Paul Zimmer, Pat MacEnulty, Gwendolyn Brooks.

Reading Time: all year-round.

Payment: in copies.

Reporting Time: 6–12 weeks.

1996; 2/yr; 500

$8/yr; $4.00/ea.

48 pp; 8 x 12

FLOATING ISLAND

Michael Sykes
P.O. Box 341
Cedarville, CA 96104

(916) 279-2337

Poetry fiction, photography in folio format, graphics/artwork.

Expansive, eclectic, very wide-ranging with center on West coast of North America—special interest in photography and graphic arts, lyric poetry and experimental prose. Volumes I-IV, First Series is now complete. Nó longer accepting unsolicited mss. No date set for the Second Series.

Diane di Prima, Gary Snyder, Michael McClure, Robert Bly, Christina Zawadiwsky, Frank Stewart, Lawrence Ferlinghetti, Joanne Kyger, Sam Hamill.

Unsolicited Manuscripts Received/Published per Year: 100/0.

Payment: in copies.

Reporting Time: 4 weeks.

Copyright held by publisher; reverts to author upon publication.

1976; irreg.; 2,000

All issues $15/ea; 40% 5 or more copies, 20% 1–4 copies

160 pp; 8½ x 11

ISSN: 0147-1686

SPD, BookPeople

THE FLORIDA REVIEW

Russell Kesler
English Department
University of Central Florida
Orlando, FL 32816
(407) 823-2038

Poetry, fiction, essays, reviews.

We publish stories with heart that aren't afraid to take risks. Experimental fiction is welcome, so long as it doesn't make us feel stupid. We look for clear, strong poems filled with real things, real people, real emotions, poems that might conceivably advance our knowledge of the human heart.

Stephen Dixon, Jane Ruiter, Liz Rosenberg, Karen Fish, Michael Martone.

Unsolicited Manuscripts Received/Published per Year: 2,500/40.

Reading Period: year–round.

Payment: 3 copies and small honorarium.

Reporting Time: 2–3 months.

Copyright held by University of Central Florida; reverts to author upon publication.

1972; 2/yr; 1,000

$7/yr ind, $11/2 yrs ind, $9/yr inst, $13/2 yrs inst; $4.50/ea; 40%

128 pp; 5½ x 8½

Ad Rates: exchange ads only

ISSN: 0742-2466

Fine Print

FLYWAY (formerly POET AND CRITIC)

Stephen Pett
203 Ross Hall

Iowa State University
Ames, IA 50011
(515) 294-2180

Poetry, fiction, literary nonfiction, reviews.

FLYWAY publishes poems, stories, excerpts from novels, personal essays, reviews (3,000 words or less), and photographs. All creative work will be accompanied by brief commentary from its author. Commentary will be requested of those whose work is accepted.

We try to be receptive to all work, asking only that it have ambition and display a sense of craft.

Michael Martone, Jane Smiley, Neal Bowers, Mary Swander, Ray Young Bear, Fern Kupfer, and Joe Geha.

Reading Period: Sept.–May.

Payment: 1 copy.

Reporting Time: 3 days–2 months.

Copyright held by Iowa State University; reverts to author upon publication.

1995–96; 3/yr; 1,000

$18/yr ind, $18/yr inst; $8/ea; 40%

96 pp; 6 x 9

Ad Rates: upon request; exchanges with other magazines

ISSN: 0032-1958

FOLIO

Department of Literature
American University
Washington, DC 20016
(202) 885-2973

Poetry, fiction, reviews, translations, black & white art & photography.

FOLIO prints quality fiction and poetry by established writers as well as those just starting out. We like to comment on submissions when time permits. Prose limit: 4,500 words. SASE required.

Henry Taylor, Linda Pastan, William Stafford, Jean Valentine, Simon Perchik, Kermit Moyer, Myra Sklarew.

Unsolicited Manuscripts Received/Published per Year: 1,300/6 stories/prose; 30 poems.

Reading Period: Aug.–April.

Payment: prizes of up to $75 awarded for best fiction and poem.

Copyright reverts to author upon publication.

1984; 2/yr; 400

$10/yr; $5/ea; 30%

70 pp; 6 x 9

DeBoer

FOOTWORK: The Paterson Literary Review (PLR)

Maria Mazziotti Gillan
Cultural Affairs Department

Passaic County Community College
1 College Boulevard
Paterson, NJ 07505-1179
(201) 684-6555

Poetry, fiction, review, graphics/artwork.

PLR is a high quality literary quarterly.

Laura Boss, William Stafford, Marge Piercy, David Ray.

Unsolicited Manuscripts Received/Published per Year: 10,000/200.

Payment: in copies.

Reading Period: Jan.–Mar.

Reporting Time: 6 months.

Copyright held by Passaic County College; reverts to author upon publication.

1979; 1/yr; 1,000

$10/yr ind, $12/yr inst; $10/ea; 40%

290 pp; 8½ x 11, perfect-bound

Ad Rates: $300/page (8½ x 11); $150/½ page (8½ x 5); $100/¼ page (4 x 2½)

FORKROADS: A Journal of Ethnic American Writing

David Kherdian
Box 159
Spencertown, NY 12165

Poems, stories, plays, profiles, studies, memoirs by and reviews of ethnic American writers.

The first multi-ethnic magazine to publish all American writers whose work is informed—at least in part—by another culture.

Luis J. Rodriguez, Michael Stephens, Lawson Fusao Inada, Piri Thomas, Norbert Krapf.

Payment: $50.00 poems & reviews; $200.00 stories, interviews. Rates negotiable.

Reporting Time: 6 weeks generally.

Copyright held by Forkroads Publishing Company.

1995; 4/yr; 5,000

$20/yr ind; $6/ea; 55%

96–122 pp; 7⅝ x 9¼

Ad Rates: Contact J.V. Johnson & Assoc., PO Box 137, Laurens, NY 13796.

THE FORMALIST

William Baer
320 Hunter Drive
Evansville, IN 47711

Contemporary metrical poetry and translations.

Devoted entirely to formal, metrical verse and publishing contemporary poetry and translations that participate in the great tradition of metrical poetry from Chaucer to Wilbur.

Howard Nemerov, Richard Wilbur, Mona Van Duyn, Derek Walcott,

Maxine Kumin, John Updike.
Unsolicited Manuscripts Received/Published per Year: 5,000+/160+.
Reading Period: year–round.
Payment: 2 copies.
Reporting Time: within 2 months.
Copyright: yes.
1990; 2/yr; growing
$12/yr, $22/2 yrs; $6.50/ea; contact publisher
128pp; 6 x 9
No advertising
ISSN: 1046-7874

THE FOUR DIRECTIONS

Joanna and William Meyer
P.O. Box 729
Tellico Plains, TN 37385
(615) 524-8612
American Indian authors, poets and writers.
To provide a forum for American Indian writers; to provide a positive publishing experience; to assist in development of Indian writers and develop a market and readership for Native American Writers.
Raven Hail, E. James Hillsburg, Whitefeather.
Unsolicited Manuscripts Received/Published per Year: Numerous/100+.
Payment: 2 cents/word for stories and articles; $10/full page poem; $5/half page poem.
Reporting Time: 4–6 weeks.
Copyright: first serial rights.
1992; 4/yr
$21/yr; $6/ea; 40%
64 pp; 8 ½ x 11
Ad Rates: $145/page; $100/½ page; $70/¼ page; inside covers: $170 back, $195 front

FRANK: An International Journal of Contemporary Writing and Art

David Applefield, Editor/Publisher
432 rue Edouard Vaillant
93100 Montreuil
FRANCE
(331) 48.59.66.58
Fax (331) 48.59.66.68
E-mail: david@paris-anglo.com
Web-Site: www.paris-anglo.com
Poetry, fiction, translations, interviews, graphics/artwork, essays, photographs.
FRANK is a highly eclectic journal open to both established and emerging talent which emphasizes internationalism. The journal encourages both literary and visual work that takes risks but does not ignore the value of intellectual traditions. Contemporary Chinese, Congolese, Turkish, Nordic, Philippino, Belgian and Pakistani writing.
Vaclav Havel, Samuel Beckett, Italo Calvino, James Tate, Allen

Ginsberg, Paul Bowles, Robert Coover, Raymond Carver, Rita Dove, Stephen Dixon, Sony Labou Tansi, Frederick Barthelme, Phillip Glass.
Unsolicited Manuscripts Received/ Published per Year: 1,000/30.
Payment: $5/page plus two copies.
Copyright held by author.
1983; 2/yr; 4,000
$30/4 issues ind, $60/4 issues inst; $9.95/ea; 33%–40%
224 pp; 5½ x 8½
Ad Rates: $1,000/page (5 x 8); $500/½ page (4½ x 3½); $300/¼ page (2½ x 3½)
ISSN: 0738-9299; ISBN: 2-908171-09-0

FREE FOCUS
Patricia D. Coscia
JAF Station
Box 7415
New York, NY 10116-4630
Women's poetry.
FREE FOCUS is a small-press magazine which focuses on the educated women of today and needs stories and poems. The poems can be as long as 2 pages or as short as 3 lines. No X-rated material. Poems should be single-spaced on individual sheets.
Patricia D. Coscia, Ed Janz.
Unsolicited Manuscripts Received/ Published per Year: 500/200.
Payment: 1 copy.
Reporting Time: 6 months.
Copyright held by editor.
1985; 2/yr; 500
$4/yr; $2/ea
20 pp; 8 x 14
Ad Rates: $1/column; $3/page
ISSN: 0447-5667

FREE LUNCH
Ron Offen
P.O. Box 7647
Laguna Niguel, CA 92607-7647
Poetry.
Unsolicited Manuscripts Received/ Published per Year: 2,500/75.
Reading Period: Sept. 2–May 31.
Copyright held by Free Lunch Arts Alliance.
1989; irregular; 1,200
Magazine is free to all serious poets living in the U.S. Send SASE for details. Will not consider more than 3 poems per submission.
Others: $12/yr; $5/ea Foreign $15/yr, $7/ea
32 pp; 5½ x 8½
Ad Rates: $100/page (4 x 8); $60/½ page (4 x 4); $35/¼ page (2 x 2)

FUEL MAGAZINE

Ms. Andy Lowry
P.O. Box 146640
Chicago, IL 60614
(312) 395-1706

Fiction, art & poetry.

FUEL is an eclectic home for risk takers and truth seekers. Academics beware—we want to be a zine, not a literary journal.

Nicole Panter, Bill Shields, Denise Dee, Larry Oberc, Dan Nielson.

Unsolicited Manuscripts Received/ Published per Year: 1,500/ 150–200.

Payment: 1 copy.

Reading Period: year round, varies as each issue fills.

Reporting Time: 2–4 weeks.

Copyright held by author.

1992; 4/yr; 3000

$10/4 copies; $3/ea

40 pp; 8½ x 5½

Ad Rates: vary, generally trade w/other publications.

Fine Print, Sugar Distribution

FURIOUS FICTIONS

Joseph Lerner
P.O. Box 423665
San Francisco, CA 94102
(415) 431-0461

"Flash" or short-short fiction.

FURIOUS FICTIONS is the leading literary journal devoted to showcasing the best new short-short or "flash" fiction in the U.S. today.

Molly Giles, Diane Glancy, Tom Whaler, Jacques Servin.

Unsolicited Manuscripts Received/ Published per Year: 6,000/60.

Reading Period: year–round.

Payment: 1 year subscription.

Reporting Time: 2 weeks–2 months.

Copyright: First serial rights.

1992; 3/yr; 1,500

$12/yr; $3.95/ea

36 pp; 8½ x 11

ISSN: 1065-7983

Ubiquity, Desert Moon, Fine Print

G

THE GALLEY SAIL REVIEW

Stanley McNail
1630 University Ave., #42
Berkeley, CA 94703
(415) 486-0187

Poetry, reviews.

GSR seeks excellence in contemporary poetry, without regard for schools, cliques, or "movements." It values sincerity and honors craftsmanship. It tries to encourage poetry that speaks to the human condition in this modern world, and to develop a wider appreciation of poetry as an essential art in society.

Martin Robbins, Michael Culross, Laurel Ann Bogen, Harold Witt, Carol Hamilton.

Payment: in copies.

Copyright held by magazine; reverts to author upon publication.

1958; 3/yr; 400

$8/yr ind, $15/2 yrs ind, $15/2 yrs inst; $3/ea; 40%

40 pp; 8½ x 5½

ISSN: 0016-4100

GAS: HIGH OCTANE POETRY

Kevin Opstedal & Tom Clark
3164 Emerson
Palo Alto, CA 94306
(415) 493-5903

Poetry.

GAS prints only premium high-octane poetry guaranteed to rid you of those psychic knocks & pings. Free cranial liposuction with fill-up.

Ed Sanders, Alice Notley, Bukowski, Dorn, Eileen Myles.

Payment: copies.

Reporting Time: 1–2 weeks.

Copyright reverts to individual authors upon publication.

1990; irregular; 100
$30/sub; $10/ea; 40%
130 pp; 9 x 7½
Ad Rates: $100/page; $50/½ page; $25/¼ page
ISSN: 1058-532X
BookPeople, Last Gasp

A GATHERING OF THE TRIBES

Steve Cannon, Angelina Lukacin, William Maxwell, Sheila Alsen, Martha Cinader
P.O. Box 20693
Tompkins Square
New York, NY 10009
Poetry, fiction, essays, reviews, interviews, graphics/artwork, photographs.
TRIBES is a multicultural magazine of writing on the arts which reflects the richness and diversity of America's cultural heritage. Also has publishing co. "FLY BY NIGHT PRESS."
Jessica Hagedorn, Ishmael Reed, Hernandez Cruz, Jayne Cortez, Al Young.
Payment: none.
Copyright held by authors.
1991; 2/yr; 3,000
$17.50/yr ind, $30/yr inst; $10/ea; 40%
80-100 pp; 8½ x 11
Ad Rates: $500/page (6¼ x 8½); $250/½ page (6¼ x 4¼)
ISSN: 1058-9112

THE GENERALIST PAPERS

Harry Smith
69 Joralemon St.
Brooklyn, NY 11201-4003
(718) 834-1212
Essays on literature, journalism and fine printing.
A lively newsletter-type format, its topics range from early American journalism to Deconstruction, often offering iconoclastic perspectives.
Richard Nason, Marshall Brooks, Alan Britt, Tristram Smith and Duane Locke.
Unsolicited Manuscripts Received/Published per year: 500/12.
Reading Period: All.
Payment: $50 to $200.
Reporting Time: one month.
Copyright held by The Generalist Association, Inc.
1989; 6 issues; 2,500
$15/yr
16 pp, 8½ x 11
Does not accept ads.
ISSN 1048-0870

GEORGETOWN REVIEW

John Fulmer
P.O. Box 6309
Southern Station
Hattiesburg, MS 39406
(601) 583-6940
Fiction and Poetry.

A literary review looking to publish honest, quality fiction and poetry.

Unsolicited Manuscripts Received/ Published per Year: 1,000–1,500/ 40–60.

Reading Period: Sept. 1–May 1.

Payment: 2 copies.

Reporting Time: 2–4 months.

Copyright reverts to author upon publication.

1993; 1/yr; 750

$10/yr; $5/ea; 55%

112 pp; 5¼ x 8¼

Ad Rates: $75/page; $32.50/½ page.

Fine Print, DeBoer

THE GEORGIA REVIEW

Stanley W. Lindberg
University of Georgia
Athens, GA 30602-9009
(706) 542-3481

Poetry, fiction, essays, reviews, artwork.

An international journal of arts and letters with a special interest in current American literary writing; seeking interdisciplinary thesis-oriented essays—not scholarly articles—and engaging book reviews, plus the best in contemporary poetry and fiction; authors range from Nobel laureates and Pulitzer Prize winners to the as-yet unknown and previously unpublished.

Rita Dove, Stephen Dunn, Czeslaw Milose, Fred Chappell, Richard Howard, Mary Hood, Louise Erdrich, Wayne Dodd, Emily Hiestand.

Unsolicited Manuscripts Received/ Published per Year: 17,000/100

Payment; $3/line for poetry; $35/printed page for prose.

Reporting Time: 8–12 weeks.

Reading Period: year-round, but no submissions accepted during June, July, or August.

Compilation copyright entered by the University of Georgia, which has purchased first serial rights; all other rights are retained by individual authors.

1947; 4/yr; 7,000

$18/yr; $7/ea; $5/sample copy

208 pp; 6¾ x 10

Ad Rates: $350/page (4¾ x 7½); $225/½ page (4¾ x 3⅝)

ISSN: 0016-8386

DeBoer, Ubiquity, Fine Print, Anderson News

THE GETTYSBURG REVIEW

Peter Stitt
Gettysburg College
Gettysburg, PA 17325-1491
(717) 337-6770

Poetry, fiction, essays, graphics/ artwork.

THE GETTYSBURG REVIEW

is an interdisciplinary magazine of arts and ideas, which features the highest quality poetry, fiction, essays, essay-reviews, and graphics by both beginning and established writers and artists. Two special interests are the publication of serial fiction and the inclusion of a full-color graphics section in each issue. Essays are in a variety of disciplines, with a wide range of subject matter.

E.L. Doctorow, Charles Simic, Philip Levine, Alison Baker, Hayden Carruth, Linda Pastan, Rita Dove, Charles Wright, Marilyn Nelson Waniek, Richard Wilbur, Joyce Carol Oates.

Unsolicited Manuscripts Received/Published per Year: 4,000/85.

Reading Period: Sept.–June.

Payment: $25/page prose; $2/line poetry; upon publication.

Copyright held by Gettysburg College; reverts to author upon publication.

1988; 4/yr; 4,200

$18/yr ind, $18/yr inst; $32/2 yrs; $45/3 yrs; $7/ea; 40%

170 pp; 6¾ x 10

Ad Rates: $225/page (5 x 7½)

ISSN: 0898-4557

Eastern News

GIORNO POETRY SYSTEMS

John Giorno

222 Bowery

New York, NY 10012

(212) 925-6372

Poetry.

Magazine in three formats: LP record, Compact Disc, and Cassette. Video Pak series is a magazine in video format.

Laurie Anderson, William Burroughs, Patti Smith, Diamanda Galas, Nick Cave.

Payment: $500 royalty advance, and 12% of the retail price of each record sold.

1972; 4/yr; 10,000

$8.98/single album; $12.98/double album; $8.98/cassette; $13.98/compact disc; $39.95/video cassette; 40%—55%

GLAS: NEW RUSSIAN WRITING

Natasha Perora; Arch Tait; Ed Hogan

c/o Zephyr Press

14 Robinson St.

Somerville, MA 02145

(617) 628-9726

Fax (617) 776-8246

Russian fiction, poetry and literary nonfiction in English translation.

The only journal whose focus is contemporary Russian writing, as well as works suppressed or hidden away during the Soviet period, presented in theme-based issues.

Vassily Grossman, Vladimir Makanin, Osip Mandelstam, Nina Sadur, Ludmila Vlitskaya.

Reading Period: Translators should query first.

Payment: Varies.

Reporting Time: Varies.

Copyright held by the authors; translations copyrighted for the translators upon publication.

1991; 2/ca; 1,200--2,500 worldwide.

$44/4 issues; $13.95/ea., 40% (5-up copies)

240 pp; 5⅝ x 8

$100/page (4½ x 7¼); $60/½ page (4½ x 3⅛)

ISSN: None; each issue or edition is assigned an ISBN number; prefix: 0-939010–(u.s.)

Inbook, Bookpeople

GLIMMER TRAIN STORIES

Linda Davies, Susan Burmeister-Brown

812 SW Washington St. #1205

Portland, OR 97205

(503) 221-0836

Quarterly short story magazine printed on acid-free, recycled stock. Each story is illustrated.

Many unknowns as well as Charles Baxter, Ellen Gilchrist, Mary McGarry Morris, Richard Bausch, Ann Beattie, Evan Cornell.

Unsolicited Manuscripts Received/Published per Year: 12,000/32.

Payment: $1000, effective 1/1/96 upon acceptance.

Reporting Time: 3 months.

Copyright reverts to author upon publication.

1991; 4/yr; 19,500

$29/yr; $9/ea; 40%

168 pp; 5¾ x 9¼

No advertising

Ingram, IPD, Pacific Pipeline, DeBoer, Ubiquity, BookPeople, ANCO

GRAB-A-NICKEL

Barbara Smith

Alderson-Broaddus College

Philippi, WV 26416

(304) 457-1700

Poetry, fiction, reviews, photographs, graphics/artwork.

GRAB-A-NICKEL is a tabloid journal of poems, fiction, book reviews, photographs and drawings. Open submissions; priority given to Appalachian writers and subject matter. There is encouragement of new writers of any age or background. It is a product of a college community's writers' workshop.

Barbara Smith, John McKernan, Eddy Pendaris, Mark Rowh, T. Kilgore Splake, Llewellyn McKernan, Jim Wayne Miller.
Unsolicited Manuscripts Received/ Published per Year: varies.
Payment: in copies.
Copyright held by author.
1977; 2–3/yr; 1,000
25¢/ea
16–20 pp; 11½ x 14

GRADIVA

Luigi Fontanella
P.O. Box 831
Stony Brook, NY 11790
(516) 632-7448 or (516) 632-7440
Poetry, essays, reviews, translation, interviews.
GRADIVA is an international journal of modern Italian literature that focuses on literary criticism and theory. All contributions are published in English or Italian. Creative works written in other languages are published with translation.
Umberto Eco, Edoardo Sanguineti, Mario Luzi, Alfredo Giuliani, Andrea Zanzotto.
Unsolicited Manuscripts Received/ Published per year: 50+/4.
Payment: in copies, subscription.
Copyright held by magazine; reverts to author upon publication.
1986; 2/yr; 3,000
$30/yr; $50/2 yrs
100 pp; 5½ x 8½
Ad Rates: $100/page (5½ x 8½); $60/½ page (5½ x 4¼); $35/¼ page (2¾ x 4¼)

GRAFFITI RAG: An Annual Anthology of New Urban Writing

Hayan Charara, Editor
Erik Fahrenkopf, Co-Editor
5647 Oakman Blvd.
Dearborn, MI 48126
(313) 846-5376
Poetry.
An annual anthology that seeks to published gifted unknowns alongside well-known poets. High-quality, perfect bound, professionally printed.
Philip Levine, Naomi Shihab Nye, Charles Burkowski, Amiri Baraka
Unsolicited Manuscripts Received/ Published per Year: 300/15–20
Reading Period: all year.
Payment: contributor copies.
Reporting Time: 2 weeks to 2 months.
Copyright held by magazine; reverts to author upon publication.
1995; 1/yr; 750
$9.95/issue; resale: $7.95
152 pp; currently 6 x 9; may change to 6½ x 8½

Ad Rates: As of yet, unknown.
ISSN: 0-8187-0227-3
DeBoer

GRAHAM HOUSE REVIEW

Peter Balakian, Bruce Smith
Box 5000
Colgate University
Hamilton, NY 13346
(315) 824-1000, ext. 262

Poetry, essays, translations, interviews.

We publish the best poetry and poetry in translation we can get. We have just begun an interview series and will publish essays in the future. We pay scrupulous attention to production, and have an international interest in selecting material.

Seamus Heaney, Derek Walcott, Madeline De Frees, David Wagoner, Maxine Kumin, Carolyn Forché.

Unsolicited Manuscripts Received per Year: 10,000.
Payment: in copies.
Reporting Time: 1–2 months.
Copyright held by magazine; reverts to author upon publication.
1976; 1/yr; 1,750
$7.50/yr ind, $7.50/inst; $7.50/ea; 20%
125 pp; 8½ x 5½

GRAIN

J. Jill Robinson, Tim Lilburn, Connie Gault, Catherine Macaulay
Box 1154
Regina, Saskatchewan, S4P3B4 CANADA
(306) 757-6310
Fax (306) 565-8554

Literary and visual art.

GRAIN publishes the best new previously unpublished fiction, poetry, and other genres from across Canada and around the world.

Unsolicited Manuscripts Received/Published per Year: Hundreds/80.
Reading Period: year–round.
Payment: $30–$100 (Canadian).
Reporting Time: 3–5 months.
Copyright remains with author.
1973; 4/yr; 1,525
$19.95/yr; $6.95/ea; 40%
144 pp; 6 x 9
Ad Rates: $250/page; $150/½ page; $100/¼ page
ISSN: 0315-7423
Canadian Magazine Publishers Association

GRAND STREET

Jean Stein
131 Varick St., Room 906
New York, NY 10013
(212) 807-6548

Poetry, fiction, essays, interviews, art.

Andrei Bitov, Kenzaburo Oe, Toni Morrison, William T. Vollmann, Paul Auster, John Ashbery, Nina Berberova.

Unsolicited Manuscripts Received/Published per Year: 3,500/10.

Reading Period: year–round.

Payment: variable.

Reporting Time: 6–8 weeks.

Copyright: one-time first-serial rights only; author retains copyright.

1981; 4/yr; 7,000

$40/yr ind, $55/yr foreign; $12.95/ea

270 pp; 7 x 9

Ad Rates: $450/page

ISSN: 0734-5496

D.A.P./Distributed Art Publishers

GRASSLANDS REVIEW

Laura B. Kennelly
NT Box 13706
Denton, TX 76203
(817) 565-2127

Poetry and fiction.

Publishes poetry and fiction from known and unknown authors chosen by students in adult learners' creative writing group. Send manuscripts only in October or March.

Peggy Little, Edward Mycue, Frances Treviño.

Unsolicited Manuscripts Received/Published per Year: 300/64.

Reading Period: Oct. & Mar. (postmarks only).

Payment: in copies.

Reporting Time: 3–4 months.

Copyright reverts to author.

1988; 2/yr; 300

$8/yr ind, $15/yr inst; $2.50/ea

90 pp; 5 x 9

Ad Rates: $20/½ page, plus subscription

GREAT RIVER REVIEW

Orval Lund
211 West Seventh St.
Winona, MN 55987
(507) 454-6564

GREAT RIVER REVIEW is accepting no unsolicited manuscripts until further notice.

GREEN FUSE POETRY

Brian Boldt
3365 Holland Dr.
Santa Rosa, CA 95404
(707) 544-8303

Contemporary free verse.

We focus on environmental themes and issues of war and peace and social justice in a 64-page, digest size format; perfect-bound.

Antler, John Brandi, Donald Hall, Dorianne Laux, Denise Lever-

tov, Laurel Speer.
Unsolicited Manuscripts Received/Published per Year: 4,000/100.
Payment: 2 copies.
Reporting Time: Within 12 weeks.
Copyright reverts to author upon publication.
1984; 2/yr; 700
3 issues for $14; $4.50
64 pp; digest; perfect-bound

GREEN MOUNTAINS REVIEW

Neil Shepard, Poetry Editor and General Editor; Tony Whedon, Fiction Editor
Johnson State College
Johnson, VT 05656
(802) 635-2356
Poetry, fiction, essays, reviews, interviews, translations, photographs.
GMR publishes work by promising newcomers and well-known writers from across the country.
Galway Kinnell, Denise Levertov, Larry Levis, David St. John, Lynne Sharon Schwartz, Grace Paley
Unsolicited Manuscripts Received/Published per Year: 2,000/60.
Reading Period: Sept.–May.
Payment: in copies.
Reporting Time: 1–3 months.
Copyright held by magazine; reverts to author upon publication.
1987; 2/yr; 1,500
$12/yr; $6/ea; 40%
144–172 pp; 6 x 9
$150/page; $75/½ page
ISSN: 0895-9307
Ubiquity, Fine Print, Armadillo

THE GREENSBORO REVIEW

Jim Clark
Department of English
Univ. North Carolina-Greensboro
Greensboro, NC 27412
(910) 334-5459
Fax (910) 334-3281
E-mail: clarkj@fagan.uncg.edu
Poetry, fiction.
Contemporary and experimental. We want to see the best being written regardless of theme, subject or style.
Ellen Herman, Peter Taylor, Greg Johnson, Peter Meinke, Lane von Herzen, Jere Hoar, Molly Giles, Robert Morgan, Greg Kuzma, Thomas Lux.
Unsolicited Manuscripts Received/Published per Year: 1,000–1,200 fictions/12–20.
Payment: in copies.
Reporting Time: 2–4 months.
Copyright held by magazine; reverts to author.
1966; 2/yr; 5–600
$8/yr, $16/2 yrs, $20/3 yrs; $4/ea
120–180 pp; 6 x 9
ISSN: 0017-4084

GULF COAST

Polly Koch, Patrick Martin
Department of English
University of Houston
Houston, TX 77204-3012

Poetry, fiction, essays, interviews, art criticism, articles.

GULF COAST encourages submission of high-quality, well-crafted work that takes risks, whether formally inventive or intensifying a form's inherent strengths, with an acute awareness of its own language—all styles & subjects.

Adam Zagajewski, Ann Beattie, Barry Hannah, Lydia Davis, Michael S. Harper, Gail Wronsky, X. J. Kennedy, Stephen Dixon, Caila Rossi, Richard Howard; interviews with Czeslaw Milosz, Walter Hopps, Amy Hempl, and others.

Unsolicited Manuscripts Received/Published per Year: 780/60

Payment: $15/poem, $30 max; $30 fiction and nonfiction; $15/art, $30 max. Plus copies

Copyright held by magazine; reverts to author upon publication.

1987; 2/yr; 1,000

$12/yr subscription, $7/ea; $5/back issue; $12/Barthelme Memorial

140 pp; 9 x 6

No ads

ISSN: 0896-2251

GULF STREAM MAGAZINE

Editor: Lynne Barrett, Associate Editors: Andrew Golden, Maidel Barrett.

FIU, North Miami Campus
North Miami, FL 33181
(305) 940-5599

Poetry, fiction, essays.

GSM publishes high quality fiction, poetry and creative nonfiction. We are open to experimental and mainstream work. No more than 5 poems. Limit prose to 25 pages.

Gerald Costanzo, Ann Hood, Stuart Dybek, Dara Wier, Sibyl James.

Unsolicited Manuscripts Received/Published per Year: 1,000/50.

Reading Period: Sept.–April.

Payment: in copies.

Reporting Time: 1–3 months.

Copyright held by magazine; First North American serial rights.

1989; 2/yr; 350

$7.50/yr; $4/ea; 40%

96 pp; 8½ x 5½

GYPSY

Belinda Subraman, S. Ramnath
10708 Gay Brewer Drive
El Paso, TX 79935
(915) 592-3701

Fiction, reviews, graphics/artwork, essays, poetry.

We are an international family of independent literary and visual artists. We seek to enlarge our family and support. Please write for current themes and guidelines. In general, we are interested in writing of lasting value, usually dealing with human rights and experience. Currently doing double issue book editions. Inquire before submitting. Prices vary.

Peter Wild, Laurel Speer, James Purdy, Albert Huffstickler, Gerald Locklin.

Unsolicited Manuscripts Received/Published per Year: 5,000±/180±.

Reporting Time: 6–12 weeks.

Copyright: Vergin Press.

1984; 2/yr; 1,000

Ad Rates: $100/page; $55/½ page; $30/¼ page

ISSN: 0176-3148

H

HABERSHAM REVIEW
David L. Greene, Lisa Hodgens Lumpkin, Co-editors
Piedmont College
P.O. Box 10
Demorest, GA 30535
(706) 778-3000
Fiction, Poetry
HABERSHAM REVIEW is a general literary journal with a regional focus (Southeastern U.S.) Each issue features an unpublished work by and an interview with a prominent Southern writer.
D.C. Berry, Judith Cofer, Rosemary Daniell, Mary Hood, Terry Kay, Frank Gannon, Judson Mitcham and David Bottoms.
Unsolicited Manuscripts Received/Published per Year: 900/40.
Payment: copies.
Reporting Time: 4 months.
Copyright held by Piedmont College; reverts to author upon publication.
1991; 2/yr; 500
$12/yr; $6/ea; 40%
96 pp; 6 x 9
Ad Rates: $500/page (5 x 8+); $250/½ page (2½ x 4)
ISSN: 1060-0469

HAIGHT ASHBURY LITERARY JOURNAL
Joanne Hotchkiss, Alice Rogoff, Will Walker
558 Joost Avenue
San Francisco, CA 94127
(415) 584-8264
The magazine began with six editors of extremely diverse socioeconomic and ethnic backgrounds. The magazine encompasses diversity of viewpoint, racial, sexual as well as style, tending to confront the

difficult and painful of human experiences as well as the higher reaches of emotional experiences. The Journal publishes both local writers and other interested writers.

Eugene Ruggles, Mona Lisa Saloy, Peter Plate, Linwood M. Ross, Laura del Feugo, Leslie Simon, Edgar Silex.

Unsolicited Manuscripts Received/Published per Year: 800/100.

Reading Period: Dec.–Mar., July.–Oct.

Payment: in copies.

Reporting Time: 4–6 months.

Copyright held by author.

1980; 1-2/yr; 3-4,000

$35/lifetime subs; $3/ea by mail; $6/2 issues; $12/4 issues

16 pp; 11 x 17¼

Ad Rates: $150/page (10 x 17); $75/½ page (7½ x 9); $50/¼ page (9 x 5); $40, $30, $20 for smaller ads

Checks payable to Alice Rogoff.

HAMBONE

Nathaniel Mackey
134 Hunolt Street
Santa Cruz, CA 95060
(408) 426-3072

Poetry, fiction, criticism, reviews, plays, translation, interviews, photographs, graphics/artwork.

Cross-cultural work emphasizing the centrifugal.

Edward Kamau Brathwaite, Susan Howe, Geoffrey O'Brien, Gustaf Sobin, Jay Wright.

Payment: copies.

Reporting Time: 1–4 months.

Copyright held by magazine: reverts to author upon publication.

1974; 1/yr; 600

$14/2 issues ind; $18/2 issues inst; $8/ea; 40%

200 pp; 5½ x 8½

ISSN: 0733-6616

Small Press Distribution

HAMMERS

Nat David
1718 Sherman #203
Evanston, IL 60201
(708) 328-7555

Poetry.

An end of the millennium irregular poetry magazine.

Beatriz Badikian, John Dickson, Michael Warr, Luis Rodriquez, Albert Huffstickler.

Unsolicited Manuscripts Received/Published per Year: 1,000/100.

Payment: 1 free copy.

Reporting Time: 1–2 months.

1990; 2/yr; 500

$5/ea; 40%

7 x 8½

THE HAMPDEN-SYDNEY POETRY REVIEW

Tom O'Grady
P.O. Box 126
Hampden-Sydney, VA 23943
(804) 223-8209

Poetry.

A small, carefully-printed correspondence among poets which attempts to print the unknown with the known.

David Ignatow, Robert Pack, Patricia Goedicke, David Huddle, Lewis Turco.

Payment: in copies.

Copyright held by Tom O'Grady; reverts to author upon publication.

1975; 2/yr; 500

$5/yr ind; $5/yr, $12/3-yr inst; $5/ea; 1990 Anthology 328 pp. $12.95; 40%

60 pp; 5 x 9

No ads

HANGING LOOSE

Robert Hershon, Dick Lourie, Mark Pawlak, Ron Schreiber
231 Wyckoff Street
Brooklyn, NY 11217
(212) 206-8465

Poetry, fiction, translation, graphics/artwork.

Our interests continue to center on finding new writers and then staying with them, often to the point of book publication. (Book mss and artwork by invitation only.)

Paul Violi, Kimiko Hahn, Steven Schrader, Donna Brook, Gary Lenhart, Sherman Alexie.

Payment: some payment to contributors.

Reporting Time: 2–3 months.

Copyright held by magazine; reverts to author upon publication.

1966; 3/yr; 1,500

$17.50/yr ind, $21/yr inst; $7/ea + $1.50 postage; 20%–40%

96 pp; 7 x 8½

ISSN: 0440-2316

Ubiquity, SPD, Fine Print

HANSON'S SYMPOSIUM: Of Literary & Social Interest

Eric Hanson
113 Merryman Court
Annapolis, MD 21401
(410) 626-0744

Poetry, fiction, essays, humor, interviews, dialogues, and various features.

A magazine of general interest, we are striving to combine the traditionally separate aspects of literary and social journals into one magazine.

Unsolicited Manuscripts Received/Published per Year: 2,000/50.

Payment: $30–$100, plus 1 copy.

Reporting Time: 2 weeks.

Copyright held by Hanson Publishing, reverts to author.
1988; 2/yr; 1,500
$5/ea; 40%
80 pp; 8½ x 11
No ads

HAWAII REVIEW

Michelle Viray
UH Mānoa
Department of English
1733 Donaghho Rd.
Honolulu, HI 96822
(808) 956-8548

Poetry, fiction, criticism, essays, reviews, plays, translations, interviews, photographs, graphics/artwork.
Ursule Molinaro, Ian MacMillan, Nell Altizer, John Unterecker, Michael McPherson, William Pitt Root, Frank Stewart.
Unsolicited Manuscripts Received/Published per Year: 1,000/100.
Payment: $10–75, plus 2 copies; more for cover art.
Reporting Time: 30–120 days.
Copyright held by magazine; reverts to author upon publication.
1973; 3/yr; 2,000
$15/yr; $5/ea
100–180 pp; 5½ x 9
Ad Rates: $100/page
ISSN: 0093-9625

HAYDEN'S FERRY REVIEW

Salima Keegan
ASU Box 871502
Tempe, AZ 85287-1502
(602) 965-1243

Poetry, fiction, nonfiction.
Nationally distributed magazine publishing quality literary art. **HFR** promotes work of emerging and established writers of fiction, poetry, and creative nonfiction.
David St. John, Ken Kesey, Maura Stanton, Raymond Carver, Norman Dubie, Rita Dove, Charles Wright, Jean Valentine, Naomi Shihab Nye, John Ashbery.
Unsolicited Manuscripts Received/Published per Year: 6,000/60.
Reading Period: year–round.
Payment: copies.
Reporting Time: 3–5 months.
Copyright reverts to author.
1986; 2/yr; 1,000
$10/yr; $6/ea
128; 6 x 9
ISSN 0887-5170

THE HEARTLANDS TODAY

The Firelands Writing Center
Nancy Dunham & Larry Smith, Managing Editors
Firelands College,
Huron, Ohio 44839
(419) 433-5560
Fax (419) 433-9696

Poetry, personal essays, fiction (4,000 wds), art and photos.

We feature a theme from the contemporary Midwest—The Heartlands Today—for each volume (annual). The writing must be set in the Midwest, though it need not treat the Midwest. We look for writing of character and place. 1996 theme: "The Mythic Midwest."

Gary Snyder, Scott R. Sanders, Carolyn Banks, Antler.

Unsolicited Manuscripts Received/Published per Year: 500/40.

Reading Period: Jan. 1–June 15th.

Payment: $10 and 2 copies, poems & photos.

$25—fiction & essays

Reporting Time: 2 months.

Copyright: we buy first rights (in some cases second), return rights to author.

1991; 1/yr; 850

$8.50/yr; $8.50/ea

160; 6 x 9

ISSN: 1066-6176

HEAVEN BONE

Steve Hirsh, Kirpal Gordon

P.O. Box 486

Chester, NY 10918

(914) 469-9018

Poetry, fiction, reviews.

Poetry, fiction, reviews with focus on surrealist, experimental and buddhist concerns.

Anne Waldman, Gerald Malanga, Diane DiPrima, Michael McClure, Charles Bukowski

Unsolicited Manuscripts Received/Published per year: 2,800/20.

Reading Period: All year.

Payment: copies.

Reporting Time: 6–40 weeks.

Copyright held by magazine; reverts to author upon publication.

1886; 1/yr; 2,500

$16.95/yr; $6.00/ea; 40%

96 pp; 8½ x 11

Ad Rates: $245/page; $130/½ page; $70/¼ page

ISSN: 1042-5381

Ubiquity, Fineprint, Desert Moon

HELLAS, A Journal of Poetry & the Humanities

Gerald Harnett

304 South Tyson Avenue

Glenside, PA 19038

(215) 884-1086

Poetry, classics, Renaissance & modern literary studies.

We provide a unique forum for the poetry, theory and criticism of poets working in meter–"The new formalism," or, as our advertising describes that movement, "The New Classicism."

Timothy Steele, Richard Moore, Joseph Malone, Frederick Turner, Dana Gioia.

Unsolicited Manuscripts Received/Published per Year: 5,000 poems, 100 articles/60-70 poems, 20-25 articles.
Copyright: First North American serial rights only.
1990; 2/yr; 700
$14/yr, $24/2 yrs; $8.75/sample (p.p.) 40%
176 pp; 6 x 9
$175/page (4 x 7); $100/½ page (4 x 3½)
ISSN: 1044-5331

HERESIES: A Feminist Publication on Art and Politics
Heresies Collective, Inc.
P.O. Box 1306
Canal Street Station
New York, NY 10013
(212) 227-2108
Essays, experimental writing, short fiction, interviews, poetry; page art, photography, graphic art, all visual arts.
HERESIES is the longest-lived feminist art journal still publishing. Thematic, political focus. "We believe that what is commonly called art can have a political impact and that in the making of art and all cultural artifacts our identities as women play a distinct role . . . A place where diversity can be articulated."
Unsolicited Manuscripts Received/Published per Year: 3,000/25–35.
Reading Period: year–round.
Payment: nominal.
Reporting Time: 8–12 months.
Copyright reverts to author upon publication.
1977; 1–2/yr; 6,000
Four issues - $27/ind, $38/inst; $8/ea; 40%
112 pp; 8½ x 11
Ad Rates: $400/page
ISSN: 0146-3411
BookPeople, Inland, Ingram, Small Changes, Fine Print, Desert Moon, Marginal Distribution

HIGH PLAINS LITERARY REVIEW
Robert O. Greer, Jr.
180 Adams St., Suite 250
Denver, CO 80206
(303) 320-6828
Fiction, essays, poetry, reviews, criticism, interviews.
Designed to bridge the gap between commercial magazines and an outstanding array of academic quarterlies. A handsomely produced literary magazine that is intended to be more broadly based than academia without being commercially "targeted." A journal designed to display the absolute best of

craft. O. Henry award winning fiction appeared as early as Vol. 1, No. 1.

Richard Currey, Nancy Lord, Marilyn Krysl, Darrell Spencer, Tony Ardizzone, Julia Alvarez, Rita Dove.

Unsolicited Manuscripts Received/Published per Year: 4,000/85.

Payment: $5/page prose; $10/page poetry.

Reporting Time: 8 weeks.

Copyright held by magazine; reverts to author upon publicaton.

1986; 3/yr; 1,100

$20/yr; $7/ea; 40%

140 pp; 6 x 9

Ad Rates: $100/page; $50/½ page

ISSN: 0888-4153

DeBoer, Ubiquity, Fine Print

HIRAM POETRY REVIEW

Hale Chatfield

Box 162

Hiram, OH 44234

(216) 569-5330

Poetry, criticism, essays, reviews, interviews. Photographs, graphics, and artwork by invitation only.

Unsolicited Manuscripts Received/Published per Year: 6,000/50.

Reporting Time: 8–24 weeks.

Copyright reverts to author upon publication.

1967; 2/yr; 500

$4/ea; 40%–60%

40 pp; 6 x 9

ISSN: 0018-2036

THE HOLLINS CRITIC

John Rees Moore

P.O. Box 9538

Hollins College, VA 24020

(703) 362-6317 or 362-8268

Poetry, critical essays, reviews, graphics/artwork.

A non-specialist periodical concentrating on the work of a single contemporary poet, fiction writer or dramatist in each issue. Cover picture, essay of about 5,000 words, brief account of author, check-list of publications, several poems and a section of brief book reviews.

Keith A. Mason, Robert Aaron Lobe, Marcyn Del Clements, Peggy A. Tartt, Michael Krebs.

Payment: $200/essay (by permission of editor only); $25/poems.

Copyright held by magazine.

1964; 5/yr; 650

$6/yr; $2/ea—US

20 pp; 7 x 10

ISSN: 0018-3644

HOME PLANET NEWS

Donald Lev and Enid Dame

P.O. Box 415

Stuyvesant Station

New York, NY 10009
(718) 769-2854

Poetry, fiction, criticism, reviews, translation, interviews, photographs, news.

We publish poetry, reviews of books, art exhibits, theater, news of the literary and small press scene, interviews and fiction. Occasional pull-out section of single poet's work.

Cornelius Eady, Norman Rosten, Will Inman, William Packard, Antler, Lyn Lifshin, Paul Genega, Richard Kostelanetz.

Unsolicited Manuscripts Received/ Published per Year: 320 (poetry)/60

Payment: in copies and subscription.

Reporting Time: Feb. 1—May 31st.

Copyright held by magazine; reverts to author upon publication.

1979; 3–4/yr; 1,000

$8/yr ind, $8/yr inst, $15/2 yrs; $2/ea; 40%

24 pp; 10 x 15

Ad Rates: $150/page (10 x 15); $75/½ page (10 x 7½); $37.50/¼ page (5 x 7½)

DeBoer

HOPEWELL REVIEW

Joseph Trimmer
c/o Arts Indiana, Inc.
409 Tyrone Dr.
Muncie, IN 47304
(317) 632-7894

Poetry, short fiction, personal essay.

HOPEWELL REVIEW is an annual collection of poetry, short fiction and personal essays by Indiana writers.

Alice Friman, Susan Neville, Dan Carpenter.

Unsolicited Manuscripts Received/ Published per Year: 1,500/40.

Payment: $35/poem; $150/short fiction, personal essay. 3 $500 awards of excellence.

Copyright held by Arts Indiana, Inc., reverts to author upon publication.

1989; 1/yr; 8,000

$6.95/ea

128 pp

ISBN 0-9647909-0-4

HOWLING DOG

M. P. Donovan
2913 Woodcock Ct.
Rochester, MI 48306
(810) 752-8511

Poetry, fiction, graphics/artwork.

Our purpose is to have an effect similar to the howl of a dog with its foot caught in a fence. We desire something that may not be pleasant or permanent, but will still be heard by everyone in the neighborhood.

John Sinclair, M. L. Liebler, Hank Malone, Larry Goodell.

Unsolicited Manuscripts Received/ Published per Year: 5,000/100.

Payment: in copies.

Reporting Time: 6 months or more.

Copyright held by authors.

1985; 2/yr; 500

$10/yr; $5/ea; 40%

64 pp; 6 x 9

Ad Rates: $80/page (4 x 8); $40/½ page (4 x 4); $20/¼ page (2 x 4)

ISSN: 0888-3521

THE HUDSON REVIEW

Paula Deitz, Frederick Morgan
684 Park Ave.
New York, NY 10021
(212) 650-0020

Poetry, fiction, criticism, essays, reviews.

We publish both new and established writers. We have no university affiliation, and we are not committed to any narrow academic aim or to any particular political perspective. We focus on the area where literature and poetry bear on the intellectual life of today.

Reading Period: nonfiction Jan. 1–Apr. 30; fiction June 1–Nov. 30; poetry Apr. 1–July 31.

Payment: 2½¢/word for prose; 50¢/line for poetry.

Reporting Time: 1–3 months.

Copyright held only on assigned reviews.

1948; 4/yr; 4,500

$24/yr; $7/ea

160 pp; 6 x 9¼

Ad Rates: $300/page (4½ x 7½); $200/½ page (4½ x 3⅝); $150/¼ page (2⅛ x 3⅝)

ISSN: 0018-702X

Eastern News

HUNGRY MIND REVIEW

Bart Schneider
1648 Grand Ave.
St. Paul, MN 55105
(612) 699-2610
E-mail: hmreview@winternet.com

Essays, reviews, interviews, and photographs.

HUNGRY MIND REVIEW publishes book reviews, essays, and forums on particular focuses. **HUNGRY MIND REVIEW** reviews large, small, and university presses, focusing on mid- and backlist titles.

Robert Bly, Jane Smiley, Kathleen Norris, Bill McKibben, Gerald Early, Maxine Hong Kingston, Michael Dorris, Quentin Crisp, E. Annie Proulx.

Unsolicited Manuscripts Received/ Published per Year: 600/0.

Payment: varies.

Copyright held by David Unowsky, dba **HMR**.
1986; 4/yr; 30,000
$14.00/yr ind; $15/yr Canada and inst; free/ea
56 pp; 9¾ x 15
Ad Rates: $1,625/page; $900/½ page; $475/¼ page; $295/⅛ page; $175/1/16 page
ISSN: 0887-5499
We distribute free of charge to over 600 independent bookstores across the U.S. and Canada.

HURRICANE ALICE: A Feminist Quarterly
Pat Cumbie, Martha Roth
Lind Hall
207 Church Street, SE
Minneapolis, MN 55455
(612) 625-1834
Reviews, essays, criticism, fiction, poetry, graphics/artwork.
HURRICANE ALICE provides a feminist review of culture. It prints reviews of books by and about women, critical essays having a feminist perspective—especially essays on literature, film, dance, and the visual arts—fiction, some poetry and graphics.
Alice Walker, Toni McNaron, Peter Erickson, Meridel Le Sueur, Susan Griffin, Pearl Cleage, Beth Brant.
Unsolicited Manuscripts Received/Published per Year: 750/60.
Reading Period: year–round.
Payment: in copies.
Reporting Time: 1–3 months.
Copyright reverts to author upon publication.
1983; 4/yr; 700
$12/yr; $10/yr students/seniors; $20/yr libraries; $2.50/ea
12–16 pp; 11 x 17
Ad Rates: $75/⅙ page; $45 (3 x 4); $20 (3 x 2)
Ubiquity, L-S Distributor, Olson, Fine Print

HYPHEN
John Boyer, Publisher; Mark Ingebretsen, Editor
c/o John Boyer
348 S. Ahrens
Lombard, IL 60148
(312) 465-5985
Fax (312) 465-5985
Fiction, nonfiction, poetry, artwork, photography
Art and literature that won't bore you senseless.
Dwight Okita, Cin Salach, Rosalind Cummings, Margriet Smulders, Michael McNeilly
Unsolicited Manuscripts Received/Published per Year: 1200/48.
Reading Period: year–round

Payment: 2 copies.
Reporting Time: 2–6 months
Copyright held by: currently changing ownership
1992; 4/yr; 1,200
$14/yr; $4/ea; 50%
Ad Rates: $250/page, $200 2x, $150 3x; $200/½ page, $150 2x, $100 3x; $150/¼ page, $100 2x, $75 3x
ISSN: 1058-3297
Fine Print, Speed Impek, Desert Moon.

I

THE ILLINOIS REVIEW (Formerly Illinois Writers Review)

Jim Elledge
4240/Department of English
Illinois State University
Normal, IL 61790-4240
(309) 438-7705

Creative writing of all genres, as well as essays and reviews.

The **ILLINOIS REVIEW** seeks poems, prose poems, short-short stories, stories, novel excerpts, one act plays, translations, essays, and book reviews. Open to mainstream and alternative, to established and unknown, and to marginalized writers. A special, double issue, of "*Prictions for the 21st Century*," with new work by David Iguatow, James Tate, Cydney Chadwick, Connie Deanovich, David Trinidad, and others available for $12.00.

Reading Period: Aug. 1–May 31.

Payment: two copies and year's subscription.

Reporting Time: 1–2 months, SASE required.

Copyright reverts to author upon publication.

1993; 2/yr; 500

Individuals and Institutions may subscribe to the journal in one of two ways: as a member of Illinois Writers, Inc.: $15/yr ind, $20/yr inst; or to the journal itself: $10/yr ind, $15/yr inst; 40%

Ad Rates: $100/page (4½ x 7); $50/½ page (4½ x 4)

ISSN: 0733-9526

Illinois Literary Publishers' Association

IMAGE: A Journal of the Arts and Religion

Publisher and Editor, Gregory Wolfe

3100 McCormick Ave.
Wichita, KS 67213
(316) 942-4291, ext. 325
Fax (316) 942-9658

Short stories, novel excerpts, poetry, memoirs, essays, interviews.

IMAGE is the only national journal dedicated to exploring and illustrating the relationship between faith and art through world-class fiction, visual art, poetry, essays, music, and other arts.

Larry Woiwode, Ron Hansen, Denise Levertov, Doris Betts, Robert Bly, Annie Dillard.

Unsolicited Manuscripts Received/Published per Year: 800/25.

Reading Period: year-round.

Payment: usually 4 copies of the journal, occasionally a fee.

Reporting Time: 3 months.

Copyright held by Hillsdale Review, Inc.

1989; 4/yr; 5,000

$30/yr, $10/ea; 40%

136 pp; 7 x 10

Ad Rates: $500/page; $300/½ page; $700/inside back cover. Discounts for multiple placements.

Ingram, DeBoer, Ubiquity

IMAGINE: INTERNATIONAL CHICANO POETRY JOURNAL

Tino Villanueva
89 Massachusetts Ave., Suite 270
Boston MA 02115
(617) 267-2592

Poetry, mostly; limited number of articles/interviews; book reviews & book notices.

Poetry in any language provided the original language text is accompanied by a English or Spanish translation. Any mode, no restrictions on form, subject or style.

Jimmy Santiago Baca, García Márquez, Gary Soto, Isabel Allende, Bernice Zamora, Frida Kahlo, Rudolfo Anaya, Luis Valdez, Luis Jiménez.

Payment: small fee plus two author's copies.

Reporting Time: 4–6 months.

Copyright reverts to authors, artist, or photographer upon publication.

1984; 2/yr; 1,000

$8/yr ind, $14/2 yrs ind, $12/yr inst, $18/2 yrs inst; $4.50/ea; newstand price; back issues vary count; 35%

75–99 pp; 6 x 9

ISSN: 0747-489X

SPD

IN THE COMPANY OF POETS

Jacalyn Robinson
P.O. Box 10786
Oakland, CA 94610
(510) 568-2531

Poetry, short stories, essays, visual art.

E. Donald Two-Rivers, Selma Glasser, Patrick Fitch.

Unsolicited Manuscripts Received/Published per Year: Approx. 350/120.

Payment: 3 copies.

Reporting Time: 3-6 months.

Copyright: US & Int'l.

1991; 6/yr; 20,000

$16/yr

approx. 62 pp; 8 x 10

ISSN: 1055-0038

INDEFINITE SPACE

Marica Arrieta, Kevin Joy
P.O. Box 90101
Pasadena, CA 91114

Poetry (some art, photos, black & white)

Favors experimental, minimalistic, philosophical, imagistic, nature, language, poetry.

Peter Ganick, John Byrum, Simon Perchik, Celestine Frost, Alan Caitlan

Reading Period: 12.

Payment: One copy.

Reporting Time: Usually one month or less.

Copyright held by poets.

1992; Once or twice/year.

$7/yr; $4/ea.

32/36 pp; 5½ x 8½

ISSN: 1075-6868

INDIANA REVIEW

Shirley Stephenson, poetry: Geoffrey Pollock, fiction:
316 North Jordan Ave.
Indiana University
Bloomington, IN 47405
(812) 855-3439

Fiction, poetry, essays, book reviews, occasional drama, interviews.

We have no prejudices of style or content, but will publish only those poems and short stories which demonstrate: 1) keen sense of craft; 2) insight into the human condition. Writers should send their best work only. We prefer stories of rich texture to those that depend on a gimmick.

Dean Young, Philip Levine, Kathy Acker, Pamela Painter, George Saunders, Martin Espada, Amy Gerstler, Ursula K. LeGuin, Maureen Seaton.

Unsolicited Manuscripts Received per Year: 5,000 (poetry and prose).

Payment: $5 per page.

Reporting Time: 2 weeks–4 months.

Copyright held by magazine; reverts to author upon publication.
1976; 2/yr; 2,000
$12/yr ind, $15/yr inst; $7/ea
200 pp; 6 x 9
Ad Rates: $150/page (6 x 9); $85/½ page (6 x 4½)
ISSN: 0738-386X
Ingram, DeBoer

INTERIM

A. Wilber Stevens, Editor; John Heath–Stubbs, English Editor; George Bruce, Scottish Editor; Associate Editors: James Hazen, Joe McCullough
Department of English
University of Nevada
Las Vegas, NV 89154

Poetry, fiction.

INTERIM prints the best poetry and short fiction we can find, plus occasional reviews. It is the revival, under its original editor, of the magazine published and edited in Seattle in 1944–55.

William Stafford, John Heath-Stubbs, X.J. Kennedy, Stephen Stepanchev, Gladys Swan.

Unsolicited Manuscripts Received/Published per Year: 3,000-3,400/60.
Reading Period: year–round.
Payment: contributor's copies plus a two-year subscription.
Copyright held by magazine; reverts to author upon publication.
1944; 2/yr; 750
$16/3 yrs; $8/yr; $14/yr inst; $5/ea; 40%
48–64 pp; 9 x 6
ISSN: 0888-2452

INTERNATIONAL POETRY REVIEW

Mark Smith-Soto
Dept. of Romance Lang.
UNC-Greensboro
Greensboro, NC 27412

Unpublished translation with contemporary original language poem. Contemporary English language poetry with international or cross cultural theme preferred, graphics.

Coleman Barks, Charles Edward Eaton, William Stafford, Pureza Canelo, Ana Istarú, Clara Janés.

Unsolicited Manuscripts Received/Published per Year: 1,200/100.
Payment: in copies.
1975; 2/yr; 400
ind.: 2 yrs $18, 3 yrs $25; libraries: 2 yrs $27, 3 yrs $40; $5/ea; 20%
100 pp; 5½ x 8½
Ad Rates: $50/page; $25/½ page

INTERNATIONAL QUARTERLY

Van Brock, Editor-in-Chief; Catherine Reid, Fiction;

Kim Garcia, Poetry; Holly Iglesias, Nonfiction
P.O. Box 10521
Tallahassee, FL 32302-0521
(904) 224-5078
Fax (904) 224-5127

Fiction, nonfiction, poetry, full color ad b&w.

IQ is a multicultural journal of contemporary work from around the world, in English and translation.

Carmen Naranjo, Guillermo Nuñez, Adonis, Dennis Brutus, Bei Dao.

Unsolicited Manuscripts Received/ Published per Year: 800/160.

Reading Period: year-round.

Payment: in copies.

Reporting Time: 6–8 weeks.

Copyright: First North American Serial rights then reverts to author.

4/yr; 5,000

$30/yr: $55/2 yrs; $75/3 yrs. $6 sample, $8/ea, $12 double issue.

180–200 pp; 7½ x 10

Perfect binding, art cover.

Full Page 4x=$515/each ad. Half page 4x=$295/each ad. Quarter page 4x=$160/each ad.

ISSN: 1060-6084

INVISIBLE CITY

John McBride, Paul Vangelisti
P.O. Box 2853
San Francisco, CA 94126
(415) 527-1018

Poetry, criticism, translation, graphics/artwork, visual poetry.

A book series, formerly tabloid, of poetry, translation, visuals and statements published whenever enough good material is available: focusing on current U.S. writing, some concrete poetry and Italian writing—focused on "the internal tension of language."

Adriano Spatola, Giulia Niccolai, Ernst Meister, John Thomas, Stanislaw Baranczak, Antonio Porta, Emilio Villa; and now DAYBOOK by Robert Crosson, with DIVISION appended, remarks, criticism & such.

Unsolicited Manuscripts Received/ Published per Year: 365/?.

Reading Period: year-round.

Payment: copies and then some.

Reporting Time: 2 months.

Copyright reverts to author upon publication.

1971; 1–2/yr; 1,000

$10/yr ind, $15/yr inst

80+ pp; 5 x 9

ISSN: 0034-2009

THE IOWA REVIEW

David Hamilton, Mary Hussmann
308 EPB
University of Iowa
Iowa City, IA 52242

(319) 335-0462

Poetry, fiction, criticism, essays, reviews, interviews.

We look for new as well as established writers and are receptive to voices beyond the academy.

Unsolicited Manuscripts Received/ Published per Year: 8,000/100.

Reading Period: Sept.–Apr.

Payment: $1/line for poetry; $10/page for prose.

Reporting Time: 2–3 months.

Copyright held by the University of Iowa; reverts to author upon publication.

1970; 3/yr; 1,500

$18/yr ind, $20/yr inst; $6.95/ea; 30%

200 pp; 6 x 9

Ad Rates: $200/page (5½ x 8½)

ISSN: 0021-065X

Ingram

IOWA WOMAN

Rebecca Childers, Editor; Debra Marquart, Poetry Editor

P.O. Box 680

Iowa City, IA 52244

(319) 351-2068

Fiction, essays, reviews, interviews, poetry, news briefs, features, ads, memoirs, graphics/artwork.

Rooted in the Midwest, **IOWA WOMAN** publishes award-winning women writers everywhere. National readership. Send SASE for annual writing contest guidelines.

Judy Ruiz, Enid Shomer, Alice Friman, Mary Swander, Lauren Slater, Sharon Ozard Warner, Linda Hasselstrom.

Unsolicited Manuscripts Received/ Published per Year: 4,000+/80+.

Payment: $5/page, copies, ad discounts.

Reporting Time: 3 months.

Copyright held by magazine; reverts to author upon publication.

1980; 4/yr; 2,500

$20/yr; $24/yr Canada; $26/yr Pan America; $30/yr inst.; 429/yr Western Europe; $32 other; samples $6.95; 30%

48 pp; 8⅛ x 10⅞

ISSN: 0271-8227

THE ITHACA WOMEN'S ANTHOLOGY

Editorial Board; Rotating board of editors.

P.O. Box 582

Ithaca, NY 14851

Poetry, fiction, translation, photographs, graphics/artwork, criticism.

THE ITHACA WOMEN'S ANTHOLOGY was originally established as an annual collection of creative work, by, for and about women. The types of work we publish include essays, interviews, criticism, journal entries, fiction, and poetry as well as graphics of all kinds. Our commitment is to provide a medium for women to creatively express their concerns, to coin varied and new voices, while emphasizing the highest in artistic quality.

Unsolicited Manuscripts Received/ Published per Year: 200/30+. From Ithaca and the New York State region.

Payment: copies.

Copyright held by magazine; reverts to author upon publication.

1976; 1/yr; 400

$6/ea; 40%

J

JACARANDA

Cornel Bonca, Bruce Kijewski, Laurence Roth

Dept. of English

California State Univ., Fullerton.

Fullerton, CA 92634

(714) 773-3163

Fiction, poetry, essays, interviews, book reviews.

We publish the best material we can find from both established and new writers. We're particularly interested now in good fiction, though we welcome all genres.

Carolyn Foshe, Heather McCugh, Charles Buttewski, Craig Raine, Louse Erdrick

Unsolicited Manuscripts Received/Published per year: 2,500/50.

Reading Period: All year round.

Payment: 3 copies.

Reporting Time: 2 months (except in summer - 4 months).

Copyright held by magazine; reverts to author upon publication.

1985; 2/yr; 1,500

$10/yr; $6/ea; 40%

140 pp, 5½ x 8

Ad Rates: $120/page; $75/½ page; $50/¼ page

ISSN: 1042-7082

Armadillo, Ubiquity

JAMES WHITE REVIEW

P. Willkie, C. Mayhood

P.O. Box 3356

Butler Quarter Station

Minneapolis, MN 55403

(612) 339-8317

Poetry, fiction, criticism, reviews, memoirs, photographs, graphics/artwork.

We are a gay men's literary quarterly.

David Feinberg, Essex Hemphill,

Lev Raphael, Assotto Saint, Stan Leventhal.
Unsolicited Manuscripts Received/ Published per Year: 1,000/100.
Reading Period: after deadlines: Feb 1, May 1, Aug 1, Nov 1.
Payment: $50/story, $10/poem.
Reporting Time: 6–8 weeks.
Copyright held by magazine; reverts to author upon publication.
1983; 4/yr; 4,500
$14/yr ind, $14/yr inst; $3/ea; 40%
20 pp; 11 x 15
Ad Rates: $400/page; $200/½ page; $120/¼ page

JEOPARDY MAGAZINE

Jason Graham, Chris Russell, Editors; Joanna Nesbit, Managing Editor; Sean Anderson, Kris Huss, Fiction Editors; Derek Martin, Non-Fiction Editor; Ken Efta, Ethan Yarbrough, Poetry Editors
132 College Hall
Western Washington University
Bellingham, WA 98225
(206) 650-3118
Nonfiction, fiction, poetry, art, photography.
Annie Dillard, Barry Lopez, Richard Hugo.
Unsolicited Manuscripts Received/ Published per Year: 1,000-1,500/100.
Payment: Two copies.
Reporting Time: 1–4 months.
Copyright reverts to author.
1963; 1/yr; 2,000
$4.75/ea
120-200 pp; book–sized

JORDAN CREEK ANTHOLOGY

Jo Van Arkel
900 N. Benton
Springfield, MO 65802
(417) 865-8731
Fiction, poetry, interviews.
We publish short stories and poetry which are literary, contemporary, experimental, humorous, or regional, with an emphasis on the Midwest to the South. No genre or formula.
John Mort, Paul Ramsey, Debra Thornton, Wilma Yeo.
Unsolicited Manuscripts Received/ Published per Year: 300/15–20.
Reading Period: Sept.–May.
Payment: copies.
Reporting Time: 6 weeks.
Copyright: first time rights.
1987; 1/yr; 500
$12/3 yrs; $4/ea; $2/resale
80 pp

THE JOURNAL

Kathy Fagan, Poetry Editor; Michelle Herman, Fiction Editor

164 West 17th Ave.
Department of English
The Ohio State University
Columbus, OH 43210
(614) 292-4076

Poetry, fiction, reviews.

THE JOURNAL attempts to provide an outlet for good writing by Ohio writers and writers from around the country. We seek out good work and attempt to attract the best new writers. The editorial staff works to publish and distribute poetry, fiction, nonfiction, and reviews, the sole criterion for which is excellence.

Maurya Simon, J. R. Hummer, Jonathan Holden, Eric Pankey, Linda Bierds, Carol Potter, Pinkney Benedict.

Reporting Time: 4–6 weeks.

Copyright held by Ohio State University.

1972; 2/yr; 1,100

$8/yr; $4.50/ea; 40%

80-100 pp; 6 x 9

ISSN: 1045-084X

JOURNAL OF NEW JERSEY POETS

Sander Zulauf, Editor; North Peterson, Sara Pfaffenroth, Wendy Jones, Associate Editors; Jane Derrick, Art Editor; Wilma Martin, Layout Editor.

214 Center Grove Rd.
County College of Morris
Randolph, NJ 07869-2086
(201) 328-5471

Poetry by New Jersey poets, essays, occasional quotations.

A magazine dedicated to the best poetry written by poets who live in New Jersey or who have lived or worked here at some time.

Kenneth Burke, Grace Cavalieri, Lesley Choyce, Alfred Starr Hamilton, Michael Weaver, Cat Doty, Joe Weil.

Unsolicited Manuscripts Received/ Published per Year: 800-1,000/75-100.

Payment: 2 copies/published poem.

Reporting Time: 6 months.

Copyright: County College of Morris.

1976; 2/yr; 900

$7/yr; $4/ea; 25%

48-64 pp; 5½ x 8½

ISSN: 0363-4205

DeBoer

K

KALEIDOSCOPE: International Magazine of Literature, Fine Arts, and Disability

Darshan C. Perusek, Ph.D., Editor-in-Chief; Gail Willmott, Senior Editor

United Disability Services

326 Locust Street

Akron, OH 44302

(216) 762-9755

Poetry, photographs, graphics/artwork, fiction, essays, reviews.

KALEIDOSCOPE Magazine has a creative focus that examines the experience of disability through diverse forms of literature and the fine arts. Works should not use stereotyping, patronizing, or offending language about disability.

Diana Hume George, Andre Dubus, Tony Ardizzone, Sandra Lindow, Sheryl L. Nelms, and Harriet Doerr.

Unsolicited Manuscripts Received/Published per Year: 500/30.

Payment: \$25–\$100 fiction, up to \$25 for body of poetry.

Reporting Time: Acknowledged within 2 weeks; up to 1 month of deadline for rejection or acceptance.

Copyright held by Kaleidoscope; reverts to author upon publication.

1979; 2/yr; 1,500

\$9/yr, \$17/2 yrs ind; \$14/yr, \$22/2 yrs inst; \$5/yr Canadian; \$8/yr International; US Funds only. \$5.00/ea; \$4/sample copy (prepaid); 20%–50%

64 pp; 8½ x 11

ISSN: 0748-8742

Ubiquity, MTS Incorporated

KALLIOPE: A Journal of Women's Art

Mary Sue Koeppel
Florida Community College
3939 Roosevelt Boulevard
Jacksonville, FL 32205
(904) 381-3511

Poetry, short fiction, reviews, interviews (3 annually), photographs, graphics/artwork.

The purpose of **KALLIOPE** is to offer support and encouragement to women in the arts. We are open to experimental forms of short fiction, poetry, prose and art as well as traditional formats. Editors like to see work that challenges the reader and addresses the complex relationships women have with each other, men, children and society.

Marge Piercy, Elisavietta Ritchie, Edith Perlman, Enid Shomer, Colette Inez, Louise Fishman, Colette, Tess Gallagher.

Unsolicited Manuscripts Received/ Published per Year: 1,000/100.

Reading Period: Sept.–April.

Payment: 3 copies or 1 yr subscription to writers and artists.

Reporting Time: 2–3 months.

Copyright held by magazine; reverts to author upon request.

1978; 3/yr; 1,600

$12.50/yr ind, $21/yr inst; $7/ea last issues; $4/ea early issues; 40%

80 pp; 7¼ x 8½

No ads

ISSN: 0735-7885

Ingram

KANSAS QUARTERLY/ ARKANSAS REVIEW

Norman Lavers, Editor; Rick Lott, Poetry editor: Debbie Chappel, Managing Editor
Dep/t. of English & Philiosphy
P.O. Box 1290
Arkansas State University
State University, AR 72467
(501) 972-3043

Fiction, essays, some poetry.

Primarily a fiction and creative nonficion magazine, international in scope (but with one corner set aside for the arts and culture of the lower Mississippi delta).

David Kirby, John Bovey, Stephen Dixon, Jonathan Holden, Peter LaSalle, Susan Fromberg Schaeffer, Jerry Bumpus, Lex Williford, Annabel Thomas.

Unsolicited Manuscripts Received/ Published per year: 5,000/180.

Reading Period: year–round.

Payment: $10/page

Reporting Time: 1–3 months.

Copyright held by magazine; reverts to author upon request.

1995; 3/yr; 1,500

$15/yr; $6/ea; 10%–40%

80+ pp; 6 x 9
Ad Rates: $100/page (4½ x 7½); $60/½ page (4½ x 3¾); $35/¼ page (2¼ x 3¾)
ISSN: 0022-8745

KARAMU

Peggy L. Brayfield
Department of English
Eastern Illinois University
Charleston, IL 61920
(217) 581-5614

Poetry, short fiction, creative nonfiction prose, black and white graphics.
Quality writing for a literate audience who enjoy fiction, poetry, and other creative pieces.
John Dickson, Sheila Golburgh Johnson, Richard Willett, Zan Bockes, John Thompson.
Unsolicited Manuscripts Received/Published per Year: Approx. 150 stories, 1,400 poems/approx. 6-7 stories, 30-35 poems.
Payment: 1 copy of issue containing work, extras at reduced price.
Reporting Time: 2-3 months, longer if work is under serious consideration.
Copyright: First serial rights.
1966; 1/yr; 400
$7.50/yr; $5/sample copy, $6/2 sample copies.
128 pp; 5 x 8
Ad Rates: inquire
ISSN: 0022-8990

THE KENYON REVIEW

David H. Lynn, Editor; Cy Wainscott, Managing Editor
Kenyon College
Gambier, OH 43022
(614) 427-3339

Poetry, fiction, essays, reviews, interviews, plays, translations, memoirs.
THE KENYON REVIEW seeks excellent writing more than any particular kind or style. We seek to present a balanced diversity of perspective/orientation. We invite offers to review books and proposals for interviews. First publication rights required. No multiple submissions read. We discourage submissions from writers who have not read a recent issue.
Hayden Carruth, Toi Derricote, Terese Svobda, Kate Braverman, Adrienne Rich, Herbert Blau, Rafael Campo, Ursula K. LeGuin.
Unsolicited Manuscripts Received/Published per Year: 5,000/60.
Reading Period: Sept.–Mar.
Payment: $10/page, prose; $15/page, poetry; $10 (translator) $5 (author)/page, translations.

Reporting Time: 3 months.
Copyright reverts to author.
1939; 3/yr; 5,000
$22/yr ind, $30/yr inst; $8/ea
185 pp; 7 x 10
Ad Rates: $285/page (4⅜ x 8); $175/½ page (4⅜ x 3⅞); exchanges considered
ISSN: 0163-075X
Inland, Ingram, DeBoer, Ubiquity

Reading Period: Jan.-Dec.
Payment: Contributors Issues (complimentary)
Reporting Time: 6 months.
Copyright held by Fairmont State College.
1993; Fall/Spring
$9/yr; $5/ea; 20%
100 pp; 6 x 9

KESTREL: A Journal of Literature and Art in the New World

Mary Dillow Stewart, Managing Editor
Val Neeman, Marty Lammon, John King, Editors
1201 Locust Ave.
Fairmont, WV 26554
c/o Fairmont State College
(304) 367-4793
Fax (304) 366-0559

Poetry, fiction, creative nonfiction, drama, artwork.
KESTREL: A New Journal, devoted to the arts, takes its name from the family of small falcons found throughout North America and elsewhere in the world.
Robert Bly, Jean Valentine, David McCaia, Margaret Gibson, Donald Hall.
Unsolicited Manuscripts Received/Published per year: 400/22.

KINESIS

Leif Peterson
P.O. Box 4007
Whitefish, MT 59937
(406) 844-3047

Fiction, poetry, essays, reviews.
The literary magazine for the rest of us.
Luci Shaw, John Leax, Lyn Lifshin, Simon Puchik
Unsolicited Manuscripts Received/Published per Year: 1,600/100.
Reading Period: Jan.–Dec.
Payment: 5 copies and 1 year subscription
Reporting Time: 6 weeks.
Copyright held by author.
1992; 12/yr; 5,000
$20/yr, $4/ea; 33%
48 pp; 8½ x 11
Ad Rates: $350/page (7¼ x 9); $200/½ page; $120/¼ page (3½ x 4½); $60/⅛ page (3½ x 2¼)
ISSN: 1056-781X
Tower Magazines, Ubiquity

KIOSK

Lia Vella, Editor-in-Chief; Jonathan Pitts, Fiction Editor; Charlotte Pressler, Poetry Editor
English Department
302 Clemens Hall
SUNY at Buffalo
Buffalo, NY 14260
(716) 645-2575

Poetry, fiction, creative non-fiction.

KIOSK welcomes submissions of creative prose and poetry. We are interested in originality and craftsmanship. We subscribe to no orthodoxy; quality is our top concern. Especially interested in new writers.

Recent issues have included Richard Russo, Sheila E. Murphy, Raymond Federman, Bonnie Jo Campbell.

Unsolicited Manuscripts Received/ Published per Year: 800/25-35.

Reading Period: Sept.–Apr.

Payment: 2 copies.

Author retains all rights.

1986; 1-2/yr; 500

$6/year or back-issues with large SASE and 6 1st class stamps.

130 pp; 5½ x 8½

No ads

KUMQUAT MERINGUE

Christian Nelson
P.O. Box 5144
Rockford, IL 61125
(815) 968-0713

Poetry and very short prose.

Dedicated to the memory of Richard Brautigan.

Gina Bergamino, Antler, Lynne Douglass, Ianthe Brautigan.

Unsolicited Manuscripts Received/ Published per Year: Thousands/130-180.

Payment: copies.

Reporting Time: 8 to 10 weeks.

1991; 2/yr; 600

$4/ea

32-40 pp; digest

L

LACTUCA

Michael Selender
159 Jewett Avenue
Jersey City, NJ 07304-2003
(201) 451-5411

Poetry, fiction, black and white art.

Our bias is toward work with a strong sense of place or experience. Writing with an honest emotional depth and writing that is dark or disturbing are preferred over safer material. Work with a quiet dignity is also desired. Subject matter is wide open and work can be rural or urban in character. We don't like poems that use the poem, the word, or the page as images or writing about being a poet/writer (though work about dead poets/writers is o.k.).

Sherman Alexie, Charles Bukowski, Joe Cardillo, Adrian C. Louis, Sheryl Nelms.

Unsolicited Manuscripts Received/Published per Year: 2000+/120.

Reading Period: year-round, but Nov.–Feb. is best. We will not be accepting new material until late 1995 or early 1996.

Payment: in copies.

Copyright held by magazine; reverts to author upon publication.

1986; 1–3/yr; 750

$10/3 issues, $17/6 issues; $4/ea; 40% bookstores, 55% distributors.

72 pp; 7 x 8½

No ads

LANGUAGE BRIDGES QUARTERLY

Eva Ziem
P.O. Box 850792
Richardson, TX 75085
(214) 530-2363

Poetry, fiction, criticism, essays, reviews, plays, translations, photographs, artwork.

LBQ is the only fully bilingual Polish-English literary magazine in the USA. All texts are printed in Polish with English translation or vice-versa. **LBQ** creates, by presenting American writers as well, a bridge between Polish and American writers, as well as readers for cross cultural dialogue.

Prof. Danuta Mostwin, Prof. Lisowski, Prof. Ewa Thompson, Valeriu Butulescu.

Unsolicited Manuscripts Received/Published per Year: 50/25.

Reporting Time: 2-3 weeks.

Copyright held by magazine.

1988; 4/yr; 250

$20/yr ind; $6/ea

24 pp; 8 x 11 ½

Ad Rates: $100/page; $50/½ page; $25/¼ page

ISSN: 1053-9913

LATIN AMERICAN LITERARY REVIEW

Yvette E. Miller
121 Edgewood Ave., 1st Flr.
Pittsburgh, PA 15218
(412) 371-9023
Fax (412) 371-9025

Criticism, essays, reviews. We now publish articles in Spanish and Portugese in addition to English.

The Journal in English devoted to the literatures of Latin America.

Payment: varies.

Reporting Time: 3 months.

Copyright held by magazine.

1972; 2/yr + special double issue; 1,200

$22/yr ind, $38/yr inst; $30/yr ind. foreign; $40/yr inst. foreign; $16/ea, back issues; 10%

150 pp; 250 pp special issue; 6 x 9

Ad Rates: $215/page (4½ x 7½); $140/½ page (4½ x 3¾); $95/¼ page (4½ x 2¼)

ISSN: 0047-4134

Ebsco, Faxon, Turner

THE LAUREL REVIEW

William Trowbridge, David Slater, Beth Richards
GreenTower Press
Department of English
Northwest Missouri State University
Maryville, MO 64468
(816) 562-1265

Poetry, fiction, creative non-fiction.

THE LAUREL REVIEW is national in scope and prints the best work received, regardless of style or author's reputation.

Patricia Goedicke, Paul Zimmer,

Nancy Willard, Jonis Agee, Albert Goldbarth.
Unsolicited Manuscripts Received/ Published per Year: 4,000/70.
Reading Period: Sept.–May.
Payment: 2 copies and subscription.
Reporting Time: 1 week–4 months.
Copyright held by GreenTower Press; reverts to author upon publication.
1960; 2/yr; 900
$8/yr, $14/2 yrs; $5/ea; 40%
124 pp; 6 x 9
Ad Rates: $80/page (6 x 9); $40/½ page (6 x 4½); exchange also
ISSN: 0023-9003

THE LEDGE POETRY & FICTION MAGAZINE

Timothy Monaghan
64-65 Cooper Ave.
Glendale, NY 11385-6150

Poetry and fiction our purpose is to publish outstanding poetry and fiction by well-known and little-known poets and writers. Excellence is our only criterion. **THE LEDGE** sponsors an Annual Poetry Chapbook Contest and Annual Poetry and Fiction Awards. Send SASE for complete guidelines.
Terri Brown-Davidson, Philip Miller, Stephanie Dickinson, Carolyn E. Campbell and Elliot Richman.
Unsolicited Manuscripts Received/ Published per Year: 3,000/50.
Reading Period: Sept.–June.
Payment: 2 copies.
Reporting Time: 3 months
Copyright reverts to author.
1988; 2/yr; 1,000
$9/yr, $15/2 yr; 20%
144 pp; 5½ x 8½
ISSN: 1046-2724
DeBoer

LIGHT QUARTERLY

Box 7500
Chicago, IL 60680

Light verse (metrical and non-metrical) satire, humor, cartoons and line drawings.
LIGHT QUARTERLY is the only publication in the United States devoted exclusively to light verse and satire.
John Updike, Donald Hall, X. J. Kennedy, William Matthews, Gavin Ewart, William Stafford, W. D. Snodgrass.
Unsolicited Manuscripts Received/ Published per Year: 1,000/2,500.
Payment: 2 copies of issue they appear in; 1 copy for foreign contributors.
Reporting Time: 1–3 months.
1992; 4/yr; 1,200
$16/yr; $6/ea; $4/back issue

32 pp; 8½ x 11
Write for ad rates.
ISSN: 1064-8186
Ubiquity

LILLIPUT REVIEW

Don Wentworth
282 Main St.
Pittsburgh, PA 15201
Poetry
Short poems, ten lines or less.
David Chorlton, Sheila E. Murphy.
Unsolicited Manuscripts Received/ Published per Year: 1,100/5% of *all* received
Reading Period: year–round.
Payment: 2 copies of issue in which work appears.
Reporting Time: 4–8 weeks.
Copyright: Magazine uses first rights, reverting to author upon publication.
1989; 12/yr; 200-250
$5/6; $1 ea. or SASE; 50%
16 pp; 4½ x 3⅝ or 3½ x 4¼

LIPS

Laura Boss
P.O. Box 1345
Montclair, NJ 07042
(201) 662-1303
Poetry.
LIPS publishes the best contemporary poetry submitted. No biases.
Michael Benedikt, Gregory Corso, Maria Gillan, Allen Ginsberg, Robert Phillips, Marge Piercy, Ishmael Reed, Stanley Barkan, Ruth Stone.
Payment: in copies.
Reporting Time: 1 month.
Copyright held by magazine; reverts to author upon publication.
1981; 2/yr; 1,000
$10/yr ind, $13/yr inst; $5/ea; 40%
88 pp; 5½ x 8½
ISSN: 0278-0933
Anton Mikofsky

LITERAL LATTÉ

Jenine Gordon, Jeff Bockman
61 East 8th Street
Suite 240
New York, NY 10003
(212) 260-5532
Short stories, poems, personal essays and art.
The highest quality prose, poetry and art distributed FREE THROUGH arts organizations, bookstores, and coffehouses in NYC.
Michael Brodsky, Stephen Dixon, Carole Maso, Carol Muske, John Updike.
Unsolicited Manuscripts Received/ Published per Year: 4,500/90.
Reading Period: year-round.
Payment: $25–$250. Subscription, gifts + copies.
Reporting Time: 3 months.

Copyright reverts to author upon publication.
1994; 6/yr; 20,000
$15/yr, $5/ea
28 pp; 11 x 17
DeBoer

THE LITERARY CENTER QUARTERLY

Ken Smith, Scott Davidson, Neile Graham, Jim Gurley
P.O. Box 85116
Seattle, WA 98145
(206) 547-2503

Reviews, essays, poetry, interviews.

We are a small quarterly hoping to offer a voice for North West writers of all genres.

John Marshall, K. C. Brown, Joseph H. Hudson.

Copyright reverts to authors.
4/yr; 2,000
$15/yr
16–32 pp; 8½ x 11
Write for ad rates and sizes

LITERARY MAGAZINE REVIEW

Grant Tracey, Editor
Department of English Language and Literature
University of Northern Iowa
Cedar Falls, IA 50614-0502
(319) 273-7207

Reviews and essays concerning literary magazines.

LITERARY MAGAZINE REVIEW is devoted almost exclusively to objective reviews of the specific contents of issues of magazines which publish at least some short fiction or poetry.

David Kirby, Ben Nyberg, Ben Reynolds.

Unsolicited Manuscripts Received/Published per year: 10/0.
Reading Period: year–round.
Payment: copies.
Reporting Time: queries only, please.
Copyright reverts to author upon publication.
1982; 4/yr; 600+
$12.50/yr; $4/ea; 40%
60 pp; 8½ x 5½
No ads
ISSN: 0732-6637

THE LITERARY REVIEW

Walter Cummins, Editor-in-Chief; Martin Green, Harry Keyishian, William Zander, Editors; Jill Menkes Kushner, Managing Editor
Fairleigh Dickinson University
285 Madison Avenue
Madison, NJ 07940
(201) 593-8564
Fax (201) 593-8564

Poetry, fiction, criticism, essays,

reviews, translation, interviews, graphics/artwork.

New writing in English and translation. We're looking for a unique blend of craft and insight.

Susan Moon, Tom Hansen, Jane Bradley, T. Alan Broughton.

Unsolicited Manuscripts Received/Published per Year: 3,500/200.

Reading Period: year–round.

Payment: 2 copies.

Reporting Time: 8–12 weeks.

Copyright held by Fairleigh Dickinson University; reverts to author upon publication.

1957; 4/yr; 2,000

$18/yr; $5/ea; 40%

128 pp; 6 x 9

Exchange ads

ISSN: 0024-4589

LITERARY ROCKET

Eileen Murphy, Printing and Marketing; Darren Johnson, Editor

P.O. Box 672

Water Mill, NY 11976

E-mail: rockusa@delphi.com

Poetry, fiction.

The **ROCKET** wants quality writing with innovative voices; voices that will take the reader into the next century, at least. Not sci-fi, but new ways to express meaning.

Lyn Lifshin, Chris Woods.

Reporting Time: 3–6 weeks.

Copyright held by Rocket Inc. reverts to author upon publication.

1993; 4/yr; 2,000

$6/yr; 40%

16 pp; 11 x 8.5

$125/page (11 x 8.5), $75 half.

ISSN: 1071-4502

LONG NEWS: In the Short Century

Barbara Henning, Art Editor; Miranda Maher, Contributing Editors: Don David, Lewis Warsh, Paul Buck, Chris Tysh, Michael Pelias, Tyrone Williams

P.O. Box 150-455

Brooklyn, NY 11215

Writing, art, poetry, experimental prose.

LONG NEWS: in the Short Century aims to publish experimental work that challenges the basic tenets of realism and expressionism.

Nicole Brossard, Fanny Howe, Sadiq Muhammad, Lorenzo Thomas.

Unsolicited Manuscripts Received/Published per year: 100/2.

Reporting Time: 60 days.

Copyright reverts to author after publication.

1991; 1/yr; 1,000

$12/2 issues, $22/4 issues; $6/ea; 40%
185 pp; 5 x 8½
CPAD: 74470-80899
DeBoer, SPD, Fine Print, Spectacular Diseases, (UK)

LONG POND REVIEW

Russell Steinke, William O'Brien, Anthony Di Franco
Suffolk Community College
533 College Rd.
Selden, NY 11784
(516) 451-4153
Poetry, fiction, essays, reviews, interviews, photographs, graphics/artwork.
LONG POND REVIEW publishes the finest work submitted by established, emergent, and beginning writers. **LPR** has been recognized as an outstanding small press in **The Pushcart Prize II** (1977–78), **IV** (1979–80), **V** (1980–81), **VI** (1981–82), **VII** (1982–83), and **IX** (1984–85).
Fred Chappell, David Citino, Colette Inez, Linda Pastan, Jim Barnes, William Stafford, Michael Blumenthal.
Payment: 1 contributor's copy.
Reporting Time: 2–6 months.
Copyright held by author.
1975; 1/yr; 500
$3/ea ind, $5/ea inst
72–88 pp; 6 x 9
Ad Rates: $75/page; $40/½ page

LONG SHOT

Nancy Mercado, Danny Shot, Lynne Breitfellow
P.O. Box 6238
Hoboken, NJ 07030
Poetry, fiction, photographs, graphics/artwork.
"Writing From The Real World."
Allen Ginsberg, Amiri Baraka, Gregory Corso, June Jordan, Tom Waits, Miguel Algarin.
Unsolicited Manuscripts Received/Published per Year: 3,000/20.
Payment: in copies.
Reporting Time: 12 weeks.
Copyright held by magazine; reverts to author upon publication.
1982; 2/yr; 2,000
$22/2 yrs; $6/ea; 40%
192 pp; 5½ x 8½
Ad Rates: $150/page (5 x 8½); $90/½ page (5 x 4¼)
ISSN: 0895-9773
DeBoer, Ubiquity, Fine Print, I.P.D., Desert Moon

THE LONG STORY

R. Peter Burnham
18 Eaton St.
Lawrence, MA 01843
(508) 686-7638
Fiction.

We are interested strictly in long stories (8,000–20,000 words, or roughly 20–50 pages)—bias is left wing and concern for human struggle for dignity etc., but quality is the main criterion.
Unsolicited Manuscripts Received/ Published per Year: 400/6-7.
Reading Period: year–round.
Payment: 2 copies.
Reporting Time: 2 weeks–2 months.
Copyright held by magazine; reverts to author upon publication.
1983; 1/yr; 1,000
$5/yr; $5/ea; 40%
160–200 pp; 5½ x 8½
ISSN: 0741-4242
Ingram

LOOK QUICK

Joel Scherzer, Robbie Rubinstein
P.O. Box 222
Pueblo, CO 81002
Poetry, fiction, reviews, photographs.
Emphasis is on free verse, blues lyrics and brief vignettes. We have also published material relating to the Beats. Not reading unsolicited manuscripts.
Payment: in copies.
Copyright held by Quick Books; reverts to author upon publication.
1975; irreg; 200
$3/ea
24–32 pp; 5½ x 8½

LOONFEATHER: A Magazine of Poetry, Short Prose & Graphics

Betty Rossi, Marsh Muirhead, Elmo Heggie
P.O. Box 1212
Bemidji, MN 56601
(218) 751-4869
Poetry, Fiction, Graphics.
LOONFEATHER is primarily but not exclusively a regional literary magazine publishing the works of both emerging and established writers. Our purpose is to promote good writing and encourage emerging artists by publishing their work; sponsoring readings, workshops, and exhibits; and supporting fellow artists/writers/organizations. Our regional focus is northern Minnesota, Minnesota, and the surrounding states and Canada.
Edith Rylander, Robert Bly, Connie Sanderson, Philip Dacey, Joyce Penchansky, Thom Ward.
Unsolicited Manuscripts Received/ Published per Year: 200/65.
Reporting Time: Within four months following deadline for submissions.
Copyright held by magazine, reverts to author upon publication.

1979; 2/yr; 200–250
$7.50/yr; $4/ea; 40%
48 pp; 6 x 9
Ad Rates: $360/page; $180/½ page; $45/¼ page
ISSN: 0734-0699

LOST AND FOUND TIMES

John M. Bennett
137 Leland Ave.
Columbus, OH 43214
(614) 846-4126

Avant-garde, experimental, visual, language, collaborative, and other beyond the pale literature. Also graphics.

More poetry than prose. Any language; emphasizing English and Spanish.

Susan Smith Nash, Al Ackerman, N. Vassilakis, S. Murphy, Jake Berry.

Unsolicited Manuscripts Received/ Published per Year: many/few
Payment: 1 copy.
Reporting Time: immediate.
Copyright retained by authors and artists.
1975; 2/yr; 350
$25/5; $6/ea; 40%
Approx. 56 pp; 8½ x 5½
Small Press Traffic, Printed Matter

LOUISIANA LITERATURE: Literature/Humanities Review

David Hanson, Editor; William Parrill, Norman German, Associate Editors
SLU 792
Southeastern Louisiana University
Hammond, LA 70402
(504) 549-5022

Poetry, fiction, reviews of Louisiana-related books, articles on LA writing and culture.

We are interested in publishing essays and photo articles on Louisiana writing, history or art, but nothing full of jargon. Creative work we will take from anywhere on any topic.

Lewis P. Simpson, Diane Wakoski, Shirley Ann Grau, Kelly Cherry, Louis Gallo.

Unsolicited Manuscripts Received/ Published per Year: 1,500/40.
Reading Period: Sept.–May.
Payment: in copies.
Reporting Time: 1 month.
Copyright held by author.
1984; 2/yr; 650
$10/yr; $5/ea; 40%
100 pp; 6½ x 9½
Query for ad rates
ISSN: 0890-0477

LULLWATER REVIEW

Marci C. Eggers
Box 22036

Emory University
Atlanta, GA 30322
(404) 727-6184

Poetry, short fiction.

LULLWATER REVIEW is Emory University's national literary journal. We provide room for new as well as experienced writers. We also publish an annual prize for poetry as well as the James Dickey Poetry contest winner.

Charles Edward Eaton, Dianna Herring, Colette Inez, R.T. Smith, Lyn Lifshen.

Unsolicited Manuscripts Received/Published per year: approx. 201/ratio

Reading Period: August-May.

Payment: 3 copies of magazine.

Reporting Time: 3 months.

Copyright held by Emory University.

1990; 2/yr; 2,000

$12/yr; $5/ea.

100 pp. (approx.); 6 x 9

$100/page

ISSN: 1051-5968

Ubiquity, B. DeBoer

LUZ EN ARTE Y LITERATURA

Veronica Miranda
P.O. Box 571062
Tarzana, CA 91357-1062
(818) 907-1454

Poetry, short stories, translations, art, etc.

LUZ is an international bilingual (Spanish/English) magazine featured mainly creative writing but also articles and interviews of writers and artists.

Carlota Caulfield, Ester de Izaguirre, Luis Benítez, Juana Rosa Pita, Enrique Jaramillo Levi.

Unsolicited Manuscripts Received/Published per Year: 1000/40

Payment: 1 copy.

Reporting Time: 3–6 months.

Copyright reverts to authors after publication.

1992; 1/yr; 1,500

$25/yr; $14/ea; 50%

100 pp; 8½ x 5½

Ad Rates: $400/page; $200/½ page; $100/¼ page

ISSN: 1067-0084

LYNX

Jane & Werner Reichhold, Co-editors
P.O. Box 1250
Gualala, CA 95445
(707) 882-2226

Renga, tanka, criticism, essays, reviews, translation, interviews, black and white graphics, features.

LYNX is for linking poets and is the only magazine dedicated to renga and tanka. Renga (linked verse) was an outgrowth of tanka, the oldest poetry form still active in Japan, and has now invaded and captured North America.

Marlene Mountain, Hiroaki Sato, Anne McKay, Lorraine Ellis Harr, David Rice.

Unsolicited Manuscripts Received/Published per Year: 400/120

Reporting Time: 1 week.

Copyright reverts to contributors.

1987; 3/yr; 300

$15/yr

80 pp; 4¼ x 11 comb-bound

ISSN: 1049-4502

LYNX EYE

Pam McCully, Kathryn Morrison
1880 Hill Dr.
Los Angeles, CA 90041
(213) 550-8522

Short stories, poetry, essays, black and white artwork.

We hope to encourage excellence by providing a showcase for the work of writers and artists, whether new or established.

Lyn Lifshin, Leonard Cirine, Julie McCracken, Vincent Zandri and Wayne Hogan.

Unsolicited Manuscripts Received/Published per year: 3,000

Reading Period: All.

Payment: $10 per piece and five copies.

Reporting Time: 8–12 weeks.

Copyright held by Buy FNASR (we copyright the serial).

1994; 4/yr; 300

$20/yr; $7/ea; $5/sample

130 pp; 5½ x 8½

$80/page; $40/½ page; $20/¼ page

ISSN: 1078-1862

THE LYRIC

Leslie Mellichamp
307 Dunton Drive SW
Blacksburg, VA 24060-5127
(703) 552-3475

Poetry.

We use rhymed verse in traditional forms, for the most part, about 40 lines max. We print only poetry, no opinions, no reviews. Our themes are varied, ranging from religious ectasy to humor to raw grief, but we feel no compulsion to shock, embitter, or confound our readers.

John Robert Quinn, Barbara Loots, Tom Riley, R.H. Morrison, Neill Megaw, Glenna Holloway, Alfred Dorn, Rhina P. Espaillat.

Unsolicited Manuscripts Received/Published per Year: 3,000/250.

$800 in prizes annually.

$12/yr; $3/ea

M

THE MACGUFFIN

Arthur J. Lindenberg
Schoolcraft College
18600 Haggerty Road
Livonia, MI 48152-2696
(313) 462-4400, ext 5292 or 5327

Poetry, fiction, essays, photographs, graphics/artwork.

We publish poetry, fiction, and essays of the highest quality. We have no biases with regard to style, but we are committed to seeking excellence. Prose submissions should be less than 4,000 words.

Joe Schall, Tom Sheehan, Wendy Bishop, Jim Daniels, Carol Morris.

Unsolicited Manuscripts Received/ Published per Year: 1,200/80.

Reading Period: Aug.–May.

Payment: 2 copies.

Reporting Time: 12 weeks.

Copyright held by Schoolcraft College; reverts to author upon publication.

1984; 3/yr; 600

$12/yr ind, $10/yr inst; $4.50/ea; 40%

144 pp; 5½ x 8½

No ads

MAGAZINE OF SPECULATIVE POETRY

Mark Rich and Roger Dutcher
P.O. Box 564
Beloit, WI 53512

Poetry, reviews, and commentary on poetry.

Speculative poetry is the equivalent to speculative fiction, that confluence of post-modernism and science fiction in the sixties and seventies of the US and UK.

Brian Aldiss, David Memmott,

Jane Yolen, Steve Rasnic Tem, Robert Frazier.
Unsolicited Manuscripts Received/Published per Year: 300-400/10.
Payment: 3¢/word; min. $3.00/poem.
Reporting Time: 1–8 weeks.
Copyright: First North American Serial Rights purchased, all rights revert to author.
1984; irregular; 200
$11/yr; $3.50/ea
22 pp; 5½ x 8½
ISBN: 8755-8785

MAGIC REALISM

C. Darren Butler
PYX Press
P.O. Box 922648
Sylmar, CA 91392-2648
Magic realism, exaggerated realism, glib fantasy.
We accept a wide range of material related to mythopoeic literature including magic realism, exaggerated realism, literary fantasy, genre/dark fantasy, and glib fantasy of the sort found in folktales, fables and myths.
Contest Rules for "MR" short fiction award available SASE.
Unsolicited Manuscripts Published per Year: 60.
Reading Period: year-round.
Payment: ¼ cent per word plus 3 copies.
Reporting Time: 3–6 months.
Copyright: held by contributers
1990; quarterly; 700
$19.50/4 issues; $5.95/ea
70 pp
ISSN: 1061-2386

THE MALAHAT REVIEW

Derk Wynand, Editor, Marlene Cookshaw, Associate Editor
Box 1700
University of Victoria
Victoria, British Columbia, CANADA V8W2Y2
(604) 721-8524
Fiction, poetry.
A "generalist" literary magazine, open to new and celebrated writers. Meticulously edited, eclectic and elegant.
Lorna Crozier, Leon Rooke, Patricia Young.
Unsolicited Manuscripts Received/Published per Year: 1,200/60.
Payment: $25 per magazine page.
Reporting Time: 3 months.
Copyright reverts to author; we buy first rights in English.
1967; 4/yr; 1,800
$25/yr (US); $7/ea (US)
132 pp; 6 x 9
ISSN: 0025-1216
Director

MANHATTAN POETRY REVIEW

Elaine Reiman-Fenton, Editor
FDR Box 8207
New York, NY 10150
(212) 355-6634

Poetry.

MANHATTAN POETRY REVIEW is dedicated to a celebration of excellence in contemporary American poetry, welcomes unsolicited manuscripts, and presents a balance of new and established poets in each issue. It was founded as a community of poets and readers to demonstrate the diversity of fine poetry in America today.

Unsolicited Manuscripts Received/ Published per Year: 1,200/50.

Reading Period: Sept.–Nov., Jan.–July.

Payment: none.

Reporting Time: 12–16 weeks.

Copyright reverts to author.

1992; $7.50 per issue, no subscriptions (foreign = U.S. $12.50)

52–60 pp; 5½ x 8½

ISSN: 885-9205

THE MANHATTAN REVIEW

Philip Fried
440 Riverside Dr., #45
New York, NY 10027
(212) 932-1854

Poetry, interviews, photographs, reviews.

We try to include American and foreign writers, and we focus on foreign writers with something to offer the current American scene. We like to think of poetry as a powerful discipline engaged with many other fields.

Peter Redgrove, Edmond Jabès, Christopher Bursk, A.R. Ammons, Stanislaw Baranczak, Bei Dao, Patricia Goedicke.

Unsolicited Manuscripts Received/ Published per Year: 400/1-4.

Payment: none.

Reporting Time: 8–10 weeks.

Copyright held by Philip Fried.

1980; 1/yr; 500

$10/ind per volume (two issues); $14/inst (2 issues)

64 pp

ISSN: 0275-6889

MÃNOA: A Pacific Journal of International Writing

Frank Stewart
English Department
University of Hawaii
Honolulu, HI 96822
(808) 956-3070 or 956-7808

Fiction, poetry, essays, reviews, interviews, translations, art, natural history essays.

US fiction and poetry, not limited to Pacific writers or themes;

also features original translations of recent work from Pacific Rim nations.

W. S. Merwin, Barry Lopez, Alberto Ríos, Naomi Shihab Nye, Norman Dubie, Arthur Sze, Janet Tan, Xvaoping Wang, David Rains Wallace.

Unsolicited Manuscripts Received/ Published per Year: 2,800/60.

Payment: copies, plus up to $20 per page prose; more for poetry.

Reporting Time: 6–16 weeks.

Copyright reverts to author on publication.

1989; 2/yr; 2,000

$20/yr ind, $26/yr inst; 50%

240+ pp; 7 x 10

Ad Rates: $200/page; $125/½ page

ISSN: 1045-7909

MANY MOUNTAINS MOVING

Naomi Horil, Marilyn Krysl
420 22nd St.
Boulder, CO 80302
(303) 545-9942
Fax (303) 444-6510

Fiction, poetry, nonfiction and art.

Publishes top-notch, previously unpublished fiction, poetry, nonfiction and art. Encourages writers and artists of all cultures to submit.

Amiri Baraka, Diane Glancy, Allen Ginsberg, Adrienne Rich, Luis Alberto Urrea

Unsolicited Manuscripts Received/Published per year: 2,000/60.

Payment: 3 copies and discount on additional copies.

Reading Period: year round.

Reporting Time: varies.

Copyright held by magazine; reverts to author upon publication.

1994; 3/yr; 2,000

$18/yr ($15/student); $6.50/ea.

192 pp; 6 x 9

Ad Rates: $150/page (5 x 8)

ISSN: 1080-6474

International Periodical Distributors, Bernhard DeBoer

THE MASSACHUSETTS REVIEW

Mary Heath, Paul Jenkins, Jules Chametzky
Memorial Hall
University of Massachusetts
Amherst, MA 01003
(413) 545-2689

Poetry, fiction, criticism, translation, interviews, photographs, graphics/artwork.

A quarterly of literature, the arts and current affairs; special art sections and special issues devoted to Feminism, Black literature, Ethnicity, Latin America, contemporary Ireland, etc. occasionally featured. S.A.S.E. with all mss & inquiries.

Ariel Dorfman, Marilyn Hacker, Seamus Heaney, Joyce Carol Oates, Octavio Paz.
Unsolicited Manuscripts Received/ Published per Year: 3,500–4,000/80–100.
Reading Period: Oct.–May
Payment: $50 prose, 35¢/line poetry ($10 min.).
Reporting Time: 3 months.
Copyright held by magazine; reverts to author upon publication when requested.
1959; 4/yr; 1,700
$15/ind, $20/inst; $5/ea + $1.00 postage; 40%
172 pp; 6 x 9
Ad Rates: $125/page (4⅛ x 7); $75/½ page (4⅛ x 3½)
Special university press rate: $100/2 full pages
ISSN: 0025-4878
DeBoer, Ubiquity, Fine Print

M/E/A/N/I/N/G

Susan Bee and Mira Schor
60 Lispenard St.
New York, NY 10013
(212) 431-3697
Art criticism and theory, artist statements, art book reviews.
A journal of contemporary art issues and theory; we publish writings by visual artists, art historians, and art critics.
Robert C. Morgan, Johanna Drucker, Charles Bernstein, Richard Tuttle, Nancy Spero, Daryl Chin, Emma Amos, Whitney Chadwick.
Unsolicited Manuscripts Received/ Published per year: 20/1 or 2.
Payment: small fee and issues for authors.
Copyright held by magazine.
1986; 2/yr; 1,000
$12/yr; $6/ea
56 pp; 8 ½ x 11
ISSN: 1040-8576
Ubiquity, SPD, DeBoer

MEDIPHORS

Eugene Radice, MD
Box 327
Bloomsburg, PA 17815
Short stories, essays, poetry, humor, photos.
A literary magazine of the health professions publishing broad work in the medicine and health field, open to general audiences for submissions and readership.
Unsolicited Manuscripts Received/ Published per year: 2,000/160.
Reading Period: all.
Payment: 2 publication copies.
Reporting Time: within 4 months.
Copyright held by 1st NA Serial Rights.
1993; 2/yr; 600
$15/yr; $5.50/ea; 20%
72 pp; 8½ x 11
ISSN: 1068-9745
Bernard DeBoer

MEN AS WE ARE

Jonathan Running Wind
P.O. Box 150615
Brooklyn, NY 11215-0615
(718) 499-2829

Fiction, poetry, essays, feature stories.

Deeply honest, vulnerable illumination of the masculine experience. A celebration and a lament of who we are today. Compassionate portrayals of our negative characteristics; models of how we can be at our highest.

James Oshinsky, Paul Milenski, David Thorn.

Unsolicited Manuscripts Received/Published per Year: 1,000/30–50.

Payment: yes.

Reporting Time: 3–6 months.

Copyright held 90 days, then reverts to author; non-exclusive anthology rights.

1994; 1/yr; 1,000

$20/4 issues; $5/ea

32 pp; 8 1/4 x 10 7/8

Ad Rates: $350/page; 3/4, 1/2, 1/4, 1/8, 1/12 page also available.

ISSN: 1067-9707

Fine Print

METAMORPHOSES

Laszlo Tikos, Editor in Chief
Melinda Kennedy, Lynn Prince, Editors
Univ. of Massachusetts
Amherst, MA 01003
(413) 545-2052
Fax (413) 545-3178

Literary translations.

Journal of the five college facility seminar on literary translations. Accepts submissions from outside as well.

Walter Kaiser, Seth Zimmermann, Ilan Stavans, Richard Wilbur, Peter Viereek

Unsolicited Manuscripts Received/Published per year: 50/25.

Reading Period: June–Aug./Jan.–Feb.

Payment: None.

Reporting Time: 1 month.

Copyright held by the authors/traslators.

$10/yr; $5/ea.

130–150 pp.

ISSN: 1068-7831

METROPOLITAIN

J. L. Bergsohn
6307 N. 31st St.
Arlington, VA 22207

Poetry and fiction.

We showcase the talents of Washington-area writers.

Hilary Tham, M. A. Schaffner, Elisavietta Ritchie.

Unsolicited Manuscripts Received/Published per Year: 700/230–50.

Payment: contributor's copy.
Reporting Time: 2–4 weeks.
Copyright reverts to author upon publication.
1991; 4/yr; 250
$8/yr; $2/ea
50 pp; 8 ½ x 5½

MICHIGAN QUARTERLY REVIEW

Laurence Goldstein
3032 Rackham Building
University of Michigan
Ann Arbor, MI 48109
(313) 764-9265

Interdisciplinary essays, fiction, poetry.

A general interest academic journal publishing essays and reviews in all areas, as well as fiction and poetry.

Donald Hall, Margaret Atwood, E.L. Doctorow.

Unsolicited Manuscripts Received/Published per Year: 3,000/40.
Payment: $8-$10/printed page.
Reporting Time: 4-6 weeks.
Copyright reverts to author after first publication.
1962; 4/yr; 1,800
$18/yr; $5/ea; 40%
160 pp; 6 x 9
Ad Rates: $100/page
ISSN: 0026-2420
DeBoer, Fine Print, Ubiquity

MID-AMERICAN REVIEW

George Looney, Editor-in-chief; Rebecca Meacham, Fiction; Tony Gardner, Poetry; Andrea Van Vorhis, Nonfiction; Jeff Gearing, Translations.
English Department
Bowling Green State University
Bowling Green, OH 43403
(419) 372-2725

Poetry, fiction, translations, essays, book reviews, interviews.

MAR publishes poetry using strong, evocative images and fresh language; fiction which is both character and language-oriented; translations of contemporary writers; essays and book reviews on contemporary authors.

Jack Driscoll, Stephen Dunn, Philip Graham, Susan Neville, Frankie Paino, Greg Pape, Alberto Ríos, Cathryn Hankla.

Unsolicited Manuscripts Received/Published per Year: 3,500+/90.
Reading Period: Sept.–May
Payment: copies and $10/page, up to $50.
Reporting Time: 1–4 months.
Copyright held by magazine; reverts to author upon publication.
1979; 2/yr; 1,000
$12/yr, $20/2 yrs; $7/ea
200 pp; 5½ x 8½
Exchange ads, 5 x 8
ISSN: 0747-8895

MID COASTER

Peter Blewett
2750 N. 45th St.
Milwaukee, WI 53210–2429

Poetry, fiction.

Unsolicited Manuscripts Received/Published per Year: 500-1,000/25

Payment: in copies.

Reporting Time: up to 8 weeks.

Copyright held by author.

1987; 1/yr; 800

$4.50/ea; 40%

36 pp; 8½ x 11

ISSN: 0892-970X

MIDLAND REVIEW

205 Morrill
Stillwater, OK 74078
(405) 744-9474

Poetry, fiction, photography, artwork, essays.

Journal of contemporary literature, literary criticism, and art.

Fritz Hamilton, Ionna-Veronica Warwick, Mark Cox.

Unsolicited Manuscripts Received/Published per Year: 400/50.

Payment: contributor copy.

1985; 1/yr; 200

$6/ea; $3/5 or more

128 pp; 6 x 9

Ad Rates: $80/page, $50/½ page, $50/¼ page

MINDPRINT REVIEW

Ron Pickup
P.O. Box 62
Soulsbyville, CA 95372
(209) 532-7045

Poetry, fiction, photographs, translations, graphics/artwork.

We publish quality prose, fiction, poetry, translations, B&W photography and graphics of both well-established and emerging writers, artists and photographers. Our submission base is Northern California, but our publication reflects a national/international cross section of work. Each issue forms a thematic focus pertaining to humanity or philosophy, but submissions are never limited to any subject, style or persuasion. Quality is our criteria for acceptance.

Rosalie Moore, John Oliver Simon, Lo Fu, Agusti Bartra, Jack Hirschman.

Payment: in copies only, upon publication.

Copyright held by magazine; reverts to author upon publication.

1983; 1/yr; 600

$7/yr ind, $7/yr inst; $6.50/ea, $7.50 by mail; 40%; consignment

128 pp; 6 x 9

Ad Rates: $240/page (4 x 7¾); $120/½ page (4½ x 4); $60/¼ page (4½ x 2½ or 2½ x 3¾)

ISSN: 1040-2233
Bookpeople

THE MINNESOTA REVIEW

Jeffrey Williams
the minnesota review
Dept. of English
East Carolina Univ.
Greenville, NC 27858
(919) 328-6388;
Fax (919) 328-4889

Poetry, fiction, criticism, essays, reviews, translations, interviews.

THE MINNESOTA REVIEW is a journal of committed writing. We are particularly interested in new work that is progressive in nature, with special commitment to the areas of socialist and feminist writing.

Jean Franco, Richard Ohmann, Michael Bérubé, Elizabeth Hahn, Joan Frank, Bruce Robbins.

Unsolicited Manuscripts Received/Published per Year: 1,500-2,000/50–75.

Payment: in copies.

Reporting Time: 60–90 days.

Copyright held by magazine; reverts to author upon publication.

1960; 2/yr; 1,600

\$12/yr ind, \$24/yr inst; \$7.50/ea

200 pp; 5½ x 8 ½

Ad Rates: \$100/page (5 x 7); \$150/2 pages; \$60/½ page (5 x 3½); \$30/¼ page (2 x 3)

ISSN: 0026-5667

MISSISSIPPI MUD

Joel Weinstein
1505 Drake Avenue
Austin, TX 78704
(512) 444-5459

Poetry, fiction, photographs, graphics/artwork.

MISSISSIPPI MUD presents lucid, elegant writing and art from the *ne plus ultra* of the American scene.

Katherine Dunn, Ursula K. Le Guin, Dionisio Martínez, Todd Grimson, Christina Zawadiwsky, Tom Spanbauer.

Unsolicited Manuscripts Received/Published per Year: 150/20.

Payment: cash, on publication, depending on length or scale.

Reporting Time: 6–8 months.

Copyright held by magazine; reverts to author upon publication.

1973; 2–3/yr; 1,500

\$19/4 issues, \$6/ea

52 pp, 11 x 17

MISSISSIPPI REVIEW

Frederick Barthelme
Southern Station, Box 5144
Hattiesburg, MS 39406
(601) 266-4321

Fiction, poetry, criticism, translation, interviews.

MISSISSIPPI REVIEW is a literary magazine published by the Center for Writers at the University of Southern Mississippi. The editors combine solicited and unsolicited works of well-known and new writers in an innovative format, producing three numbers a year. Although **MR** publishes mostly fiction and poetry, the editors are interested in literature in translation, interviews, and literary criticism.

Elizabeth Tallent, William Gibson, E.M. Cioran, Amy Hempel, Tama Janowitz.

Unsolicited Manuscripts Received/ Published per Year: 1,200/30-40.

Reading Period: Will not be reading new mss until January 1997.

Payment: in copies.

Reporting Time: 8–12 weeks.

Copyright held by magazine; reverts to author upon publication.

1976; 2/yr; 2,000

$15/yr; $12/ea

120 pp; 5½ x 8½

Ad Rates: $100/page; $50/½ page; exchange

ISSN: 0047-7559

DeBoer, Fine Print

THE MISSOURI REVIEW

Speer Morgan, Greg Michalson
University of Missouri
1507 Hillcrest Hall
Columbia, MO 65211
(573) 882-4474

Poetry, fiction, essays, reviews, interviews, special features of literary interest, cartoons.

Reading Period: year–round.

Payment: $20/page; (average) up to $500.

Reporting Time: 10–12 weeks.

Copyright held by the University of Missouri; reverts to author upon request.

1978; 3/yr; 6,500

$19/yr; $7/ea; 30%

224 pp; 6 x 9

Ad Rates: $250/page

ISSN: 0191-1961

ISBN: 1-879758

MOBIUS

Fred Schepartz
1250 E. Dayton #3
Madison, WI 53703
(608) 255-4224

Short fiction, poetry, occasional essays.

Fiction and poetry which uses social change as a primary or secondary theme. Doesn't have to be overtly political as long as it has something to say. Otherwise anything goes.

William Steigerwaldt, Gay Davidson, R. Russell, Bonnie Brown, Andrea Musher.
Payment: Copies.
Reporting Time: 8-10 weeks.
Copyright: Reverts to author upon publication.
1989; 4/yr; 1,500
$12/yr ind, $3.50/ea; 40%
32pp; 8 ½ x 11
Ad Rates: $150/page (7½ x 10); $80/½ page (3 x 9)

MODERN HAIKU

Robert Spiess
P.O. Box 1752
Madison, WI 53701
(608) 233-2738
Haiku, essays, reviews.
We publish only quality haiku in which felt-depth, insight and intuition are evident. Good university and public library subscription list includes foreign.
Paul O. Williams, Geraldine Little, William J. Higginson, Cor van den Heuvel, Wally Swist, Patricia Neubauer, James Kirkup.
Unsolicited Manuscripts Received/Published per Year: 14,000/850.
Payment: $1/haiku on acceptance; $5/page for articles.
Reporting Time: 2 weeks.
Copyright held by Robert Spiess; reverts to author upon publication.
1969; 3/yr; 700
$16.25/yr; $5.65/ea
108 pp; 5½ x 8½
ISSN: 0026-7821

THE MONOCACY VALLEY REVIEW

William Heath, Editor
Dept. of English
Mount Saint Mary's College
Emmitsburg, MD 21727
(301) 447-6122
Fiction, poetry, photographs, graphics, artwork, criticism, interviews, essays. Our motto is: "the magazine that is always local but never provincial." We welcome singular voices and particular visions that create a real world and dramatize what matters.
Holly St. John Bergon, Roser Caminals, Mary Noel, John Grey, Roberta Bevington, Barbara Petoskey, Maxine Combs.
Reading Period: Dec.–Jan.
Payment: $10-25 for each poem, story, or artwork accepted (funds permitting).
$8/2 issues; $5/ea

MONOGRAPHIC REVIEW/ REVISTA MONOGRAFICA

Genaro J. Pérez, Janet Pérez
Department of Classical and

Modern Languages
Texas Tech University
Lubbock, Texas 79409-2071
(806) 742-3145
Fax (806) 742-3306

Literature and criticism of the Hispanic world.

A professional journal of criticism in the Hispanic literatures, monographic in character, devoted to areas neglected by mainstream journals. Recent topics: The Erotic, The Comics, Women Poets, Science Fiction, Detective Fiction

David W. Foster, John Dowling, Manuel Andújar, Noel Valis, Paul Ilie.

Unsolicited Manuscripts Received/Published per Year: 50/25.
Reading Period: Aug. and Sept.
Payment: complimentary copy.
Reporting Time: 2 months.
Copyright: Perez & Perez
1985; 1/yr
$40/yr
pp vary
ISSN: 0885-7512

MOSAIC: A Journal for the Interdisciplinary Study of Literature

Dr. Evelyn J. Hinz
208 Tier Building
University of Manitoba
Winnipeg, Manitoba, R3T 2N2 CANADA
(204) 474-9763
Fax (204) 261-9086
E-mail: ejhinz@bldgarts.lan1.umanitoba.ca

Interdisciplinary study of literature.

MOSAIC publishers original scholarly articles which both theorize and demonstrate the way that insights from other disciplines can be use to elucidate literary works and issues, and vice versa.

Unsolicited Manuscripts Received/Published per Year: 200/30–32.
Payment: none.
Reporting Time: 4 months.
Copyright held by magazine.
1967; 4/yr; 1,000
$24/yr; $42/2 yrs; $53/3 yr (US/CANADA); $7/sample
138 pp; 6 x 9
Ad Rates: $150/page; $90/half page (B/W)
ISSN: 0027-1276
Hignell Printers (CANADA)

MOTHER EARTH INTERNATIONAL JOURNAL

Herman Berlandt, Editor
Maureen Hurley, Co-editor
Fort Mason Cultural Center
Bldg. D
San Francisco, CA 94123
(415) 776-6602

Fax (415) 776-3206

Seven major issues involving entries from 90 nationalities.

MOTHER EARTH is an international journal of English translations presenting the poet's perspective on the current political and ecological crisis.

(China) BEI DAO; (Egypt) MUHAMMED AFIFI MATAR; (Nigeria) WOLE SOYINKA; (Israel) YEHUDA AMICHAI: (Mexico) HOMERO ARIDJIS

Unsolicited Manuscripts Received/Published per Year: 200/35.

Reading Period: throughout the year.

Payment: free copies.

Reporting Time: 3 months.

Copyright held by magazine; reverts to author upon publication.

1992; 2–4; 1750

$18/yr; $5/ea; 50–60%

48 pp; 11 x 15 (tabloid)

Ad Rates: $300/page; $50/⅛ page

ISSN: 0 942405-74-3

EBSCO and Boer

MOUNT OLIVE REVIEW

Pepper Worthington, Editor; Janie Jones Sower, Assistant Editor; Susan Kurjiaka, Assistant Editor; Happy Taylor, Circulation Manager

634 Henderson Street

Mount Olive, NC 28365

(919) 658-2502

Poetry, fiction, criticism, essays, reviews, plays, interviews, photographs, graphics/artwork.

The **MOUNT OLIVE REVIEW** is a cutting-edge phenomenon with an emphasis on combining academic scholarship and creative, mainstream literature. The journal is theme oriented each year and welcomes book reviews, essays, short stories, poetry, interviews, and criticism as they all relate to the stated theme.

Copyright held by Mount Olive College

1987; 1/yr; 3,500

40%

300+ pp; 7 x 10 ½

Ad Rates: $150/page (10 x 6); $75/½ page (5 x 3); $35/¼ page (3 x 2)

ISSN: 0893-8288

MR. COGITO

John M. Gogol

Humanities

Pacific University

Forest Grove, OR 97116

Poetry, photographs, graphics/artwork.

Poetry in English, including translations; photographs, graphics. We like poems that surprise and move us with their language, sound and invention. **MR COGITO** specializes in publishing translations of East Central European poetry: i.e., Polish, Russian, Ukrainian Lithuanian, Latvian, Estonian, Czech, Slovak, Bulgarian, Rumainian, Greek, Serbian, Croatian, and German. Also interested in Native American poets and poems on Native American themes.

Baranczak, Herbert, Martinaitis, Cholin, Frajlich, Krynicki, Swirszczynska, Musial, Ficowski, Jastrun, Sujica, Poswiatowska, Orban, Richter, Marcenas, etc.

Unsolicitated Manuscripts Published per Year: 1%.

Reading Period: year–round.

Payment: 1 copy.

Reporting Time: 1–3 months.

Copyright held by magazine; all but anthology rights revert to author upon publication.

1973; irregular; 500

$10/3 issues; $3.50/ea

24–28 pp; 4¼ x 11

ISSN: 0740-1205

Ebsco, Faxon, Dawson

MUAE: A Journal of Transcultural Production

8 Harrison St., Ste. 3
New York, NY 10013
(212) 431-1291
Fax (212) 925-5684

Art/Fiction/Poetry/Cultural Criticism/Essays/Translations.

An annual journal of Asian and Asian diasporic culture, with special emphasis on Korea and the Korean diaspora.

Lawrence Urma, Miran Kim, Nam June Paik, Kimiko Hahn, Heinz Insu Fenkl.

Unsolicited Manuscripts Received/Published per year: 20/5.

Reading Period: January–March.

Payment: Varies.

Reporting Time: 3 months.

Copyright held by Kaya Production (has one-time right to print).

1995; 1/yr; 2,500

$19.95

272 pp; 7¼ x 9

Ad Rates: $150/page; $75/½ page; $50/¼ page; call about exchange agreements.

ISSN: 1074-830X

D.A.P./Distributed Art Publishers; SPD/Small Press Distribution.

N

NASSAU REVIEW

Dr. Paul A. Doyle, Managing Editor
English Dept.
Nassau Community College
State University of New York
Garden City, NY 11530
(516) 572-7792

Poetry, fiction, criticism, essays.

Unsolicited Manuscripts Received/Published per Year: 600–700/30–35.

Reading Period: Sept.–Feb.

Payment: none.

Reporting Time: 5–7 months.

Copyright held by Nassau Community College; reverts to author upon publication.

1964; 1/yr; 1,200

Free.

92–95 pp; 6½ x 9½

THE NEBRASKA REVIEW

James Reed, Fiction Editor; Susan Aizenberg, Poetry Editor
212 FA
University of Nebraska, Omaha
Omaha, NE 68182-0326
(402) 554-2771

Poetry, fiction.

TNR publishes quality literary fiction and poetry, material that transcends mere technical proficiency.

Carolyne Wright, Joseph Geha, Joan Joffe-Hall, E.S. Goldman, David Hopes, Erin Belieu, Cris Mazza, Pamela Stewart

Unsolicited Manuscripts Received/Published per Year: 1,500/6-10 fiction; 45-50 poetry.

Reading Period: January–May.

Payment: 1 year subscription plus contributor's copies.

Reporting Time: 3–5 months (longest for poetry.)

Copyright held by magazine; reverts to author upon publication.

1972; 2/yr; 500

$9.50/yr; $5.00/ea; 40%
80 pp; 5½ x 8½
Ad Rates: $45/page (3⅝ x 6¼); $25/½ page (3⅝ x 3)
ISSN: 8755-514X

NEGATIVE CAPABILITY

Sue Brannan Walker, Ron Walker
62 Ridgelawn Dr., East
Mobile, AL 36608
(334) 343-6163

Poetry, fiction, essays, reviews, interviews, photographs, graphics/artwork, original music, bagatelles. Annual poetry & fiction contest: $1,000 award for each.

NEGATIVE CAPABILITY is a creative journal whose emphasis is joy—not merely laughter, though we encourage humor, but the joy that arrives through insight into oneself and others, the world and our all too human condition.

John Brugaletta, Vivian Shipley, Marge Piercy, Jimmy Carter, John Updike, Diane Wakoski, Leo Connellan, X. J. Kennedy.

Unsolicited Manuscripts Received/Published per Year: 2,000/400.
Reading Period: Sept.—May.
Payment: 1 copy.
Reporting Time: 6 weeks.
Copyright held by magazine; reverts to author upon publication.
1981; 3/yr; 1,000
$18/yr ind, $24/yr inst; $5/ea; 40%
200+ pp; 5¼ x 8¼
Ad Rates: $100/page (4½ x 8); $50/½ page (4 x 4); $25/¼ page (4 x 2½)
ISSN: 0277-5166

NEW AMERICAN WRITING

Maxine Chernoff, Paul Hoover
369 Molino Ave.
Mill Valley, Ca 94941

Poetry, fiction, essays, plays, graphics.

Nathaniel Mackey, Lyn Hejinian, Charles Simic, Ron Padgett, Bob Perelman, Robert Creeley, John Ashbery, Wanda Coleman.

Unsolicited Manuscripts Received/Published per Year: 1,500/50.
Reading Period: Sept.–Dec. and Mar.–June.
Payment: $5/page, when available.
Reporting Time: 1–3 months.
Copyright held by OINK! Press, Inc.; reverts to author upon publication.
1971; 2/yr; 5,000
$18/3 issues; $7/ea; libraries and foreign orders: $24/3 issues, $9/ea; 40%
150 pp; 5½ x 8½
Ad Rates: $150/page (5 x 8); $100/½ page (2¼ x 4)
ISSN: 0893-7842
Ingram, SPD, Ubiquity, Total

NEW DELTA REVIEW

c/o Department of English
Louisiana State University
Baton Rouge, LA 70803-5001
(504) 388-4079

Poetry, fiction, essays, interviews.

NDR is a literary journal published by the Creative Writing Program at LSU. We publish both extablished and new writers. We offer the Eyster Prizes, which honor Warren Eyster, teacher, author, and faculty advisor to **NDR**'s predecessors.

James English, Julie McCracken, Virgil Suarez, Mircea Cartarescu, and an interview with Pulitzer Prizewinner Robert Olen Butler.

Unsolicited Manuscripts Received/Published per Year: 2,000/45.

Reading Period: year–round.

Payment: in copies; Eyster Prize awarded to 1 poet and 1 fiction writer per issue.

Copyright: First North American; reverts to author upon publication.

1984; 2/yr; 500

$7/yr; $4/ea; 40%

100 pp; 6 x 9

Ad Rates: from other literary magazines.

NEW ENGLAND REVIEW

Stephen Donadio
Middlebury College
Middlebury, VT 05753
(802) 388-3711, ext 5075

Fiction, poetry, essays, reviews, translations, interviews-open to memorable writing of all kinds.

NEW ENGLAND REVIEW has been a mainstay of the American literary community for almost twenty years. Now located at Middlebury College, under new editorship, and newly affiliated with University Press of New England, **NER** is committed to the exploration of all forms of contemporary cultural expression, in the United States and elsewhere. In addition to original literary work in traditional genres, the magazine welcomes speculative and interpretive essays, critical reassessments, statements by visual artists, and letters from abroad.

Arnost Lustig, Ann Beattie, Stephen Dunn, Donald Hall, Edward Hirsch, W. D. Wetherell, Miroslav Holub, Samuel F. Pickering.

Reading Period: Sept. – June.

Payment: $10/minimum.

Reporting Time: 5–7 weeks.

Copyright held by author.

1978; 4/yr; 3,000

$23/yr ind, $30/yr inst; $7/ea; 40%

180 pp; 6 x 9

Ad Rates: $300/page (7 x 10); $150/½ page (7 x 5); $100/¼ page (3½ x 5)
ISSN: 0736-2579

NEW HOPE INTERNATIONAL

Gerald England
20 Werneth Ave.,
Gee Cross, Hyde, Cheshire SK14 SNL ENGLAND
0161-351-1878

Poetry, short fiction, b & w artwork

NHI WRITING publishes poetry from traditional to avant-garde, including translations. **NHI REVIEW** covers books, mags, cassettes, PC-software, etc.

Lisa Kucharski, B. Z. Niditch, Mary Rudbeck Stanko.

Unsolicited Manuscripts Received/Published per Year: 5000/150
Payment: in copies only.
Reporting Time: usually within 2–3 months.
Copyright: First British Serial Rights.
1980; 2–6/yr; 1,500
$20/yr; $4/ea (Sterling only, payable to G. England)
36 pp
ISSN: 0260-7958

NEW LAUREL REVIEW

Lee Meitzen Grue
828 Lesseps St.
New Orleans, LA 70117
(504) 947-6001

Poetry, fiction, criticism, essays, reviews, translation, interviews, graphics/artwork, whatever is interesting.

NEW LAUREL REVIEW publishes poetry, fiction, translation, articles; work of sound scholarship which is alive. We hope to continue showing the best writing by nationally accepted writers with that of fresh new talent not seen before.

Enid Shomer, Sue Walker, Martha McFerren, James Nolan, Nahid Rachlin.

Reading Period: Sept.–May.
Reporting Time: varies.
Copyright held by author.
1971; 500
$9/yr ind, $11/yr inst.
125 pp; 6 x 9
ISSN: 0145-8388

NEW LETTERS

James McKinley, Editor; Robert Stewart, Managing Editor; Glenda McCrary, Administrative Assistant
University of Missouri, Kansas City
Kansas City, MO 64110
(816) 235-1168 or 235-1120

Poetry, fiction, reviews, photographs, graphics/artwork.

NEW LETTERS, an international literary quarterly, publishes contemporary writing, including that of well-known writers and fresh, new talents and interviews with Nobel Laureates and Pulitzer Prize Winners. Also publishes photographs and graphics; notable discoveries of overlooked gems. e.g., Theodore Roethke interview, Countee Cullen memoir, and Richard Wright, archival material.

Jim Harrison, Jorie Graham, William H. Gass, Tess Gallagher, Luisa Valenzuela, Margaret Atwood, Thomas Berger, William Burroughs, Rosellen Brown, Lisel Mueller, Amiri Baraka, John Updike, Annie Dillard.

Unsolicited Manuscripts Received/Published per Year: 5,000/100.

Reading Period: Oct. 15–May 15.

Payment: small honorarium and copies.

Reporting Time: 6–18 weeks.

Copyright held by magazine; reverts to author upon publication.

1934; 4/yr; 2,500

$17/yr ind, $20/yr inst; $5/ea; 40%–50%

128 pp; 6 x 9

Ad Rates: $150/page (4 x 6⅞); $100/½ page (4 x 3⅛)

Ingram, Ubiquity

NEW MYTHS: MSS

Robert Mooney
SUNY Binghampton
Box 530
Binghampton, NY 13901
(607) 777-2168

Poetry, fiction, essays, photographs, graphics.

Special emphasis on publishing the best work of young and unestablished writers with the work of well-known writers.

Andrew Hudgins, Dianne Benedict, Gerald Stern, William Stafford, Linda Pastan.

Payment: whenever funds allow.

Reporting Time: 2–8 weeks.

Copyright reverts to author upon publication.

1961; 2/yr; 1,000

$8.50/yr ind, $14/yr inst; $5.50/ea

Ad Rates: $500/page; $250/½ page

NEW NOVEL REVIEW

Lynne Diamond-Nigh
New Novel Review
Elmira College
Elmira, NY 14901
(607) 735-1898
Fax (607) 735-1701

French, Hispanic and Anglo-American new novel. Fiction issue every 2 years.

Refereed journal dedicataed to French, Hispanic and Anglo-American new novel and related

visual arts. Comparative and interdisciplinary work welcome.
Lois Oppenheim, Alasdair Gray, Eberhard Calle-Gruber, Michel Butor, Valerie Minogue.
Unsolicited Manuscripts Received/ Published per year: 30/5.
Reading Period: all—slow in summer.
Payment: 0.
Reporting Time: 3.
Copyright held by NNR.
1993; 2/yr; 100
$16/yr ind, $22/yr inst; $8/ea
100 pp; 6 x 9
ISSN: 1070-844

NEW ORLEANS REVIEW

Ralph Adamo
Box 195
Loyola University
New Orleans, LA 70118
(504) 865-2295
Poetry, short fiction, translations, literary & film criticism, artwork.
Payment: please inquire
Reporting Time: 3 months
1968; 4/yr; 1,000
$21/yr inst, $18/yr ind; $9/ea.
100-160 pp; 6 x 9
ISSN: 0028-6400

THE NEW PRESS

Robert Balogh, President; Joseph Sullivan, Editor-in-Chief; Evie-Ivy Biber, Poetry Editor; Carol Blair-Wolfe, Art Editor
63-44 Saunders Street, Suite 3, Rego Park, NY 11374
(718) 459-6807
Fax (718) 275-1646
Poetry, short stories, essays, line drawings.
A literary quarterly that stresses poetic vision and voice. For the literate mind. Work should be accessible and enjoyable to an intelligent reader.
Unsolicited Manuscripts Received/ Published per Year: 750/100.
Payment: 2 copies; $100 prizes for published essay and fiction cntest winners; $200 first prize, $75 second prize, five 2-year subs as third prize for poetry contest winners.
Reporting Time: 2–3 months.
Copyright: First time serial rights; reverts to author.
1984; 4/yr; 2,000
$15/yr; $4/ea; 40%
48 pp; 8½ x 11
$100/page; $65/½ page; $40/¼ page; $20/business card
ISSN: 0894-6078
Ubiquity

the new renaissance

Louise T. Reynolds, Patricia Michaud, Michal Anne Kucharski

9 Heath Road
Arlington, MA 02174

Fiction, poetry; lead articles; stories & poetry including bilingual translations; reproduction of paintings, sculpture, mixed media, photographs; commentary, graphics, illustrations, essays, reviews.

We offer a forum for idea/opinion pieces on political/sociological pieces, and publish a wide variety of styles, statements, tones, and visions in fiction, poetry and art. Since we take a classicist position, we avoid the trendy and the fashionable, for the most part, but our range is so broad it includes contradictory statements within a single issue. There is, however, an emphasis on the human condition.

Tom Ruane, Marvin Mandell, Bennett Capers, Richard Lynch, J. Patrick Lewis, Albino Pierro, (Lugi Bonaffini, translator) Joan Colby Ann Struthers

Unsolicited Manuscripts Received/ Published per Year: 1,000+/25-30.

Reading Period: Jan.–Feb. and Sept.–Oct.

Payment: After publication.

Reporting Time: 6–15 weeks, poetry; 20–50 weeks, prose. One month for queries. All fiction/ poetry submissions are tied into our award programs for work published in a 3-issue volume of *tnr*. Independent judges. Winners from Vol. IX will be announced in the Spring 1996. Submitting periods: Sept./Oct. & Jan./Feb. Entry fee for subscribers: $10 per submitting period, U.S. Non-subscribers: $15 per submitting period. Recent issue or 2 back issues or extend subscription by one issue.

Copyright held by magazine.

1968; 2/yr; 1,500

$19.50/3 issues; $21/3 issues (CANADA); $23/3 issues; $8.50/sample of most recent issue.

144–192 pp; 6 x 9

ISSN: 0028-6575

NEW VIRGINIA REVIEW

Mary Flinn, Editor; Margaret Gibson, Poetry Editor.
1306 East Cary St., 2A
Richmond, VA 23219
(804) 782-1043

Poetry, fiction, essays.

NEW VIRGINIA REVIEW: a trice yearly collection of new poetry, fiction, and essays that strives to publish the best possible work being done by contemporary authors both unknown and widely recognized. Special issues forthcoming. Nature and poetry at the end of the century; New Russian prose in translation.

Richard Bausch, Peter Taylor, Mandy Sayer, Mona Van Duyn, Rachel Hadas.

Unsolicited Manuscripts Received/ Published per Year: 6,000+/40.

Payment: $10/printed page, $25 minimum for poems, upon publication.

Copyright held by magazine, and individual writers; reverts to author upon publication.

1979; 3/yr; 3,000

$15/yr; $6/ea; 50% w/no return discount on back issues w/subscriptions.

160–200 pp; 6½ x 10

No ads

ISSN: 0-939233-00-2

NEXT PHASE

Kim Guarnaccia
5A Green Meadow Dr.
Nantucket, MA 02554
(508) 325-0411
Fax (508) 325-0056

Fiction, commentary, reviews, poetry.

Whether your interest lies in innovative ways to save our planet, social science fiction, or winning poetry, **NEXT PHASE** offers a unique compilation of the best of the small press in a well designed format.

Dr. Timothy Leary, D.F. Lewis, Allen Ginsberg.

Unsolicited Manuscripts Received/ Published per Year: 150/25.

Payment: 3 contributors copies.

Reporting Time: 6 weeks.

Copyright reverts to author.

1989; 3/yr; 1,900

$10/yr; $18/2yr

52 pp; 8½ x 11

Ad Rates: $100/page; $60/½ page; $40/¼ page

Fine Print, Ubiquity, Desert Moon, IPD, Ingram

NIGHT ROSES

Allen T. Billy, Sandra Taylor
P.O. Box 393
Prospect Heights, IL 60070
(708) 392-2435

Poetry, some art.

We like to publish romance poetry, flower poetry, ghost images of past or future and odds and ends of interest.

Genoa, Mary R. De Maine, Ken Stone, Jane Camron.

Unsolicited Manuscripts Received/ Published per Year: 1,500/150.

Reading Period: Sept.–July.

Payment: copy of issue.

Reporting Time: 4–12 weeks.

Write for guidelines before submitting work.
Copyright belongs to authors.
1986; 2–4/yr; 250
$10/3 issues; $4/sample; $5/Current New issues per copy
44–56 pp; 5⅜ x 8½

NIMROD: International Journal of Prose & Poetry

Francine Ringold
University of Tulsa
600 S. College
Tulsa, OK 74104
(918) 631-2000

Poetry, fiction, prose, translation, photographs, graphics/artwork, interviews.

NIMROD seeks vigorous writing that is neither wholly of the academy nor of the streets. Fall issues feature the winners and finalists of the Nimrod/Hardman Literary Awards Competition and spring issues are thematic. Past thematic issues include "Arabic Literature," "China Today," "India: A Wealth of Diversity," "Oklahoma Indian Markings," "Clap Hands and Sing: Writers of Age," "Australian Literature: Then and Now" "O! Canada," "Article Circle."

Wendy Stevens, Tess Gallagher, Denise Levertov, Gish Jen, Sharon Sakson, Alvin Greenberg, Janette Turner Hospital, Charles Johnson, Stanley Kunitz.

Unsolicited Manuscripts Received/Published per Year: 2000 fiction and poetry/2%.
Reading Period: year–round.
Payment: $5/page up to $25 plus two copies; also $1,000 to first place winners in our fiction and poetry competition, $500 for second place.
Reporting Time: 3–6 months.
Copyright of entire magazine held by the University of Tulsa. Rights to individual stories revert to authors.
1956; 2/yr; 4,000–4,500
$15.00/yr; $8.00/ea
160 pp; 6 x 9
Ad Rates: $200/page; $100/½ page
ISSN: 0029-053X

96 INC

Vera Gold and Julie Phipps, Editors
P.O. Box 15559
Boston, MA 02215
(617) 267-0543
Fax (617) 267-6725

Fiction, poetry, interviews, graphics/artwork.

96 INC, the parent organization of the Kenmore Writers Group, was formed to foster the publication of original literary works, with an emphasis on new writers; to sponsor public and private readings; and to train students of high school and other ages.

Payment: 4 copies of magazine and free sucsbription. Modest fee when funds are available.

Copyright reverts to author upon publication.

1992; 2/yr; 3,000

$10/yr; $4/ea; 40%; consignment

50 pp; 8½ x 11

Ad Rates: $100/page (8½ x 11); $75/½ page (4¼ x 5½); $50/¼ page (2⅛ x 2¾)

DeBoer

NIT & WIT

Harrison McCormick, Marie Aguirre
P.O. Box 627
Geneva, IL 60134
(312) 232-9496

Poetry, fiction, essays, reviews, interviews, photographs, graphics/artwork.

NIT & WIT is a full-spectrum cultural arts magazine with regular features on art, music, dance, theatre, film, architecture, photography, reviews, essays, fiction and poetry.

Philip Graham, June Brinder, Gordon Lish, Sharon Sheehe Stark.

Payment: none.

Reporting Time: 2–3 weeks.

Copyright held by author.

1977; 6/yr; 6,000

$12/yr; $2/ea; 40%–50%

68 pp; 8½ x 11

Ad Rates: $750/page (7⅛ x 10); $390/½ page (4 11/16 x 7⅜); $210/¼ page (3½ x 4 15/16)

NO ROSES REVIEW

Carolyn Koo, Davis McCombs
1322 N. Wicker Park
Chicago, IL 60622

Poetry, 10 pp max.

Barbara Guest, Lyn Hejinian, Leslie Scalapino, Susan Wheeler, Rosmarie Waldrop, Charles Bernstein, Ron Silliman, Donald Revell.

Payment: in copies.

Reporting Time: 2–3 months.

Copyright reverts to author upon publication.

1992; 2/yr; 350

$12/yr; $6/ea

60 pp

ISSN in application.

THE NORTH AMERICAN REVIEW

Robley Wilson
University of Northern Iowa
Cedar Falls, IA 50614
(319) 273-6455

Poetry, fiction, criticism, essays,

reviews, graphics/artwork.

Oldest magazine in North America, publishing fiction and nonfiction, poetry and reviews. Winner in 1981 and 1983 of National Magazine Award for fiction. Nonfiction frequently has ecological/environmental slant.

Unsolicited Manuscripts Received/ Published per Year: 20,000 poetry, 3,000 prose/30-35 poems, 55-65 prose.

Reading Period: Jan.–Apr. 1, Fiction.

Payment: $10/published page; 50¢/line for poetry, $20 minimum.

Reporting Time: 1–3 months.

Copyright by University of Northern Iowa; reverts to author upon publication.

1815; 6/yr; 4,700

$18/yr; $4/ea

48+ pp; 8⅛ x 10⅞

Ad Rates: $500/page (7 x 10); $200/⅓ page (2¼ x 10)

ISSN: 0029-2397

Eastern News

NORTH ATLANTIC REVIEW

John Gill
15 Arbutus Lane
Stony Brook, NY 11790-1408
(516) 751-7886

Fiction, Essays.

General fiction, with a special section in each issue devoted to literary or social issues.

Lewis Turco, Burton Raffel, Walter Cummins, Richard Eberhart, David Ignatow, Archibald MacLeish, James Dickey, May Swenson, David Slavitt, Richard Wilbur, Louis Simpson.

Unsolicited Manuscripts Received/ Published per Year: 1,600/40.

Reading Period: year–round.

Reporting Time: 4–5 months.

Copyright held by author.

1989; 1/yr; 1,000

$10/yr; 40%

300; 7 x 9½

$200/page; $125/½ page; $75/¼ page

ISSN: 1040-7324

NORTH CAROLINA LITERARY REVIEW

Alex Albright
English Dept., ECU
Greenville, NC 27858
(919) 328-4876 or (919) 328-6041
Fax (919) 328-4889

Articles, essays, interviews, reviews, photos, w/NC focus.

A magazine of literature, culture, and history, for serious readers found as often in bookstores and libraries as in universities.

Fred Chappell, A.R. Ammons, Leon Rooke, Janet Lembke, James Applewhite, Fielding

Dawson, Michael Rumaker, Paul Metcalf, Elaine Gottlieb.

Unsolicited Manuscripts Received/ Published per Year: 110/6.

Payment: $50–$500.

Reporting Time: 6 weeks on queries; no unsolicited fiction or poetry, please.

Copyright: First rights held by magazine; returned to author on request.

1992; 1/yr; 1,200 paid

$17/2 issues; $11.50/ea ppd.; Returnable/NR 30–40%

224 pp; 7½ x 10

Ad Rates: $200/page; $125/½ page; $75/¼ page

ISSN: 1063-0724

Ebsco, Faxon, Cox, Swets

NORTH DAKOTA QUARTERLY

Robert W. Lewis, Editor; William Borden, Fiction Editor; Jay Meek, Poetry Editor

University of North Dakota, Box 7209

Grand Forks, ND 58202

(701) 777-3322

Poetry, fiction, criticism, essays, reviews, graphics.

An interdisciplinary journal in the arts and humanities. Recent and forthcoming special issues on Yugoslav culture, Egypt, and Hemingway.

Sherman Paul, Kathleen Woodward, Philip Booth, Naguib Mahfouz, Carol Shields, Martin Espada, Jane Mead, Weldon Kees, Mary Oppen.

Unsolicited Manuscripts Received/ Published per Year: 1,000/125.

Payment: in copies.

Reporting Time: 1–3 months.

Copyright by University of North Dakota.

1910; 4/yr; 1,000

$20/yr; $5/ea; $10 for special issues; 20%

200 pp; 6 x 9

ISSN: 0029-277X

NORTHEAST ARTS

Mr. Leigh Donaldson

J.F.K. Station

P.O. Box 6061

Boston, MA 02114

Poetry, reviews, fiction.

NORTHEAST ARTS is an arts literary journal, featuring original poetry, short fiction, essays, photography, black & white art and reviews.

Otto Laske, S.P. Luttrell, Sebastian Lockwood.

Unsolicited Manuscripts Received/ Published per Year: 2,000/100.

Payment: 2 copies.

Reporting Time: 2–3 months.

Copyright: one-time use, rights revert to creator.

$10/yr; $4.50/ea
26-32 pp; 6½ x 9½
Ad Rates: $75/page (5 x 8); $45/½ page (5 x 4½) or $50/½ page (2½ x 8)

NORTHEAST CORRIDOR

Susan Balée, Editor; Peggy Finn, Fiction Editor; Jeffrey Loo, Janna King, Poetry Editors
Beaver College
450 S. Easton Rd.
Glenside, PA 19038
(215) 572-2870
Short stories, poetry, drama, personal essays, interviews, black & white photos, line art.
NORTHEAST CORRIDOR is a literary magazine focusing on the work of writers and artists in the Northeastern United States. We seek excellent fiction, poetry, plays, essays, black and white line art and photography.
Eleanor Wilner, Glen Weldon, Kermit Moyer, Frederick Morgan, Geoffrey Clark.
Unsolicited Manuscripts Received/Published per Year: 900/40–60.
Reading Period: Sept.–May.
Payment: $10/per poem; $25/story or essay; $100 for best of each genre in issue.
Reporting Time: 3 months or less.
Copyright held by NEC until publication; then it reverts to author.
1993; 2/yr; 1,000
$20/libraries; $10/ind; $5.00/ea; $3.00
90-150 pp; 6½ x 9
Ad Rates: $200/page
Fine Print

THE NORTH STONE REVIEW

James Naiden, Editor
Anne Duggan, Associate Editor
Jack Jarpe, Assistant Editor
Box 14098
Minneapolis, MN 55414
(612) 721-8011
Fax (401) 789-3793
E-mail: nstone.@uol.con
Poetry, fiction, criticism, book reviews, art work.
A literary magazine whose editors try to find the best writing possible and publish it.
Robert Bly, X. J. Kennedy, David Ignatow, Ralph Mills, Jr., Maura Stanton
Unsolicited Manuscripts Received/Published per year: 600/50–60.
Reading Period: All year round.
Payment: 2 copies.
Reporting Time: Promptly to three months.
Copyright held by magazine.
1971; various; 1,750

$20/2 issues; $10/single copy
260–310 pp; 5½ x 8½
Ad Rates: query first
ISSN: 1-887341-03-X
Bernhard DeBoer

NORTHWEST LITERARY FORUM

Ce Rosenow, Nancy Hune
3410 NE. Sandy Blvd.
#143
Portland, OR 97213

Haiku, poetry, fiction, interviews.

We are a quarterly which integrates haiku and its related forms with poetry and short fiction.

Vincent Tripi, Michael Dylan Welch, Lyn Lifshin, Errol Miller, Jim Kacian; Interviews: Ann Charters, Sam Hamill.

Unsolicited Manuscripts Received/Published per Year: 800/130.

Reading Period: year-round.

Payment: 1 copy of journal.

Reporting Time: 1–2 months.

Copyright reverts to author upon publication.

1992; 4/yr
$15/yr; $4/ea; 60%/40%
44 pp; 8½ x 5½
ISSN: 1062-3353

NORTHWEST REVIEW

John Witte, Hannah Wilson
369 PLC
University of Oregon
Eugene, OR 97403
(503) 346-3957

Poetry, fiction, criticism, essays, reviews, translation, interviews, graphics/artwork.

NORTHWEST REVIEW is a tri-annual publishing poetry, fiction, artwork, interviews, book reviews and comment. We have no other criterion for acceptance than that of excellence. We are devoted to representing the widest possible variety of styles and perspectives (experimental, feminist, political, etc.), unified within a humanist framework. "A publication to which the wise and honest, and literate, may repair!"—William Stafford.

Joyce Carol Oates, Madeline DeFrees, Alan Dugan, Morris Graves, Raymond Carver.

Unsolicited Manuscripts Received/Published per Year: 4,000/90.

Payment: in copies.

Reporting Time: 8–10 weeks.

First serial rights held by magazine; reverts to author upon request.

1957; 3/yr; 1,100
$20/yr; $7/ea; 20%–40%
160 pp; 6 x 9
Ad Rates: $160/page (6 x 9)
ISSN: 0029-3423

THE NOTRE DAME REVIEW

Valerie Sayers, Editor
Julia Cosmides, Managing Editor
Creative Writing Program
English Dept.
Univ. of Notre Dame
Notre Dame, IN 46556
(219) 631-6952

Fiction, poetry, interviews, book reviews.

A magazine devoted to publishing both established and fledgeling authors of innovative and provocative poetry and prose.

Seamus Heaney, Robert Hass, Czeslaw Milosz, Denise Levertoy, John Peck.

Unsolicited Manuscripts Received/Published per year: 130/10.

Reading Period: Sept.-April.

Payment: Vary.

Reporting Time: 1–3 months.

Copyright held by authors.

1995; 2/yr; 2,000

$15/yr ind, $20/yr inst; $8/ea; 20$pct$

160 pp; 6 x 9

Ad Rates: $120/page (5 x 8); $65/½ page

ISSN: 1082-1864

B. DeBoer

NOW & THEN, THE APPALACHIAN MAGAZINE

Jane Harris Woodside, Nancy Fischman
CASS/ETSU
Box 70556
Johnson City, TN 37614
(423) 929-5348
Fax (423) 929-6340

Anything to do with the Appalachian scene.

NOW & THEN reflects the complexity of life in the Appalachians. Our articles, interviews, essays, short stories, poems, and photographs provide insight into frequently overlooked aspects of the Appalachian region.

Ruth Moose, Jeff Daniel Marion, Sharyn McCrumb, Howard Dorgan, Gurney Norman.

Unsolicited Manuscripts Received/Published per year: 100/8--10.

Reading Period: August, December, & April.

Payment: $15/typeset page.

Reporting Time: 4–5 months.

Copyright held by: Center for Appalachian Studies & Services

1984; 3/yr; 1,000

$15/yr; $4.80/ea; 40%

40 pp; 11 x 8½

ISSN: 0896-2693

Center for Appalachian Studies & Services.

O

OASIS, a literary magazine

Neal Storrs, Editor & Publisher; Eugene Storrs, Assistant Editor
1833 10th Street SW
Largo, FL 34648
(813) 587-9552

Poetry, fiction, essays, translation.

First, last and only consideration is quality of writing. Genres, target audiences, don't apply. Strongly interestedin translations. Mailings, Neal Storrs, Bookstores in Tampa Bay area. Want nothing more than to stay on present course.

James Sallis and Susan Medenica.

Payment: $5/poem; $15–$50/prose work.

Reporting Time: no more than ten days.

Copyright: Neal Storrs, reverts to author upon publication.

1992; 6/yr; 150

$25/yr ind, $25/yr inst; $4.95/ea

70 pp; 7 x 10

ISSN: 1064-6299

OBJECT LESSON/ Weighted Anchor Press

Joshua S. Beckman
44 Laurelcrest Rd.
Madison CT 06443

Fiction, poetry, one act plays, essays, essays on art, interviews, black and white artwork, artists books, letters.

OBJECT LESSON is open to all styles of writing no length requirements.

Alice Mattison, Lance Olsen, Harry Brody, Paul Beckman.

Unsolicited Manuscripts Received/ Published per Year: 1,200/50.

Reading Period: year–round.

Payment: in copies.

Reporting Time: 6–8 weeks.

Copyright: Object Lesson, reverts to author on publication.

1990; 3/yr; 500

$20/yr; $8/ea

300 pp; 5½ x 7, perfect bound

Ad Rates: $100/page (6½ x 5); trades avail.
ISSN: 1061-429X

130 pp; 6 x 9
Ad Rates: $200/page (4½ x 7⅛); $100/½ page (4½ x 3½)
ISSN: 0888-4412

OBSIDIAN II: Black Literature In Review

Gerald Barrax, Joyce Pettis
Box 8105
Department of English
North Carolina State University
Raleigh, NC 27695-8105
(919) 737-3870

Poetry, fiction, criticism, essays, reviews.

OBSIDIAN II is a biannual review for the study and cultivation of creative works in English by Black writers worldwide, with scholarly critical studies by all writers on all aspects of Black literature, book reviews, poetry, short fiction, interviews, bibliographies, bibliographical essays, and very short plays in English.

Houston A. Baker, Jr., Gayl Jones, Wanda Coleman, Raymond R. Patterson, Gerald Early.

Payment: none.

Copyright held by Department of English, North Carolina State University; reverts to author upon publication.

1986; 2/yr; 500

$12/yr ind, $12/yr inst; $5/ea; 40%

ODESSA POETRY REVIEW

Jim Wyzard
RR 1, Box 39
Odessa, MO 64076

Poetry.

Ester Leipen, Rod Kessler, Rochelle Lynn Holt, Marian Park.

Payment: varies with quality of work.

Copyright held by Jim Wyzard; reverts to author upon publication.

1984; 4/yr; 500–700

$16/yr; $4/ea; 40%

150 pp; 5½ x 8½

No ads

THE OGALALA REVIEW (formerly EPIPHANY)

Gordon Grice
P.O. Box 628
Guymon, OK 73942

Fiction, poetry, translations, creative nonfiction.

TOR specializes in literary fiction, nonfiction, and poetry.

Alicia Ostriker, R. S. Gwynn, Enid Shomer, David Citino, Trent Busch.

Unsolicited Manuscripts Received/ Published per Year: 2,000/12.
Reading Period: Feb.–Aug.
Payment: 2 copies, small honorarium when funds permit.
Reporting Time: 1–4 months.
Copyright: One time publishing right—copyright reverts to author.
1990; 1/yr; 400
$5/ea
Format varies
Ad Rates: $100/page (5 x 8); $60/½ page (5 x 3¾)

THE OHIO REVIEW

Wayne Dodd
209 C Ellis Hall
Ohio University
Athens, OH 45701-2979
(614) 593-1900
Poetry, fiction, essays, reviews.
THE OHIO REVIEW publishes the best in contemporary American poetry, fiction, book reviews, and essays.
Marianne Boruch, Bim Ramke, Mary Oliver, Donald Revell, Leonard Kriesel.
Unsolicited Manuscripts Received/ Published per Year: 2,000/20.
Reading Period: Sept.–May 31.
Payment: $1/line (poetry), $5/page (prose).
Reporting Time: 90 days.
Copyright held by magazine; reverts to author upon request.
1971; 3/yr; 2,700
$16/yr, $40/3yrs; $6/ea; 40%
144 pp; 6 x 9
Ad Rates: $175/page (4¼ x 7¼); $100/½ page (4¼ x 3¼)
ISSN: 0360-1013
Ingram, DeBoer, Ubiquity, Michiana News Service

ON THE ISSUES (The Progressive Woman's Quarterly)

Merle Hoffman, Ronni Sandroff
97-77 Queens Blvd.
Forest Hills, NY 11374
(718) 459-1888, ext. 208
Women's issues.
The women's magazine you've been looking for (but never thought you'd find). **ON THE ISSUES** engages your mind, heart, and principles. It features unexpurgated discussions of points of view too controversial for the mainstream medium. Focuses on feminism today, women's health, relationships, campus politics, ecology, animal rights, global humanism, and women in the arts.
Louise Armstrong, Phyllis Chesler, Andrea Dworkin, Liz Holtzman, Mary Hunt, Julia Kagan, Cong. John Lewis, Andrea Peyser, Ar-

lene Raven, Elayne Rapping, Rep. Pat Schroeder, Anne Mollegen Smith, John Stoltenberg, Alice Vaachs.
Payment: negotiated.
1991; 4/yr
$14.95/yr, add $10/inst; $3.95/ea; 30%
64 pp; 8⅜ x 10⅞
Ad Rates: $660/page, B/W only (color add'l $250).
ISSN: 0895-6014
Eastern News

ONTARIO REVIEW

Raymond J. Smith, Joyce Carol Oates
9 Honey Brook Dr.
Princeton, NJ 08540
Poetry, fiction, essays, interviews, photographs, graphics.
Maxine Kumin, Albert Goldbarth, Russell Banks, Alicia Ostriker, Tom Wayman.
Unsolicited Manuscripts Received/Published per Year: 1,500/25.
Payment: $10/page.
Reporting Time: 6 weeks.
Copyright held by magazine; reverts to author upon publication.
1974; 2/yr; 1,100
$12/yr; $6/ea; 40%
128 pp; 6 x 9
Ad Rates: $125/page (4¼ x 7); $75/½ page (4¼ x 3¼); $50/¼ page (2 x 3¼)
ISSN: 0316-4055
Ingram, Ubiquity

ONTHEBUS

Jack Grapes
P.O. Box 481266
Bicentennial Station
Los Angeles, CA 90048
(213) 651-5488
Poetry, fiction, translations, essays, interviews, book reviews.
Open to all kinds, experimental to neo-narrative to Bohemian-language-confessional haiku! 6-10 poems max, fiction 1,500 max.
Joyce Carol Oates, Charles Bukowski, Ai, David Mura, Wanda Coleman, Kate Braverman, Norman Dubie.
Unsolicited Manuscripts Received/Published per Year: 3,500/200.
Reading Period: March.–June; Sept–Novemver.
Payment: 1 copy.
Reporting Time: 2 months–2 years.
Copyright reverts to contributors.
1989; 2/yr; 3,200
$28/3 issues; $11/ea; 20-40%
336 pp; 8½ x 5½
Ad Rates: $300/page (7¼ x 4¼); $200/½ page; $125/¼ page
ISSN: 1043-884X
DeBoer, Bookpeople, SPD, Fine Print

ORO MADRE

Loss Pequeño Glazier
P.O. Box 143
Getzville, NY 14068-0143

Poetry, fiction, criticism, reviews, graphics.

ORO MADRE seeks to present writings with attention to details of the poem's status and the uncertain edges of the poetic act; of interest also, electronic poetries and the language of electronic communication; it also focuses on coverage of the small press world through reviews, interviews, and articles on small press activities and trends.

Alejandro Muguia, Jack Hirschman, Robert Anbian.

Reading Period: year–round.

Payment: in copies.

Reporting Time: 2 months.

Copyright held by author.

1981; irreg; 500

$14/yr ind, $20/yr inst; $3.50/ea; 40%

48 pp; 5½ x 8

Ad Rates: $40/page (5 x 7½); $25/½ page (5 x 3¾)

OSIRIS

Andrea and Robert Moorhead
Box 297
Deerfield, MA 01342
(413) 774-4027

Poetry, photographs, graphics/artwork.

OSIRIS is a multi-lingual poetry journal publishing contemporary work in English, French, and German. Poetry in other languages such as Hungarian, Portuguese, and Danish appears in a bilingual format.

Robert Marteau, Hélèn Dorion, Eugenio de Andrade, Peter Nim, Jana Hayes.

Unsolicited Manuscripts Received/Published per Year: 150-200/6-8.

Payment: in copies.

Reporting Time: 4 weeks.

Copyright reverts to author upon publication.

1972; 2/yr; 500

$12/yr; $6/ea

40 pp; 6 x 9

Ad Rates: $125/page (5½ x 8½)

ISSN: 0095-019X

OSTENTATIOUS MIND

Patricia D. Coscia
JAF Station Box 7415
New York, NY 10116-4630

Poetry; all types except x-rated.

OSTENTATIOUS MIND is designed to encourage the intense writer, the cutting reality. The staff deals in the truth of life: political, social, and psychological. SASE for submission guidelines.

Payment: 4 copies.

Reporting Time: as soon as possible.
1987
$2/ea
10 pp; 7 x 8
225 pp; 7 x 9
Ad Rates: $100/page (7 x 9); $75/½ page (3½ x 4½)
ISSN: 8756-4696

OTHER VOICES

Lois Hauselman, Editor; Ruth Canji, Tina Peano, Assistant Editors
University of IL at Chicago
Dept. of English (M/C 162)
601 S. Morgan St.
Chicago, IL 60607-7120
(312) 413-2209
Fiction, interviews.
A Prize-winning (IAC), independent market for quality fiction, we are dedicated to original, fresh, diverse stories and novel excerpts. We've won 15 IAC awards in 11 years, plus a CCLM/GE Younger Writers Award in 1988.
David Evanier, Rolaine Hochstein, Edith Pearlman, Stephen Dixon, Karen Karbo.
Unsolicited Manuscripts Received/Published per Year: 1,000/40-50.
Reading Period: Oct.–April 1.
Payment: gratuity plus copies.
Reporting Time: 10–12 weeks.
Copyright held by magazine; reverts to author upon publication.
1985; 2/yr; 1,500
$20/yr ind, $24/2 yr inst; $7/ea; 40%, 50% to distributors

OUTERBRIDGE

Charlotte Alexander
112 E. 10th St.
New York, NY 10003
Poetry, fiction.
Craft first. Regular special themes, i.e., urban, rural, Southern. Slight bias to new voices and less published writers. Personal replies. Anti pure polemic. Theme projects: interdisciplinary (biology, physics, music, astronomy, etc.); nature, animals, ecology, environment; broad theme of love and friendship agape to eros.
Stuart Ackerman, Walter McDonald, Candida Lawrence, Thomas Swiss, Tom Lish, Laurie Calhoun, Louise Budde De Lourentis.
Unsolicited Manuscripts Received/Published per Year: 500+/30+.
Payment: 2 copies.
Reporting Time: 2–2½ months, except July–Aug.
Copyright held by magazine; reverts to author upon publication.
1975; 1/yr; 800
$5/yr; $5/ea
120 pp; 8½ x 5
ISSN: 0739-4969

OWEN WISTER REVIEW

(Editors rotate yearly)
P.O. Box 4238, University Station
University of Wyoming
Laramie, WY 82071
(307) 766-3819

Prose (to 3,000 words), B & W artwork, poetry (no line limit).

Student produced magazine, but publishes a mixture of student and small press authors. Perfect-bound, slick paper, high quality printing. Built to last.

Gerald Locklin, Richard Kostelanetz, W.D. Ehrhart, Cathy Lynn, Laurel Speer, Rane Arroyo.

Unsolicited Manuscripts Received/ Published per Year: 500+/75-100.

Reading Period: Sept.–Mar.

Payment: 1 copy, 10% off additional copies.

Reporting Time: 1–4 months. Do not read over the summer.

Copyright reverts to author upon publication.

1978; 2/yr; 500

$15/yr; $7.50/ea; Inquire

approx. 100 pp; digest

THE OXFORD AMERICAN

Marc Smirnoff
P.O. Box 1156
Oxford, MS 38655

THE OXFORD AMERICAN is a general interest literary magazine originating from the South. We appeal to the intelligent, but non–academic, general reader.

John Grisham, Larry Brown, Eudora Welty, John Updike, Donna Tartt.

Payment: $250–500 per essay, review, story; $60–75 per poem.

Reporting Time: 1–2 months.

Copyright held by magazine, but reverts to author upon publication.

1993; 6/yr; 25,000

$24/yr; $4.50/ea; 40%

128 pp; 8 3/16 x 10 7/8

Ad Rates: 4 color full page $2400; 1/2 page $1870
$1800 B/W (7 1/8 x 9 13/16);
$1170/1/2 page (7 1/8 x 4 13/16);
$450/1/6 page (2 1/4 x 4 13/16)

Ingram, Ubiquity, ICD

OYEZ REVIEW

Sarah L. Kisar
Roosevelt University
430 S. Michigan Ave.
Chicago, IL 60605
(312) 341-2017

Poetry, fiction, photographs.

OYEZ REVIEW is an award-winning, university-based magazine in its 27th year of publication. Each issue contains a number of poems and short stories written by people from various parts of the country and

many different walks of life. The writings are diverse in content; all have universal appeal.
Ronald Wallace, David Martin, Barry Silesky, John Jacob, Brooke Bergan.
Payment: none.
Reporting Time: 6 months.
Copyright held by magazine; reverts to author upon publication.
1967; 1/yr; 400
$4/ea; 40%
110 pp; 5½ x 8½
No ads

P

THE PACIFIC REVIEW

James Brown, Faculty Editor
Department of English
California State University
5500 University Pkwy.
San Bernardino, CA 92407-2397
(714) 880-5824
Fax (714) 880-5894

Poetry, fiction, essays, plays, translation, interviews.

THE PACIFIC REVIEW is an academic-based journal of the verbal and visual arts, edited by graduate and undergraduate students at CSUSB. An annual publication now in its thirteenth year, **THE PACIFIC REVIEW** attempts to reflect aspects of its unique position in Southern California whenever possible, but without compromising its goal to serve as a vehicle for both emerging and established creative voices—from and about any area.

Unsolicited Manuscripts Received/Published per Year: 200-300/15.
Reading Period: Sept.–Feb. 1.
Payment: in copies, upon publication.
Copyright held by magazine; reverts to author upon publication.
1983; 1/yr; 750
$6/yr ind, $7/inst; $4/ea; 40%
102 pp; 6 x 9
Ad Rates: $150/page (5 x 7½); $100/½ page (5 x 3¾); $50/¼ page (2½ x 3¾)

PAINTBRUSH: A Journal of Contemporary Multicultural Literature

Ben Bennani
Division of Language and Literature
Truman State University
Kirksville, MO 63501
(816) 785-4185

Poetry, fiction, criticism, essays, reviews, interviews, translation, photographs, graphics/artwork, by and on one single writer per volume.

Publishes serious but innovative writers—especially neglected ones.

William Stafford, Richard Eberhart, Ngugi wa Thiongo, N. Scott Momuday, Amy Tan.

Unsolicited Manuscripts Received/Published per Year: 300/50.

Payment: in copies or $10/page when available.

Reporting Time: 4–6 weeks. Please inquire about special needs before submitting.

Copyright held by magazine; reverts to author upon publication.

1974; 1/yr; 500

$15/yr ind, $20/yr inst; 40%

200+ pp; 5½ x 8½

Ad Rates: $150/page

ISSN: 0094-1964

PAINTED BRIDE QUARTERLY

Marion Wrenn, Kathy Volk Miller
230 Vine Street
Philadelphia, PA 19106
(215) 925-9914

Poetry, fiction, criticism, essays, reviews, plays, photographs, graphics/artwork.

PAINTED BRIDE QUARTERLY is a journal of literary and visual arts associated with the Painted Bride Art Center in Philadelphia. We publish both local and national writers and artists; the emphasis is on quality. We like crafted, articulate writing in any genre.

Naomi Shihab Nye, Eugene Howard, Etheridge Knight, Tina Barr, Robert Bly, Marnie Mueller.

Reading Period: Sept.–June.

Payment: copies and 1 year subscription, $5/piece.

Reporting Time: 3 months.

Copyright reverts to author.

1973; 4/yr; 1,000

$16/yr ind, $20/yr inst; $6/ea; 50%

80 pp; 5 x 8½

Ad Rates: $75/page; $50/½ page; $25/¼ page

PAISLEY MOON PRESS/OPEN UNISON STOP

Michael Spring, P. Notzka
P.O. Box 95463
Seattle, WA 98145

Poems, prose, reviews.

Joyce Odam, Stephen Kessler, Judson Crews, Carolyn Stoloff.

Payment: 1 copy.

Reporting Time: 1 day–3 months.

300

$10/yr; $3/ea
5½ x 8½
No ads

PANDORA
Meg MacDonald
2063 Belford
Holly, MI 48442
Poetry, fiction, graphics/artwork.
Character-oriented science fiction and fantasy by new and established writers. We emphasize character intensive fiction rather than nuts and bolts SF or stock-plot fantasy.
W. Gregory Stewart, Beckett Gladney, Deborah Wheeler, Roger Dutcher.
Payment: 1¢-2¢/word; $10 and up on illus; $3.50 and up on cartoons and fillers.
Closed to unsolicited manuscripts at this time.
Copyright held by author. We buy First North American serial rights usually.
1978; 2/yr; 500
$12/2, $6/ea (US); $14/2, $7/ea (CANADA); $20/2, $10/ea (overseas); *US funds please!*
112 pp; 5½ x 8½; color cover
ISSN: 0275-519X
Faxon

PANHANDLER
Laurie O'Brien
English Department
University of West Florida
Pensacola, FL 32514-5751
(904) 474-2923
Poetry and short fiction.
THE PANHANDLER is a magazine of contemporary poetry and fiction. We want poetry and stories rooted in real experience in language with a strong colloquial flavor. Works that are engaging and readable stand a better chance with us than works that are self-consciously literary. Annual poetry chapbook competition: Winner receives $100 plus 50 copies. Send SASE for details.
Walter McDonald, Malcolm Glass, Enid Shomer, David Kirby, Joan Colby.
Unsolicited Manuscripts Received/ Published per Year: 4,000+/70-80.
Reading Period: year–round, slower in summer.
Payment: in copies.
Reporting Time: 4–6 months.
Copyright held by University; reverts to author upon publication.
1976; 2/yr; 500
$10/yr, $18/2yrs; both include winning chapbook; 40%
64 pp; 6 x 9
ISSN: 0738-8705
Ebsco

PAPER BAG

M. Brownstein
P.O. Box 268805
Chicago IL 60626-8805

Guidelines included.

Literary arts publication: all forms of poetry—looking for original and strong images, black-and-white illustrations, and short short fiction (under 500 words).

Claudette Bess, Jean Townes.

Unsolicited Manuscripts Received/Published per Year: 500/30.

Payment: 1 copy.

Reporting Time: 2 minutes–1 month.

Copyright: no.

1988; 4/yr; 200+

$12/yr; $3/ea

20–30 pp; 5½ x 4¾

THE PAPER SALAd Poetry Journal

R. L. Moore
P.O. Box 520061
Salt Lake City, UT 84152-0061

Poetry.

Digest sized, flat spined about 100 pages about 30 poets, sometimes color cover, annual.

Rich Cronshey, Glenn Parker.

Unsolicited Manuscripts Received/Published per Year: 500/30+.

Reading Period: year–round.

Payment: 1 copy upon publication.

Reporting Time: about 2 months.

Poets retain copyright.

1990; 1/yr; 400

$7.25/ea

100 pp; digest

Ad Rates: contact me and we'll work something out.

PARABOLA: The Magazine of Myth & Tradition

656 Broadway
New York, NY 10012
(212) 505-6200

Essays, reviews, interviews, retellings of traditional myths and stories, photographs, graphics/artwork.

PARABOLA's focus is on myth and the world's cultural and spiritual traditions. Accordingly, **PARABOLA**'s approach to literature involves an emphasis on myths, legends, folktales, and oral transmission. **PARABOLA** primarily publishes articles and interviews which deal with mythology, comparative religion, and contemporary spirituality. Each issue focuses on a central theme.

P.L. Travers, Peter Brook, Eknath Easwaran, Frederick Franck, Robert Lawlor, Rhich Nhat Hanh, Chinua Achebe.

Payment: sliding scale.

Reporting Time: 3 months.

Copyright held by author.

1976; 4/yr; 41,000

$20/yr; $6/ea; 40%
128 pp; 6½ x 10
Ad Rates: $815/page (5¹⁄₁₆ x 8⁵⁄₁₆); $545/½ page (5¹⁄₁₆ x 4⅛); $310/¼ page (2⁷⁄₁₆ x 4⅛)
ISSN: 0362-1596

THE PARIS REVIEW

George Plimpton, Fiction Editor; Richard Howard, Poetry Editor
541 E. 72nd St.
New York, NY 10021

Fiction, poetry, literary non-fiction.

Focus on best of emerging and established poets, writers and artists. Always on the look-out for lively newcomers.

Joseph Brodsky, Carolyn Kizer, Rick Bass, E.L. Doctorow, Alice Munro, Joanna Scott.

Unsolicited Manuscripts Received/ Published per Year: 20,000/35.
Payment: varies.
Reporting Time: 8–10 weeks.
Copyright held by Paris Review Inc.; reverts to author upon publication.
1953; 4/yr; 12,000
$34/yr; $10/ea
304 pp; 5½ x 8¼
Ad Rates: $1,000/page; $700 non-profit
ISSN: 0031-2037
Random House

PARIS TRANSCONTINENTAL

Claire Larriere
Institut du Monde Anglophone
Sorbonne Nouvelle, 5
Rue de L'Ecole de Medecine
75006 Paris, FRANCE

Short stories exclusively, unpublished. 2000 to 4500 words.

A forum for writers of excellent stories whose link is the English language, wherever spoken. **PARIS TRANSCONTINENTAL** hopes to introduce the best among today's authors, wherever they hail from.

Stephen Dixon, Jayan Ya Mahapatra, Joyce Carol Oates, Albert Russo, Alan Sillitoe, Michael Wilding, etc.

Unsolicited Manuscripts Received/ Run per semester: 500.
Reading Period: Oct.–June.
Payment: 2 copies of issue.
Reporting Time: 2–3 months.
Copyright is in name of individual authors.
2/yr; 1,000
FF 140/yr; FF 75/ea or $20/yr; $11/ea, or £14/yr; £8/ea
128 pp
Ad Rates: none
ISSN: 1146-5948

PARNASSUS

Herbert Leibowitz
205 West 89th St. Apt 8F

New York, NY 10024-1835
(212) 362-3492
FAX (212) 875-0148

Criticism, essays, poems, reviews, photographs, graphics/artwork.

Devoted to the in-depth analysis of contemporary books of poetry. **PARNASSUS** seeks essays and reviews that are themselves works of art. The ideal reviewer is a poet with his or her own particular point of view. **PARNASSUS** publishes special issues on music, poetry in translation, the long poem, poetry and prose; includes paintings, illustrations and photographs.

Seamus Heaney, Ross Feld, Alice Fulton, William Logan, Helen Vendler, Mary Karr.

Unsolicited Manuscripts Received/ Published per Year: 250–300/1–2.

Payment: $25–$250.

Reporting Time: varies.

Copyright held by Poetry in Review Foundation; reverts to author upon request.

1972; 2/yr; 2,500

$27/yr ind, $46/yr inst; $10-15/ea

250–500 pp; 6 x 9¼

Ad Rates: $250/page (6 x 9¼); $150/½ page (5 x 4)

ISSN: 0048-3028

Small Press Distribution

PARTING GIFTS

Robert Bixby
3413 Wilshire Dr.
Greensboro, NC 27408

Poetry, fiction.

Unsolicited Manuscripts Received/ Published per Year: 2,000/80-100.

Reading Period: Jan.–May, but mss. welcome anytime.

Payment: 1 copy.

Copyright held by March Street Press; reverts to author upon publication.

1988; 2/yr; 100

$8/yr; $4/ea; 40%

40 pp; 5½ x 8½

ISSN: 1043-3325

PARTISAN REVIEW

William Phillips, Editor-in-Chief; Edith Kurzweil, Editor
236 Bay State Rd.
Boston, MA 02215
(617) 353-4260

Essays, criticism, reviews, fiction, poetry, translation, interviews.

PARTISAN REVIEW examines the central issues of contemporary culture and social thought. It publishes critical essays on the arts and politics, new fiction and poetry, and book reviews.

Octavio Paz, Cynthia Ozick, Doris Lessing, Joseph Brodsky,

Czeslaw Milosz, Donald Revell, George Konrad.
Unsolicited Manuscripts Received/ Published per Year: 1,000/5 (fiction); 1,000/10-15 (poetry).
Reading Period: year–round.
Payment: varies.
Reporting Time: 2 months.
Copyright held by Partisan Review, Inc; reverts to author upon publication.
1937; 4/yr; 8,150
$22/yr ind, $32/yr inst; $7.50/ea;
160 pp; 6 x 9
Ad Rates: $200–$250 page (4¼ x 7⅜); $120/½ page (4¼ x 3½); $75/¼ page (2 x 3½)
ISSN: 0031-2525
Eastern News

PASSAGES NORTH

Anne Ohman Youngs
Dept. of English
Northern Michigan University
Marquette, MI 49855
(906) 227-2700
Poetry, fiction, interviews.
PASSAGES NORTH publishes high quality writing by established and emerging writers.
Tony Hoaglund, Thomas Lux, Jim Daniels, Tess Gallagher, Richard Jackson.
Unsolicited Manuscripts Received/ Published per year: 1,000/NA.
Reading Period: Sept.-May.
Payment: Copies.
Reporting Time: 1–2 months.
Copyright held by magazine; reverts to author upon publication.
1979; 2/yr.
$15/yr; $7.50/ea.
128 pp.
Ad Rates: $200/page; $100/½ page; $50/¼ page.
ISSN: 0278-0829

PASSAIC REVIEW

Richard Quatrone
Forstmann Library
195 Gregory Avenue
Passaic, NJ 07055
Poetry, fiction, plays, photographs, graphics/artwork.
PASSAIC REVIEW is an independent magazine that publishes the best work submitted to it. Emphasis is on strong, clear, direct writing.
Antler, Ronald Baatz, Amiri Baraka, Allen Ginsberg, Eliot Katz, Wanda Phipps.
Payment: none.
Reporting Time: 1–52 weeks.
Copyright held by magazine; reverts to author upon publication.
1979; 2/yr; 500
$6/yr ind, $10/yr inst; $3.75/ea; 40%
48–54 pp; 5 x 8½
Ad Rates: $80/page (5 x 8½);

$40/½ page (2¾ x 4¼); $20/¼ page (1⅜ x 2⅛)
ISSN: 0731-4663

PEMBROKE MAGAZINE

Shelby Stephenson
Box 60, PSU
Pembroke, NC 28372
(919) 521-4214, ext. 433

Poetry, fiction, criticism, reviews, plays, interviews, graphics/artwork.

Open to poetry, fiction, essays, interviews, and artwork.

A.R. Ammons, Fred Chappell, Barbara Guest, Robert Morgan, Betty Adcock.

Payment: none.

Reporting Time: up to 3 months.

Copyright held by magazine; reverts to author upon publication.

1969; 1/yr; 500–800

$5/yr; $5/ea; (surface mail add .50 to each rate)

250 pp; 6 x 9

Ad Rates: $40/page; $25/½ page

THE PENNSYLVANIA REVIEW

Rick Sides, Editor; Maria McLeod, Poetry Editor; Julie Albright, Fiction Editor; Kathleen Veslany, Non-fiction Editor
English Department, 526 CL
University of Pittsburgh
Pittsburgh, PA 15260
(412) 624-6506

Poetry, fiction, criticism, essays, reviews, translations, interviews, graphics/artwork, photos (b&w).

Publishing the finest contemporary fiction, poetry, nonfiction and illustrations, *Choice* calls **THE PENNSYLVANIA REVIEW** a "fine small literary magazine . . . highly recommended."

Cornelius Eady, Dorothy Barresi, Christopher Buckley, Joyce Carol Oates,Linda Pastan.

Unsolicited Manuscripts Received/Published per year: 800–1,000/20–25.

Payment: in copies.

Reporting Time: 8–12 weeks.

Copyright held by Univ. of Pittsburgh; reverts to author upon publication.

1985; 2/yr; 600; 1994; Vol. 6 #2, forthcoming January 1995 (new tabloid size).

$7/yr; $3.50/ea; 40%

32 pp; 11 x 15

Ad Rates: $180/page (9 x 13); $90/½ page (6 x 9); $45/¼ page (4 x 6)

ISSN: 8756-5668

PEQUOD

Mark Rudman
N.Y.U. English Dept., 2nd floor
19 University Pl.

New York, NY 10003

Poetry, fiction, criticism, essays, translation.

Past issues of **PEQUOD** have featured Irish, Scandinavian, Russian, Israeli, Ukranian, and British poetry. Recent issues have included a special issue on literature and the visual arts, a focus on the long poem, and two issues on the subject of mourning.

Thomas Bernhard, Louise Glück, Donald Hall, Jane Kenyon, Joyce Carol Oates, Charlie Smith, David St. John, John Updike.

Unsolicited Manuscripts Received/ Published per Year: 2,600/varies.

Reading Period: Oct.–Apr.

Payment: some payment to contributors.

Copyright held by magazine.

1974; 2/yr; 1,000–2,000

$12/yr ind, $20/2 yrs ind; $18/yr inst, $34/2 yrs inst; $10/ea

200 pp; 5½ x 8½

Ad Rates: $150/page (5½ x 8½); $200/2 pp

ISSN: 0149-0516

DeBoer

PEREGRINE: The Journal of Amherst Writers & Artists

Pat Schneider
P.O. Box 1076
Amherst MA 01004
(413) 253-3307

Poetry, fiction, cover graphics/artwork.

PEREGRINE is the journal of Amherst Writers & Artists, an organization dedicated to the belief that good writing is honest and unpretentious. We believe literature is related to the speech of home and workplace, and to the meanings discovered in ordinary lives.

Jane Yolen, Barbara Van Noord, Steven Reil.

Unsolicited Manuscripts Received/ Published per Year: 500/15.

Payment: in copies upon publication.

Copyright held by Amherst Writers & Artists Press, Inc.; reverts to author upon publication.

1983; 1/yr; varies

$5 plus $2 postage/ea; 40%

Sample copy $4 postage included

64 pp; 5½ x 8¼

Ad Rates: contact magazine for information

ISSN: 0890-662X

PERMAFROST

c/o English Department
203 Fine Arts Building
University of Alaska
Fairbanks, AK 99775
(907) 474-7193

Poetry, fiction, creative nonfiction, black & white photographs/art.

PERMAFROST seeks to promote excellence in contemporary literature and welcomes submissions in this vein. Although the magazine is regionally based, material need not refer to Alaska. Manuscripts from the lower 48 states, Hawaii, and international submissions (in English) are welcomes. **PERMAFROST** also sponsors the Midnight Sun Poetry Chapbook Contest (entry fee $10) and the Midnight Sun Fiction Contest (entry fee $10) [Chapbook winning manuscript (20–25 pp.) receives 25 copies. Fiction contest winner (10–40 pp) receives $50.]

Reading Period: Aug.–May.

Payment: 2 copies.

Reporting Time: 4 months, 6 months for mss. received in Summer.

Copyright held by author.

1975; 1/yr; 400 journal; 50 chapbook

$7/yr; 40% disc. to booksellers

115 pp; 5 x 8

Ad inquiries welcome.

PIEDMONT LITERARY REVIEW

William Reuben Smith
Piedmont Literary Society
3750 Woodside Ave.
Lynchburg, VA 24503
(804) 384-2027

Poetry, fiction, graphics/artwork, newsletter.

We publish mainly poetry, short stories; approximately 40 poems, 1 story per issue. We need short stories of around 1,500 to 2,000 words. Traditional to free verse—we publish established poets and many first timers.

Wm. Stafford, X.J. Kennedy, Harold Witt, Enid Shomer, Judson Jerome.

Unsolicited Manuscripts Received/ Published per Year: 500/75.

Payment: in copies.

Reporting Time: 5 days–3 months.

Copyright held by magazine; reverts to author upon publication.

1976; 4/yr; 300

$15/yr; $4/ea domestic

50 pp; 5½ x 8½

ISSN: 0257-357X

PIG IRON

Jim Villani
P.O. Box 237
Youngstown, OH 44501 Phone: (216) 747-6932
FAX (216) 747-0599

Poetry, fiction, essays, translation, interviews, photographs, graphics/artwork.

Special emphasis on popular culture, genres, and new literature in a highly visual and cerebral format. Publishes issues around special themes: recent issues have featured Family, Classical Antiquity, Third World, Labor, The Epistolary Form & theLetter, The Viet Nam Era, Surrealism. Most recent edition is the American Dream.

Jim Sanderson, Andrena Zawinski, Larry Smith, Jack Remick, Laurel Speer, Marian Steele, GAry Fincke, Miriam Goodman, Arlene Zekowski.

Unsolicited Manuscripts Received/ Published per Year: 6,000/85.

Payment: $5/page.

Reporting Time: 4 months.

Copyright held by editors; reverts to author upon publication.

1975; 1/yr; 1,500

$11/1 issue; $20/2 issues

$11.95/ea; 40%

128 pp; 8½ x 11

ISSN: 0362-5214

THE PITTSBURGH QUARTERLY

Frank Correnti, Editor; James Deahl, Canadian Editor; Lyn Ferlo, Art Editor

36 Haberman Ave.

Pittsburgh, PA 15211-2144

Canadian address:

237 Prospect St. South

Hamilton, Ontario

Canada L8M ZZ6

(412) 431-8885

Per issue: short short stories (up to 4,000 words), poetry, interviews, reviews, features, (essays, etc).

THE PITTSBURGH QUARTERLY is a community writing project which networks (publishes) writers from all parts of the US, Canada, and overseas. We emphasize personal expression and craft over ideology.

John Wylam, Andrena Zawinaki, Marilyn Bates Patricia Harrington Wyson, Joseph Bathanti, Susan Terris.

Unsolicited Manuscripts Received/ Published per Year: 400/100.

Payment: 2 copies.

Reporting Time: 4 months.

Copyright reverts to author upon publication. Acknowledge **TPQ** in future publication.

1991; 4/yr; 600

$12/yr; $14/overseas; $4/ea; 10 or more 40%

76 pp; 5½ x 8½

Ad Rates: $100/full page (4½ x 7½); $50/½ page; $25/¼ page

ISSN: 1054-6340

Central Wholesale (Pittsburgh PA 15203)

PIVOT

Martin Mitchell

250 Riverside Dr. #23

New York, NY 10025
(212) 222-1408
Poetry.
Now in its 45th year, **PIVOT** publishes the work of both seasoned and new poets. It has a reputation for "firsts" of admirable performance.
Philip Appleman, Eamon Grennan, William Matthews, Grace Schulman, W. D. Snodgrass, Robert Wrigley.
Unsolicited Manuscripts Received/ Published per Year: 500/25.
Reading Period: Jan. 1–June 1.
Payment: in copies.
Reporting Time: 2–4 weeks.
Copyright held by Sibyl Barsky Grucci; reverts to author upon publication.
1951; 1/yr; 1,500–3,000
$5/ea
76 pp; 6 x 9
Ad Rates: $125/page; $70/½ page; $40/¼ page

THE PLASTIC TOWER
Carol Dyer, Roger Kyle-Keith
P.O. Box 702
Bowie, MD 20718
Poetry, reviews, artwork.
Your basic poetry line, highly eclectic and user-friendly. Friendly to writers, too! Digest sized, black and white graphics and reviews.
Unsolicited Manuscripts Received/ Published per year: 5,000/200.
Reading Period: year round.
Payment: Copies.
Reporting Time: 3–4 months.
Copyright held by magazine.
1989; 4/yr; 200
$8/yr; $2.50/ea.
50 pp; Digest.
ISSN: 1066-6044

PLOUGHSHARES
Don Lee, David Daniel
Emerson College
100 Beacon St.
Boston, MA 02116
(617) 578-8753
Poetry, fiction, translation.
A magazine of new writing edited on a revolving basis by prominent poets and writers to reflect different and contrasting points of view.
Rosellen Brown, James Welch, Sue Miller, Al Young, Tobias Wolff, Marie Howe, Christopher Tilghman, Alberto Ríos, Carolyn Forché.
Unsolicited Manuscripts Received/ Published per Year: 5,000/200
Reading Period: Aug. 1–March 31.
Reporting Time: 3–5 months.
Copyright reverts to author upon publication.

1971; 3/yr; 6,000
$19/yr ind, $22/yr inst; $8.95/ea; 20%–40%
252 pp; 5½ x 8½
Ad Rates: $300/page (4½ x 7); $200/½ page (4½ x 3¼);
ISSN: 0048-4474
DeBoer, Fine Print, Ingram Periodicals, L-S Distributors

THE PLUM REVIEW

M. Hammer, Christina Daub
P.O. Box 3557
Washington, DC 20007

Poetry, poetry book reviews, interviews.
All-poetry magazine featuring the best in contemporary poetry by both established and emerging poets from around the world.
Joseph Brodsky, Mark Strand, Marge Piercy, Robert Bly, Donald Hall, Linda Pastan, Jane Hirshfield.
Unsolicited Manuscripts Received/Published per Year: 3,000+/50–60.
Reading Period: Sept.–May.
Payment: 1 copy.
Reporting Time: 1 to 2 months.
1991; 2/yr; 1,000
$14/yr; $7/ea
120 pp; 6 x 9 flat-spined
Ad Rates: $200/page; $125/½ page
DeBoer

POEM

Nancy Frey Dillard
English Department
University of Alabama in Huntsville
Huntsville, AL 35899
(205) 895-6320

Poetry.
High quality mature poetry. No bias as to form or theme. Particular regard given to less well known poets.
Charles Edward Eaton, John Ditsky, Stephen Lang, R.T. Smith, Alison Reed.
Unsolicited Manuscripts Published per Year: 100-120.
Payment: in copy.
Reporting Time: 1 month.
Copyright held by Huntsville Literary Association.
1967; 2/yr; 400
$10/yr; $5/ea
70 pp; 4½ x 7½
No ads

POET LORE

Sunil Freeman
Poet Lore, The Writer's Center
4508 Walsh St.
Bethesda, MD 20815
(301) 654-8664

Poetry, criticism, essays, reviews, translation, graphics/artwork.
POET LORE publishes original poems of all kinds. The editors

continue to welcome narrative poetry and original translations of contemporary world poets. **POET LORE** publishes reviews of poetry collections and critical essays of contemporary poetry.

Walter McDonald, Sharon Olds, Leonard Nathan, Peter Wild, Albert Goldbarth.

Unsolicited Manuscripts Received/Published per Year: 1,500/150.

Payment: 2 copies.

Reporting Time: 3 months.

Copyright held by The Writer's Center; reverts to author upon publication.

1889; 4/yr; 600

$15/yr ind, $24/yr inst; $4.50/ea; 40%

80 pp; 6 x 9

Ad Rates: $100/page (5½ x 8); $55/½ page (5½ x 4)

ISSN: 0032-1966

Faxon, Ebsco, McGregor, Boley

POETIC SPACE: POETRY AND FICTION

Don Hildenbrand, Editor; Thomas Strand, Fiction Editor

P.O. Box 11157

Eugene, OR 97440

Poetry, fiction, reviews, interviews, graphics/artwork, theater and film reviews. Chapbook and Anthology now available; for information send SASE.

Patty McDonald, Albert Huffstickler, William Meyer, Crawdad Nelson, Arthur Winfield Knight, Spenser Reese, Sesshu Foster.

Unsolicited Manuscripts Received/Published per Year: 500+/50.

$4/issue, $7/2 issues; $13/4 issues: $5/anthology 1987-1991; $6 poetic space chapbook # 1.

POETICS JOURNAL

Lyn Hejinian, Barrett Watten

2639 Russell St.

Berkeley, CA 94705

(510) 548-1817

Criticism, essays, reviews.

POETICS JOURNAL is an irregularly published journal of contemporary poetics by poets and prose writers as well as by other artists, critics, linguists, and political theorists. It features essays, articles, and investigatory reviews. Individual issues focus on topics including "close reading", "poetry and philosophy", "women and modernism", "non-narrative", etc.

Ron Silliman, George Lakoff, Rae Armantrout, Kofi Natambu, Leslie Scalapino.

Unsolicited Manuscripts Received/Published per Year: 40-50/3.

Payment: in copies.

Reporting Time: 2–4 weeks.

Copyright held by author.
1982; irreg.; 600
$10/ea; 25%–40%
144 pp; 6 x 9
ISSN: 0731-5236
SPD, Sun & Moon

POETPOURRI

Comstock Writer's Group; Kathleen Bryce Niles, Coordinator; Jennifer B. MacPherson, President
907 Comstock Ave.
Syracuse, NY 13210
(315) 475-0339

Poetry only.

Perfect-bound 100 pp, put out twice yearly. We accept poetry on the basis of quality, not reputation. We do not accept porno, sentimental, greeting card verse and very few haikus or religious verse. Well crafted poetry, free or formal, written in understandable, grammatically correct English—metaphor, fresh, vivid imagery enjoyed.

Gayle Elen Harvey, Robt. Cooperman, Kathryn Howd Machan, Linda Keegan, John Engle, Jr.

Unsolicited Manuscripts Received/Published per Year: thousands/300.

Payment: copy, prize money.

Reporting Time: usually 2–4 weeks, with comments.

Copyright reverts to author.
1986; 2/yr; 500
$8/yr; $15/2 yrs; $4/ea
100–125 pp; 5½ x 8½

POETRY

Joseph Parisi
60 West Walton St.
Chicago, IL 60610
(312) 255-3703

Poetry, reviews, essays.

For over 80 years **POETRY** has been the most widely read monthly of verse. From Auden to Ashbery, Pound to Pinsky, Stevens to Soto—voices famous and new.

Adrienne Rich, A.R. Ammons, Richard Kenney, J.D. McClatchy, Sharon Olds.

Unsolicited Manuscripts Received/Published per Year: 80,000/300.

Reading Period: year–round.

Payment: $2/line for verse; $20/page of prose.

Reporting Time: 3–4 months.

Copyright held by Modern Poetry Association; reverts to author upon request.

1912; 12/yr; 7,600
$27/yr ind, $30/yr inst; $3.00/ea
64 pp; 5½ x 9
Ad Rates: $280/page (3¾ x 7); $174/½ page (3¾ x 3½); $111/¼ page (1¾ x 3½)

ISSN: 0032-2032
DeBoer, Ingram, Michiana News Service, Ubiquity

POETRY CANADA

Barry Dempster, Poetry Editor; Bob Hilderley, Prose Editor
P.O. Box 1061, 221 King St. E.
Kingston, Ontario K7L 4Y5 CANADA
(613) 548-8429
Fax (613) 548-1556
Poetry essays on poetry, reviews of poetry books.
Bill Bissett, Maggie Helwig, Daniel David Moses.
Unsolicited Manuscripts Received/ Published per Year: 2,400/20.
Payment: after publication.
Reporting Time: 4 months.
Copyright: We retain first North American Serial Rights.
1980; 4/yr; 700
$16/4; $4.55/ea
36 pp; tabloid
Ad Rates: available upon request.
ISSN: 0709-3373

THE POETRY CONNECTION

Sylvia Shichman
13455 SW 16 Court #F-405
Pembroke Pines, FL 33027
(904) 431-3016
Listings of poetry publications and contests, songwriting, greeting card/performing arts publications/organizations. Poetry printing assistance, mailing list of poets, writers, and song writers! TPC members receive info on how to sell their poetry/books and obtain assistance in getting poetry published.
THE POETRY CONNECTION/ Magical Circle lists poetry readings and sponsors poetry meetings/socials!
Sylvia Shichman, Editor/Publisher of **THE POETRY CONNECTION**, has been named Poet Laureate of Century Village.
1978; 12/yr; 200
$7/sample issue; $22/yr.
Multiple pp; 8½ x 11
Ad Rates: $5 per listing; $60 1/yr.

POETRY EAST

Richard Jones
802 W. Belden
English Department
DePaul University
Chicago, IL 60614
(312) 362-5114
Poetry, translations, fiction, art, interviews, reviews.
POETRY EAST publishes issues dedicated to particular poets or topics. We are also interested in reading essays on poetics, the relationship between art and the

world. We are also looking for translations and ideas for feature/symposia.

Gerald Stern, Ruth Stone, Jack Grapes.

Unsolicited Manuscripts Received/Published per Year: 5,000/200–300.

Payment: in copies, honoraria.

Reporting Time: 3 months.

Copyright reverts to author, but we reserve the right to include work in anthologies.

1980; 2/yr; 1,500

$12; $8

200 pp; 5½ x 8½

Ad Rates: $100/page; $50/½ page

ISSN: 0197-4009

DeBoer, Fine Print

POETRY FLASH

Joyce Jenkins, Editor; Richard Silberg, Associate Editor

P.O. Box 4172

Berkeley, CA 94704

(510) 525-5476

Criticism, essays, reviews, interviews, photographs, poetry.

POETRY FLASH, A Poetry Review and Literary Calendar, publishes the most complete literary calendar of the West available. Also reviews of books, magazines, readings, and events, as well as interviews, occasional essays, photos, general commentary and information on submissions and publications for poets.

Keith Abbott, Marilyn Chin, Catalina Cariaga, Kathleen Fraser, Jack Marshall, Jack Foley, Dorianne Laux, Tony Barnstone.

Unsolicited Manuscripts Received/Published per Year: 1,500/50.

Reading period: year–round.

Payment: subscription to $25; $50 to $100 maximum.

Reporting Time: 3 months.

Copyright held by author.

1972; 12/yr; 20,000; free to public places

$15/yr ind, $16/yr inst

24–36 pp; 11½ x 15

Ad Rates: $500/page (10 x 13¾); $250/½ page (10 x 7); $125/¼ page (6½ x 5) or $130/5 x 7

ISSN: 0737-4747

THE POETRY MISCELLANY

Richard Jackson, Michael Panori, Richard Seehuos

University of Tennessee at Chattanooga

Department of English

Chattanooga, TN 37402

(615) 624-7279 or 755-4629

Poetry, essays, reviews, translation, interviews.

We are very much a miscellany in the traditional sense of that word; we publish a variety of "types" of poetry.

John Ashbery, Marvin Bell, William Matthews, Tomaz Salamun, Mark Strand.
Payment: none.
Reporting Time: 10 weeks.
Copyright held by magazine; reverts to author upon publication.
1971; 2/yr; 1,100
$5/yr ind; $5/ea
20 pp; tabloid
Ad Rates: $100/page; $65/½ page; $40/¼ page

POETRY MOTEL

Ed Gooder, Ellen Seitz-Ryan, Bud Backen, Patrick McKinnon
1228 E. 3rd St.
Duluth, MN 55805
Poetry.
General poetry magazine open to all from "beginners" to "pros."
Todd Moore, Linda Wing, Robert Peters.
Unsolicited Manuscripts Received/Published per Year: 1,000/100
Reading Period: year–round.
Payment: varies.
Reporting Time: 1 week to never.
Copyright: yes.
1984; varies; 1,000
$15.95/3 issues; $5.95/ea; $49.00 lifetime
52 pp; 8 x 7
No ads

POETRY NEW YORK: A Journal of Poetry and Translation

Burt Kimmelman, Tod Thilleman, Emmy Hunter
P.O. Box 3184
Church St. Station
New York, NY 10008
Poetry, translations of poetry, artwork.
About 9 x 6, perfect bound, about 80 pp.
Bonnefoy, Bronk, Creeley, Di Prima, Heller, Mac Low, Rothenberg.
Unsolicited Manuscripts Received 4 poems max./Published per Year: 400/5–10.
Reading Period: spring and fall
Payment: 1 copy.
Reporting Time: 4 months or more.
Copyright belongs to author.
1985; 1/yr; 1,500
$5/ea; 500
80 pp; 9 x 6
Ad Rates: swap ads
DeBoer

THE POETRY PROJECT NEWSLETTER

Mitch Highfill
The Poetry Project
St. Mark's Church
131 E. 10th St.
New York, NY 10003
(212) 674-0910

Poetry, criticism, essays, reviews, listings.

Bernadette Mayer, Anselm Hollo, Robert Creeley, Kofi Natambu, Paul Violi, James Schuyler, Nicole Brossard.

Reading Period: Sept.–May.

Payment: none.

Reporting Time: 4 weeks.

Copyright held by author.

1967; 4/yr; 4,000

$20/yr

24 pp; 8½ x 11

Ad Rates: $200/page (7 x 10); $130/½ page (7 x 5 or 3½ x 10); $100/⅓ page (3½ x 5 or 7 x 2½); $60/⅙ page (3½ x 2½); $40/1/12 page; Discounts for nonprofits.

POETS ON

Ruth Daigon
29 Loring Ave.
Mill Valley, CA 94941
(415) 381-2824

Poetry.

POETS ON is a semi-annual poetry magazine. Theme-oriented, exploring basic human concerns through insightful, significant, well-crafted poetry. We publish recognized poets as well as unknown poets.

Robert Cooperman, Michael Bugeja, Marge Piercy, Lyn Lifshin, Barbara Crooker, James Broughton.

Unsolicited Manuscripts Received/Published per Year: 5,000+/85.

Reading Period: Sept.–Nov. 30; Feb.–April 30.

Payment: in copies.

Reporting Time: 2–3 months.

Copyright reverts to author.

1977; 2/yr; 500

$8/yr; $5/ea

48 pp; 5½ x 8½

PORTLAND REVIEW

Aaron Mahony
P.O. Box 751
Portland, OR 97207
(503) 725-4433

Fiction, poetry, essays, plays, photographs, graphics/artwork.

The **PORTLAND REVIEW** is the triannual Arts and Literature Magazine of Portland State University. It draws material mainly from the Pacific Northwest, but is open to submissions from outside the region.

Unsolicited Manuscripts Received/Published per Year: 700/100.

Payment: 1 copy.

Reporting Time: 2–4 months.

Copyright held by author.

1953; 2/yr; 1,000

$8/yr; $6/ea + $1 postage

80 pp; 9 x 12

PORTLANDIA REVIEW OF BOOKS

Tami Parr
3439 NE Sandy Blvd. #174
Portland, OR 97232
(503) 797-2962

Fiction, poetry, reviews, essays, art and graphics.

PORTLANDIA REVIEW OF BOOKS foregrounds the Pacific Northwest's thriving literary scene by highlighting its authors, publishers and regional friends.

Mark Berlin, Deborah Lambert, Lyn Lifshin, Judy Myers.

Unsolicited Manuscripts Received/Published per year: 250+/50+

Reading Period: year-round.

Payment: copies.

Reporting Time: 1 month.

Copyright held by magazine.

1995; Quarterly; 2,500

$12/yr; $3/ea; 60%

24 pp; 11 x 17

$300/page; $150/½ page; $75/¼ page; inquire for other sizes.

Small Changes

POTATO EYES

Roy Zarucchi, Carolyn Page
Nightshade Press, P.O. Box 76
Troy, ME 04987
(207) 948-3427

Canadian and US poetry, short stories, reviews of poetry, black and white art, contemporary essays. Now guest edited by Parks Lanier, Redford University English professor. Send SASE to Prof. Lanier for themes but all poetry & short fiction is welcome. Submissions to: English Box 6935, Radford Univ., Radford, VA 24142-6935.

A semi-annual literary arts journal focusing on poetry, short fiction and art work from/about the Appalachians from Alabama to Quebec. This is a primary, but not exclusive focus. Nightshade Press, of which **POTATO EYES** is an imprint, also publishes a NIGHTSHADE NIGHTSTAND READER which contains short stories, as well as single author short story collections. Send those submissions to Maine address, c/o Carolyn Page.

Earl Braggs, Barbara Presnell, Elizabeth Cohen, Jack Coulehan, M.D., Ina Cofelt, Edward M. Holmes, and L. L. Harper.

Unsolicited Manuscripts Received/ Published per Year: 1,600/200+.

Reading Period: year–round.

Payment: in copies.

Reporting Time: 8 weeks.

Copyright held by publisher, reverts to author upon publication.

1989; 2/yr; 800

$11/yr; $7.95/ea; 40%

104 pp; 5½ x 8½
ISSN: 1041-9926

POTOMAC REVIEW

Eli Flam
P.O. Box 354
Port Tobacco, MD 20677
(703) 556-0578

Fiction, poetry, essays, reportage, criticism and visuals.
A questing mainstream quarterly literary & pubic interest journal.
Hilary Tham, Richard Peabody,
Roland Flint, Lyn Lifshin, Elisavietta Ritchie.
Unsolicited Manuscripts Received/Published per Year: 2,000/100.
Reading Period: year–round.
Payment: 1 copy.
Reporting Time: 60 days.
Copyright held by author.
1994; 4/yr; 1,000
$15/yr; $4/ea; 40%
80–100 pp; 5½ x 8½
ISSN: 1073-1989

POTPOURRI

Polly W. Swafford, Senior Editor; Terry Hoyland, Poetry Editor
P.O. Box 8278
Prairie Village, KS 66208
(913) 642-1503

Fiction, nonfiction, poetry.
POTPOURRI is a not-for-profit, quarterly literary magazine.
POTPOURRI publishes a broad genre of short stories, poetry, adventure, travel, essays by both professional and novice writers.
David Ray, Pattiann Rogers, F.D. Reeve, Lance Olsen, Lloyd van Brunt, Anne Paolucci.
Unsolicited Manuscripts Received/Published per Year: 2,700/300.
Reading Period: year-round.
Payment: in copies.
Reporting Time: 8–12 weeks.
Copyright: yes.
1989; 4/yr; 3,000
$15/yr; $3.95/sample copy, includding shipping and handling
68 pp; 8 x 10 magazine
Ad Rates: Contact publisher for different rates/sizes.

POULTRY, A Magazine of Voice

Jack Flavin, Brendan Galvin, George Garrett
P.O. Box 4413
Springfield, MA 01101
(413) 732-0435

Parodies, satire, put-ons, put-downs of contemporary poetry, lit & litbiz.
Bruce Berlind, John Ciordi, Carolyn Kizel, Fred Chapell, David Graham, Lola Haskins, Peter Makuck.
Unsolicited Manuscripts Received/Published per Year: 500/80.

Payment: 10 free copies.
Reporting Time: six months.
Copyright: first publishing rights.
1979; 2/yr; 1,400
$6/yr; $3/ea; $5 for libraries

PRAIRIE FIRE

Andris Taskans, Managing Editor
423-100 Arthur St.
Winnipeg, Manitoba, R3B 1H3 CANADA
(204) 943-9066
Fiction, poetry, essays, book reviews.
A Canadian magazine with a western perspective, featuring new writing and special issues on topics such as ethnic writing, women's writing, genre writing and more.
Sandra Birdsell, Carol Shields.
Unsolicited Manuscripts Received/Published per Year: 1,200/120.
Reporting Time: 3–4 months.
Copyright reverts to author upon publication.
1978; 4/yr; 1,200
$24/yr; $8.95/ea; 30%
128 pp; 6 x 9
ISSN: 0821-1124
Canadian Magazine Publishers Association

PRAIRIE JOURNAL/of Canadian Literature

Prairie Journal Trust
P.O. Box 61203, Brentwood P.O.
Calgary, Alberta, T2L 2K6 CANADA
Short fiction, poetry, review, essays, drama.
Literary small press publication. No US stamps (submissions will not be read or returned without sufficient Canadian postage for return.)
Fred Cogswell, Lorna Crozier, Mick Burrs, Robin Mathews, Bruce Hunter, John V. Hicks, Shaunt Basmajian, George Amabile, Gary Hyland, Glen Sorestad, Peter Baltensperger, Dennis Cooley.
Unsolicited Manuscripts Received/Published per Year: 200/20.
Payment: Honouraria.
Reporting Time: 3–6 weeks.
Copyright for author.
1983; 2/yr; 600
$12/yr; $6/ea; 40%
60 pp; 7½ x 8
Ad Rates: negotiable
ISSN: 0827-2921

PRAIRIE SCHOONER

Hilda Raz
201 Andrews Hall
University of Nebraska
Lincoln, NE 68588-0334
(402) 472-0911
Poetry, fiction, essays, reviews, translation.
PRAIRIE SCHOONER, a liter-

ary quarterly, publishes the best writing available from beginning and established writers: short stories, poems, interviews, imaginative essays of general interest, and reviews of current books of poetry and fiction. Scholarly articles requiring footnote references are generally not published by **PRAIRIE SCHOONER**.

Marilyn Hacker, Reginald Shepherd, Ursula Hegi, Antonya Nelson, Marvin Bell, Richard Jackson.

Unsolicited Manuscripts Received/ Published per Year: 4,800/120.

Reading Period: Sept.–May.

Payment: 12 annual writing prizes and grant funds, when available; copies also.

Reporting Time: 3 months.

Copyright held by magazine; reverts to author upon request.

1926; 4/yr; 3,100

$22/yr ind, $25/yr inst; $7.25/ea; $5/Back issues; 40%

200 pp; 6 x 9

Ad Rates: $150/page (4¾ x 7½)

ISSN: 0032-6682

Ingram

PRIMAVERA

Editorial Board

Box #37-7547

Chicago, IL 60637

(312) 324-5920

Poetry, fiction, photographs, graphics/artwork.

PRIMAVERA focuses on the experiences of women; publishes both established and unknown writers. Literary quality is the most important consideration.

Diane Seuss-Brakeman, Pamela Gemin, Megan Olden, Candyce Barnes.

Unsolicited Manuscripts Received/ Published per Year: 1,000/25–30.

Payment: in copies.

Reporting Time: 2 weeks–3 months.

Copyright held by magazine; reverts to author upon publication.

1975; 1/yr; 1,000

$10/yr; $10/ea

5½ x 8½

No ads

ISSN: 0364-7609

THE PROLIFIC FREELANCER

Brian S.Konradt

P.O. Box 554

Oradell, NJ 07649, Dept. LM

(201) 262-3277 (voice)

E-mail: bskcom@village.ios.com

Interviews, how-to, news, markets.

A literary trade magazine focusing on freelancing in both the paper and electronic environment.

David Colozzi, Merry Harris, Kim Tobias.

Unsolicited Manuscripts Received/ Published per Year: 300/140.
Reading Period: Jan.–Dec.
Payment: $15–100; per article.
Reporting Time: 1 month; queries 2–4 weeks.
First North American Rights & Second Reprint Rights.
1992; 4–6/yr; 2,000+
$30/yr; $5/ea
16 pp; 8½ x 11
Ad rates: $30/3 x 5; $40/5 x 7; $60/7 x 5½; $95/8½ x 11
BSK

PROSODIA: A New College of California Poetics Journal

Gloria Frym
Poetics Program
New College of California
766 Valencia St.
San Francisco, CA 94110
(415) 626-0884
Fax (415) 626-5541

Poetry, and short prose.
PROSODIA is produced every Spring by students of the Poetics Program. Each year, a theme is chosen. The 1994 theme was "Peripheral Vision." The 1995 theme was "Birthmarks."
Will Alexander, David Meltzer, Harryette Mullen, Leslie Scalapino, Anne Waldman, Alice Notley.
Reading Period: January–April.
Payment: 2 copies.
Reporting Time: 2 months.
Copyright held by Prosodia.
1990; 1/yr; 750
$7/ea; 2–4 10%, 5–9 20%, 10+ 40%
100 pp; 9 x 6
Ad Rates: $125/full page; $65/½ page; $25/¼ page
Small Press Distribution

THE PROSPECT REVIEW

Peter A. Koufos
557 10th St.
Brooklyn, NY 11215
(718) 788-5709

Poetry, fiction.
TPR is a literary journal committed to daring; bridging a gap between the unacknowledged poet and writer with those in academia for cultural unity.
E. Ethelbert Miller, Richard Burgin, Jana Harris, Gina Bergamino.
Unsolicited Manuscripts Received/ Published per Year: many/20.
Payment: copies.
Reporting Time: on or near issue release date.
Copyright reverts to authors upon publication.
1990; 2/yr
$12/yr; $6/ea
86 pp; 6 x 8
Ad Rates: Available on request
ISSN: 1049-0426
DeBoer

PROVINCETOWN ARTS

Christopher Busa
650 Commercial Street
Provincetown, MA 02657
(508) 487-3167

Poetry, fiction, reviews, essays, translation, interviews, photographs, graphics/artwork.

The documentary voice of the artists and writers who visit Cape Cod, **PROVINCETOWN ARTS** focuses on the phenonmenon of the art colony, not as geographical locus, but as a point of view. A large proportion of this annual book-length magazine emphasizes visual art, exploring the relation of visual art to language.

Alan Dugan, Stanley Kunitz, Susan Mitchell, Mark Doty, Cyrus Cassells, Henri Cole.

Unsolicited Manuscripts Received/Published per Year: 1,200/varies.

Reading Period: Aug.–Feb.

Payment: $25–$125 per poem; $125–300 per story (fiction & nonfiction).

Reporting Time: 2–4 months.

Copyright: Provincetown Arts, Inc.

1985; 1/yr; 8,500

$10/yr; $6.50/sample; 40%

184 pp; 9 x 12

Ad Rates: $950/page; $550/½ page; $400/⅓ page

Ingram, IPD, Publishers Circulation Corp.

PUCK: THE UNOFFICIAL JOURNAL OF THE IRREPRESSIBLE

Brian Clark, Violet Riverrun
47 Noe St. #4
San Francisco, CA 94114-1017
(415) 255-9765
Internet: bcclark@igc.apc.org
www: http://www.armory.com ~jay/permeable.htm

Fiction, essays, reviews, graphics, poetry.

A radical reinterpretation of consensus reality. Color covers, 96 pages, 8½ x 11, printed offset, appearing thrice a year.

Dan Pearlman, Paul DiFilippo, Lance Olsen

Unsolicited Manuscripts Received/Published per Year: 1,000's/dozens.

Payment: copies and honararium

Reporting Time: 2 weeks–2 months.

Copyright: yes.

1984; 3/yr; 5,000

$17/yr; $6.50/ea; 40%–55%

80 pp; 8½ x 11

Ad Rates: Write, call, or e-mail for rates

ISSN: 1071-7633

Fine Print, Desert Moon, Ubiquity, Bookpeople, Inland, IDP, AK, Tower

PUCKERBRUSH REVIEW

Constance Hunting
76 Main St.
Orono, ME 04473
(207) 581-3832

Fiction, poetry, reviews, criticism, interviews, essays, graphics/artwork, photographs.

The special focus is on Maine literature and literary figures. The intent is to publish fiction, poetry and reviews by contemporary Maine writers. The purpose is both to reveal and to encourage the literary energy in this isolated state. "Puckerbrush" = new growth.

Deborah Pease, James Laughlin, Leo Connellan, Farnham Blair, Kate Barnes.

Unsolicited Manuscripts Received/ Published per Year: 200/35.

Payment: in copies.

Copyright held by magazine; reverts to author upon publication.

1978; 2/yr; 450

$8/yr; $4/ea; 40%

75 pp; 8½ x 11

Ad Rates: inquire

PUDDING MAGAZINE: THE INTERNATIONAL JOURNALS OF APPLIED POETRY

Jennifer Bosveld
Pudding House Writers
Resource Ctr., 60 N. Main St.
Johnstown, OH 43031
(614) 967-6060

Poetry, short-short stories, essays, articles on writing and applied poetry.

Focus on poetry's use, though it needs no "use." Each issue unlike the one before.

John Bennett, Jeanne Lohman, Wilma Elizabeth McDaniel, Ron Moran, Ed Baccia.

Unsolicited Manuscripts Received/ Published per year: 100,000+/ 150.

Reading Period: 12 months.

Payment: Copy of the issue.

Reporting Time: Overnight unless traveling.

Copyright held by magazine; reverts to author upon publication.

1980; 2-3/yr; 2,000

$18/3 issues; $6.95/ea (direct mail only)

40–120 pp; 5½ x 8½

Ad Rates: Accepts no advertising.

Direct from publisher only

PUERTO DEL SOL

Kathleene West, Poetry; Antonya Nelson, Kevin McIlvoy, Fiction; Chris Burnham, Essay
Box 30001, Dept. 3E
New Mexico State University
Las Cruces, NM 88003-9984
(505) 646-2345

Poetry, fiction, novel sections, criticism, essays, reviews, translation, interviews, photographs, graphics/artwork.

Though our emphasis is on Southwest writers, forty percent of each issue is the poetry, short fiction, artwork, etc. of artists from all over the United States.

Marilyn Hacker, Alison Joseph, Virgil Suarez, Dagoberto Gilb, Judith Ortiz Cofer, Ricardo Aguilar Melantzón, José Antonio Burciaga, Christopher McIlroy.

Unsolicited Manuscripts Received/Published per Year: 1,000/25 fiction, 35-45 poetry, 5-10 essay.

Reading Period: Sept.–March 1.

Payment: copies.

Reporting Time: 12–20 weeks.

Copyright held by magazine; reverts to author upon publication.

1960; 2/yr; 1,400

$10/yr ind, $10/yr inst; $8/ea; 40%

250 pp; 6 x 9

Ad Rates: $150/page; $90/½ page; $60/¼ page

ISSN: 0738-517X

QUIXOTE

Morris Edelson, Melissa Bondy
1812 Marshall

Q

QUARRY WEST

Kenneth Weisner
c/o Porter College
University of California
Santa Cruz, CA 95064
(408) 459-2155; (408) 459-2951 (messages)

Poetry, fiction, essays, graphics/artwork.

QUARRY WEST combines quality design, graphics, production with about 95 pages of poetry and fiction, plus essays and reviews. We value intensity of voice and variety in form, content, intent. "A controversy of poets." We do symposiums, also: #22, Rexroth; #25, Neruda; #29/30, Dissident Song: Contemporary Asian American Anthology.

Marilyn Chin, Francisco X. Alarcón, Bill Knott, Lucille Clifton, Bruce Weigl.

Unsolicited Manuscripts Received/Published per Year: 800/20.

Payment: 2 contributor's copies.

Copyright held by magazine; reverts to author upon request.

1971; 2/yr; 1,000

$15/yr; $10/ea; $3.50/back issue; 40%

110 pp; 6¾ x 8¼

Ad Rates: inquire

ISSN: 0736-4628

THE QUARTERLY

Gordon Lish, Dana Spiotta, Jodi Davis
650 Madison Ave.
New York, NY 10022
(212) 888-4769

Fiction, poetry, essay, humor.

A wide-open venue with particular hospitality for the unaffiliated. Fastest, fairest readings.

Unsolicited Manuscripts Received/Published per Year: 25,000/200.
Reading Period: year–round.
Payment: author copies.
Copyright held by magazine; reverts to author upon publication.
1987; 4/yr; 15,000
$30/4 issues
D. A. P. total circulation

QUARTERLY REVIEW OF LITERATURE

Contemporary Poetry Series
Theodore and Renee Weiss
26 Haslet Ave.
Princeton, NJ 08540

Poetry.

QRL, a new concept in poetry, publishes 4 to 6 prize-winning books of poetry in each volume, chosen through international competition. Called "the most significant event in years" and "the best bargain in poetry" and applauded as "brilliant." Each issue includes: complete books of poetry, long poems, poetic plays,
a book of poetry translation, plus introductory essays, photographs, and biographies of each author.

Wislava Szymborska, David Schubert, Nancy Esposito, Larry Kramer, Julia Mishkin.

Reading Period: May and Nov.
Payment: $1,000 plus 100 copies per winning manuscript. Please write for more information, with SASE.
Reporting Time: 2 months or less.
Copyright held by magazine.
1943; 1/yr; 3–5,000
$20/2 volumes ind paper, $20/cloth volume inst; $10/ea; 10%
350 pp; 5½ x 8½
Ad Rates: $300/page; $175/½ page
ISSN: 0033-5819

QUARTERLY WEST

M. L. Williams and Lawrence Coates
317 Olpin Union
University of Utah
Salt Lake City, UT 84112
(801) 581-3938

Fiction, poetry, reviews, translation.

We try to publish the best in poetry and fiction, both mainstream and experimental. We conduct a biennial novella competition and also publish reviews and translations. We're not a western genre magazine. Biennial Novella Competition; send S.A.S.E. for details. We accept multiple submissions (just tell us, please).

Andre Dubus, Francine Prose, Ron Carlson, Marvin Bell, Stephen

Dobyns, William Stafford, Philip Levine, C.E. Poverman, Antonya Nelson.
Unsolicited Manuscripts Received/ Published per Year: 1,000+/40.
Reading Period: year–round.
Payment: fiction $25–$50; poems and reviews $15–$50 each + 2 copies and 1 yr sub.
Reporting Time: 4–12 weeks.
Copyright held by magazine; reverts to author upon request.
1976; 2/yr; 1,000
$11/yr; $6.50/ea; 25%–40%
200 pp; 6 x 9
Ad Rates: $150/page (4⅜ x 7⅞); $85/½ page (4⅜ x 4)
ISSN: 0194-4231

QUIXOTE

Morris Edelson, Melissa Bondy
1812 Marshall
Houston, TX 77098
(713) 529-7944
Poetry, fiction, criticism, essays, translation, interviews.
Social criticism/satire/mucking around.
D. A. Levy, Pablo Neruda, Tuli Kupferberg, Steve Kowitt, Curt Johnson.
Payment: in copies.
Reporting Time: 6 months.
Copyright held by author.
1965; 12/yr; 300
$15/yr; $2/ea
40–100 pp; 4 x 5–11 x 17

R

RACCOON

David Spicer
P.O. Box 111327
Memphis, TN 38111-1327

Poetry, fiction, criticism, essays, reviews, translation, interviews, photographs.

A journal of contemporary literature, with poetry, fiction, essay.

Maurya Simon, Pattiann Rogers, David Romtvedt, Jay Meek, Frank Russell.

Payment: poetry–1 year subscription; prose–$50 and 1 copy.

Reporting Time: 6 weeks–3 months.

Copyright reverts to author upon publication.

1977; 3/yr; 500

$12.50/yr; $5/ea; 40%

ISSN: 0148-0162

SPD, Ebsco, Faxon

RAFTERS

Matt Uhler
Calder Square
P.O. Box 10929
State College, PA 16805-0929
(814) 867-4073

Poetry, short fiction, short shorts.

An open forum for literary expression that's attempting to appeal to a large audience and impact the literary market.

Bruce Weigl, Thomas E. Kennedy, Dave Kress.

Reading Period: all year.

Payment: contributor's copy.

Reporting Time: 3–5 months.

Copyright held by author.

1996; 4/yr; 500

70 pp.

RAG MAG/Black Hat Press

Beverly Voldseth
Box 12

Goodhue, MN 55027
(612) 923-4590

Poetry, fiction, essays, reviews, plays, photographs, graphics/artwork.

Small ecletic lit mag.

Theme issues through 1997

Send SASE for guidelines.

Carol Susco, Lynne Burgess, Myra Sullivan, Benj. Mahle, Brian Raszka.

Unsolicited Manuscripts Received/Published per Year: 800/80.

Reading Period: Jan.–Mar.

Payment: in copies.

Reporting Time: 1 week–2 months.

Copyright held by magazine; reverts to author upon publication.

1982; 2/yr; 300

$10/yr. $6/ea

112 pp; 6 x 9

Ad Rates: $35/page (4 x 7⅜); $20/½ page (4 x 3½); $10/¼ page (4 x 1¾); will exchange ads

ISSN: 0742-2768

RAMBUNCTIOUS REVIEW

M. Alberts, N. Lennon, R. Goldman, E. Hausler

1221 West Pratt Boulevard
Chicago, IL 60626

Poetry, fiction, photographs, graphics/artwork.

We are an annual literary arts magazine devoted to the publication of new and established writers and artists. We sponsor annual poetry and fiction contests and theme issues. Our next issue is focused on "Secrets."

Elizabeth Eddy, Richard Calisch, Hugh Fox, Richard Kostelanetz.

Unsolicited Manuscripts Received/Published per Year: 1,000/15.

Reading Period: Sept. 1–May 31.

Payment: 2 issues.

Copyright held by magazine; reverts to author upon publication.

1982; 1/yr; 450

$12/3 issues; $4/sample

48 pp; 7 x 10

No ads

Ingram

RARITAN

R. Poirier, Editor; Suzanne K. Hyman, Managing Editor

31 Mine St.
New Brunswick, NJ 08903
(908) 932-7887 or 7852

Criticism, essays, reviews, poetry, fiction. A comprehensive critique of contemporary culture.

Stanley Cavell, Clifford Geertz, Vicki Hearne, Edward W. Said.

Unsolicited Manuscripts Received/Published per Year: 250/7.

Payment: $100/article.

Reporting Time: 2 months.

Copyright reverts to author in 6 months.

1981; 4/yr; 3,500

$16/yr, $26/2 yrs ind, $20/yr, $30/2 yrs inst; $5/ea; $6/back issues; 40%–50%

160 pp; 6 x 9

Ad Rates: $275/page (4½ x 7½)

ISSN: 0275-1607

DeBoer, Ingram

THE RAVEN CHRONICLES

Kathleen Alcala, Phoebe Bosché, Phil Red-Eagle, Annie Hansen, Arthur Tulee, John Olson, Jody Aliesan, Stephan Magcosta, D.L. Birchfield, Tiffany Midge.

P.O. Box 95918

Seattle, WA 98145

(206) 328-1676:

Fax (206) 543-1104

Poetry, essays, interviews, fiction, reviews, artwork (b/w), cartoons.

TRC is designed to promote multicultural & transcultural arts and literature. We provide a forum for critical discussion of multicultural art forms.

Sherman Alexie, Charles Johnson, Elizabeth Woody, David Whited, Carter Revard.

Unsolicited Manuscripts Received/Published per Year: 1200/100.

Reading Period: Jan.– Nov.

Payment: 2 copies of issue and $10–40 (varies with each issue).

Reporting Time: 3–6 months.

Copyright held by author/artists: though we copyright work in each issue.

1990; 3/yr; 3,500

$15/yr U.S.; $20/yr foreign; $3 to $4.50, 50%

48 to 64 pp; 8½ x 11

Ad Rates: (call for information; will barter) Business Card Size: $25; ½ page; $150; full page; $350.

ISSN: 1066-1883

Small Changes in Pacific Northwest

READER'S BREAK

Gertrude S. Eiler

P.O. Box 40

Jamesville, NY 13078

(315) 423-9268

Short stories, poetry.

Established to be a vehicle for writers of talent and ability whether previously published or not.

Edwidge Danticat, L. E. McCullough, Bradley White, Ann T. Beacham, Edith C. Johnson, James Mathews, Judith Graham.

Unsolicited Manuscripts Received/Published per Year: 500/Approx. 56

Payment: one copy of book in which author's story appears.
Reporting Time: 1–3 months.
Copyright: One time copyright. Rights revert to author.
1990; book only
$18.95 per book; 40%
250± pp; 8½ x 5½

$20/3 issues; $35 inst & overseas; $7.50–$10 ea; 40%
150 pp; 8½ x 11
Ad Rates: $300/page; $175/½ page; $75/⅓ page (4 x 5¼)
ISSN: 0883-0126
Ubiquity, Fine Print, Last Gasp, Armadillo, DeBoer, Desert Moon, Central Books (UK)

RED BASS

Jay Murphy
105 W. 28th St.
New York, NY 10001
(212) 239-7470

Poetry, essays, graphics/artwork, criticism, reviews, translation, interviews, fiction, plays, photographs.

RED BASS illuminates the interface between art and politics in a series of thematic book/magazines, usually of a cross-cultural, interdisciplinary nature.

Robert C. Morgan, Luisa Valenzuela, James Purdy, Carolee Schneemann, Etel Adnan.
Unsolicited Manuscripts Received/Published per Year: We are not accepting unsolicited manuscripts.
Payment: in copies, sometimes in cash as funds allow.
Reporting Time: 3 months.
Copyright held by magazine; reverts to author upon publication.
1981; 2/yr; 3,000

THE RED CEDAR REVIEW

Laura Klynstra, Tom Bissell
Department of English
17C Morrill Hall
Michigan State University
East Lansing, MI 48824
(517) 355-9656

Poetry, fiction.

We recommend reading past issues before submission. We publish the highest quality of fiction and poetry from our submissions; we seek no particular style or form. Tend to the conventions of English; i.e. use good grammar, write clean prose. Please include SASE for response.

Jim Harrison, Margaret Atwood, tom Paine, Jim Cash, Stuart Dybeck, Diane Wakoski.
Unsolicited Manuscripts Received/Published per Year: 300/25.
Reading Period: year–round.
$10/yr; $5/ea; $2/sample, 40%
Faxon, Ebsco

RE*MAP MAGAZINE

Todd Baron
8270 Willoughby Ave.
Los Angeles, CA 90046

RENEGADE

Michael Nowicki, Miriam Jones, Larry Snell
P.O. Box 314
Bloomfield Hills, MI 48303

Poems, essays, short stories, plays.
Open literary magazine.
Unsolicited Manuscripts Received/Published per Year: 500/10–20.
Payment: contributor's copy.
Reporting Time: 2 weeks–6 months.
1989; 2/yr; 100
$9.90/yr; $5/ea
24 pp; 11 x 8½
Ad Rates: free

REPRESENTATIONS

Stephen Greenblatt, Carla Hesse, Co-Chairs; Editorial Board
English Department
University of California
Berkeley, CA 94720
(510) 642-4671

Criticism, essays, translations.
REPRESENTATIONS publishes critical essays on interdisciplinary topics; disciplines included are literature, political theory, art history, and anthropology, and roughly 50 percent of the work published is literary criticism. Of the balance, literary methodology is a substantial influence in essays in other fields such as history, political theory, anthropology, etc.
Unsolicited Manuscripts Received/Published per Year; 400/28
Payment: none.
Reporting Time: 8–16 weeks.
Copyright held by University of California Press.
1983; 4/yr; 2,200
$36/yr ind; $80/yr inst; $24/yr student
152 pp; 7 x 9¾
Ad Rates: $285/page
ISSN: 0734-6018
DeBoer

RESONANCE

Evan and Patty Pritchard
P.O. Box 215
Beacon, NY 12508
(914) 838-1217

Essays, graphics/artwork, poetry, review, photographs, fiction, interviews, music and humor.
RESONANCE is a journal of all forms of creative expression inspired by personal spiritual experience. It strives to create a popular forum for communication between artists, scientists and the spiritual community,

however it does not promote or denigrate any other organizations, spiritual, educational or otherwise. It is a forum for individual spiritual insight.

Heather Hughes-Calero, Susan Hanniford Crowley. Interviews with Chris Williamson, Madeleine L'Engle, Arun Gandhi, Pete Seeger, David Lanz, Joan Houston, others.

Unsolicited Manuscripts Received/ Published per Year: 700/10.

Payment: 1 copy.

Reporting Time: 8 weeks.

Copyright held by Evan and Patty Pritchard—compilation only; reverts to author upon publication.

1987; 3/yr; 2,000

$10/yr; $3/ea; 40%

52 pp; 8½ x 11

$100/½ page; $50/¼ page; $25/⅛ page

Ubiquity, Homing Pigeon, Armadillo, L-S Distributors, Book Tech, New Leaf

RESPONSE: A Contemporary Jewish Review

Yigal Schleifer, David R. Adler, Michael R. Steinberg

27 W. 20 St. 9th fl.

New York, NY 10011

(212) 620-0350

Fax (212) 929-3459

Unsolicited Manuscripts Received/ Published per Year: 200-300/15.

REVIEW: THE AMERICAS SOCIETY

Alfred J. Mac Adam, Daniel Shapiro, Editors

Americas Society

680 Park Ave.

New York, NY 10021

(212) 249-8950

Fiction, poetry, criticism, essays, reviews, translations, interviews, articles on visual arts and music.

REVIEW presents the best of Latin American literature in English translation. It contains a review section as well as major articles on the Latin American visual and performing arts.

Unsolicited Manuscripts Received/ Published per Year: 75–100/5.

Payment: $100 and up.

Copyright held by the Americas Society (present); Center for Inter-American Relations (back issues).

1967; 2/yr; 5,000

$16/yr ind, $25/yr inst; $9/ea

100 pp; 8½ x 11

Ad Rates: $700/page (7¾ x 9¾); $400/½ page (5 x 7)

Total, Ingram, Inland

REVIEW OF CONTEMPORARY FICTION

John O'Brien, Steven Moore
Campus Box 4241
Illinois State University
Normal, IL 61790-4241

Criticism, essays, reviews, translation, interviews.

Each issue is devoted to criticism on one or two contemporary novelists.

Upcoming issues are devoted to Carole Maso, Raymond Queneau, Edmund White.

Gilbert Sorrentino, Robert Creeley, Paul Metcalf, Carlos Fuentes, Toby Olson.

All manuscripts are by invitation only.

Reporting Time: 2 weeks.

Copyright held by magazine; reverts to author upon publication.

1981; 3/yr; 2,800

$17/yr ind, $26/yr inst; $8/ea; 10%–40%

200 pp; 6 x 9

Ad Rates: $250/page (5 x 7½)

ISSN: 0276-0045

Inland, SPD

RFD

Short Mountain Collective
P.O. Box 68
Liberty, TN 37095
(615) 536-5176

Poetry, fiction, essays, reviews, interviews, photographs, graphics/artwork.

RFD focuses on rural gay men in related areas of human growth and consciousness and is an open forum for new ideas, radical views and controversial issues. The scope includes articles on alternative lifestyles, homesteading skills, collectives, gardening, cooking, contact letters, poetry, fiction, prisoner section, book reviews and graphics.

Harry Hay, Bru Dye, Louise Hay, Robin Walden, Jan Nathen Long.

Unsolicited Manuscripts Received/Published per Year: 50/20.

Payment: 1 copy of issue published in.

Reporting Time: 1–6 months.

Copyright held by author.

1974; 4/yr; 3,700

$32/yr ind 1st class, $20/yr ind 2nd class; $20/yr inst; $6/ea; 40%

80 pp; 8½ x 11

Ad Rates: $350/page (8½ x 11); $185/½ page (4¼ x 11 or 8½ x 5½); $98/¼ page (4¼ x 5½)

ISSN: 0149-709X

RHINO

Kay Meier, Don Hoffman
1808 N. Larrabee St.
Chicago, IL 60614

(312) 787-9125
Fax (312) 794-6243
Poetry, occasional stories.
Small annual poetry journal.
John Dickson, Michael Davidson, Esteban Torres-Guzman, Simon Perchik, Roberts Swann.
Unsolicited Manuscripts Received/ Published per Year: 100/25.
Reading Period: Sept.–Nov.
Reporting Time: 6 mo.–1 yr.
Copyright held by author.
1992; 1/yr; 100.
$6/ea.
80 pp; 5 x 8

RIVER CITY (formerly **MEMPHIS STATE REVIEW**)
Paul Naylor
English Department
The University of Memphis
Memphis, TN 38152
(901) 678-4591
Poetry, fiction, essays, interviews. No novel excerpts.
The magazine sponsors the River City Writing Awards in fiction: 1st prize $2,000; 2nd prize $500; 3rd prize $300. Send SASE for details.
Fred Busch, Marvin Bell, Mona Van Duyn, Pattiann Rogers, Luisa Valenzuela, John Updike.
Unsolicited Manuscripts Received/ Published per Year: 1,000/40.
Reading Period: Sept.–May.
Payment: varies.
Reporting Time: 1 month.
Copyright reverts to author.
1980; 2/yr; 1,000
$12/yr; $7/ea
100 pp; 7 x 10
Ad Rates: $40/page

RIVER OAK REVIEW
Etta L. Worthington
P.O. Box 3127
Oak Park, IL 60303
(708) 524-8725
Fax (708) 848-9729
Short fiction, creative nonfiction, poetry.
Rooted in the innovative literary tradition of the Midwest, we seek to publish work that is compelling accessible, and important, produced by established and emerging writers.
Eric Pankey, Kathleen Norris, Anne Calcagno, Ronald Wallace, Mary Swander.
Unsolicited Manuscripts Received/ Published per Year: 500/50.
Reading Period: year-round.
Payment: copies; miminal payment if grant money available.
Reporting Time: approx. 3 months.
Copyright held by magazine, rights revert to author.
1993; 2/yr; 450

$12/yr, $6/ea; 40%
112 pp; 6 x 9, perfect bound
Ad rates: $200/full page; $100/½ page
ISSN: 1074-3693
Ubiquity, Bernard DeBoer

RIVER STYX

Richard Newman, Quincy Troupe, Michael Castro
3207 Washington
St. Louis, MO 63103-1218
(314) 533-4541
Poetry, fiction, interviews, photographs, graphics/artwork.
RIVER STYX is a multicultural journal of poetry, prose and graphic arts publishing works by both established and up and coming writers and artists, significant for their originality, quality, and craftsmanship.
Sharon Olds, Grace Paley, Derek Walcott, Marilyn Hacker, Carl Phillips.
Unsolicited Manuscripts Received/Published per Year: 1,500+/50-60.
Reading Period: Sept. and Oct.
Payment: $8/page for literature: $10/page for photographs or drawings.
Copyright held by Big River Association; reverts to author upon publication.
1975; 3/yr; 1,000
$20/yr ind, $28/yr inst; $7/ea; 33%
112 pp; 5½ x 8½
Exchange ads
ISSN: 0149-8851
Ingram

RIVERWIND

C. A. Dubielak, Audrey Naffziger
Hocking College
Nelsonville, OH 45768
(614) 753-3591, ext 2375
Poetry, fiction, nonfiction.
RIVERWIND is more interested in publishing the new poet, the good poet, the challenging, the true as opposed to the well-established and/or predictable. Quality, please. Beginning with our 1993 edition, the focus of Riverwind will be on Appalachian Writers (Ohio, W. Virginia, Kentucky, etc.), themes, characters and concerns.
Simon Percik, James Riley.
Unsolicited Manuscripts Received/Published per Year: 200/30-50.
Payment: copies.
Reporting Time: 4 weeks–3 months. No summer submissions.
Copyright held by author.
1982; 1/yr; 400
$2.50/yr; $2.50/ea; 60%
80 pp; 6 x 9

ROSEBUD™

Rod Clark
Box 459

Cambridge, WI 53523
(608) 423-9609
Short stories, poems, non-fiction narrative, articles.
Each issue features five rotating themes, such as "En Route" and "Mothers Daughters, Wives." Stories, articles, profiles and poems . . . of love, alienation, travel, humor, nostalgia and unexpected revelation.
Unsolicited Manuscripts Received/Published per Year: 4,000/80.
Reading Period: year-round.
Payment: $45 per piece, plus 3 additional awards $150 each.
Reporting Time: 10 weeks.
Copyright returned to the writer.
1993; 4/yr; 7,000
$18/yr; $30/2yr; $5.50/ea; 20%
120 pp; 7⅝ x 10¼
Ad Rates: $500/page (x4 $350); $300/½ page (4x $20)
ISSN: 1072-1681
Eastern News, institutional subscriptions EBSCO, FAXON

S

SAGUARO

Charles Tatum
315 Douglass Bldg
The University of Arizona
Tucson, AZ 85721
(520) 621-7551

Fiction, poetry, essays, autobiography and biography, no reviews.

Bilingual (Eng/Span) magazine dedicated to writing by and about Chicano/Latinos. **SAGUARO** seeks works by both established and unknown writers.

Bernice Zamora, Sandra Cisneros, Joel Huerta, Carmen Tafolla, Maria Herrera-Sobek, Max Aguilera-Hellweg.

Unsolicited Manuscripts Received/ Published per Year: 200/20.

Payment: in copies.

Reporting Time: variable.

Copyright held by Mexican American Studies & Research Center; reverts to author upon publication.

1984; 1/yr; 500

$10/2 issues; $6/ea; 20–40%

100 pp; 6 x 9

No ads

ISSN: 0885-5013

SAIL Studies in American Indian Literatures

Robert M. Nelson, Production Editor Joseph Bruchac, Poetry/Fiction Editor
Box 112
University of Richmond
Richmond, VA 23173

Poetry, fiction, criticism, essays, translations, interviews, letters, announcements, contributing notes, scholarly articles and reviews.

SAIL is the only peridical focusing exclusively on literature *by*

American Indian authors. **SAIL** publishes reviews and scholarly articles as well as poetry, fiction, interviews, autobiography and other nonfiction; also translations/transcriptions of oral texts and performances. We are seeking funds to expand publication of translations and original-language texts, and to permit printing of graphics and half-tones.

Joseph Bruchac, Maurice Kenny, Lance Henson, Charlotte DeClue, Karoniaktatie.

Copyright held by Sail, reverts to author upon publication.

1989; 4/yr; 350

$12/yr ind, $16/yr inst

100+ pp; 5½ x 8½

SALAMANDER: A Magazine for Poetry, Fiction, & Memoirs

Jennifer Barber

48 Ackers Ave.

Brookline, MA 02146

(617) 232-4647

Poetry, fiction, memoirs, translations, black-and-white artwork.

Salamander specializes in publishing highly accomplished work by writers who deserve a wider audience.

Jane Brox, Ira Sadoff, Reetika Vazirani, Andrew Hudgins, Michael Collins.

Unsolicited Manuscripts Received/Published per year: 1,000/40.

Reading Period: Only in a grant year - $25 per 2 pgs.

Reporting Time: 4 months.

Copyright held by magazine; reverts to author upon publication.

1992; 2/yr; 1,000

$12/yr; $6/ea; 40%

80 pp; 5½ x 8½

Ad Rates: $150/page (4½ x 7½)

ISSN: 1063-3359

Bernhard DeBoer, Inc.

SALMAGUNDI

Robert and Peggy Boyers, Editors; Thomas S.W. Lewis, Associate Editor, Marc Woodworth, Assistant Editor

Skidmore College

Saratoga Springs, NY 12866

(518) 584-5000, ext 2302

Poetry, fiction, criticism, essays, reviews, translation, interviews.

SALMAGUNDI is an international quarterly of the humanities and social sciences publishing essays and book reviews on literature, contemporary politics, film, dance, and current ideas. General issues also feature original fiction, poetry, photographs and interviews.

George Steiner, Nadine Gordimer, Seamus Heaney, Tzvetan Todorov, William Gass, David Rieff.

Unsolicited Manuscripts Received/Published per Year: 2,000/15-20.

Payment: none.

Reporting Time: 1–5 months.

Copyright held by Skidmore; reverts to author upon publication.

1965; 4/yr; 4,850

$18/yr ind, $25/yr inst; $7/ea

160–230 pp; 8½ x 5½

Ad Rates: $150/page (4 x 7); $85/½ page (4 x 3½)

DeBoer

SAN DIEGO WRITERS' MONTHLY

Charles Harrington Elster, Michael T. McCarthy

3910 Chaman St., Suite D

San Diego, CA 92110

(619) 226-0896;

Fax (619) 223-0226

Quincy Troupe, William Murray, Elizabeth George, Joseph Wambaugh, Raymond Feist.

As San Diego's only monthly literary magazine, our goal is to inform, represent, and entertain while promoting writing from all San Diegans, established and aspiring. Our publication crosses all genres and includes a variety of columns, interviews, essays, features, reviews, fiction and poetry written chiefly by county residents.

Payment: $5/poem, $10–25 for fiction/nonfiction.

Reporting Time: 4–5 weeks.

Copyright held by author, although magazine asks for one time North American Serial Rights.

1991; 12/yr; 700

$23/yr ind and inst; $3/ea

36 pp; 8½ x 11

Ad Rates: $375/page (7 x 9½); $300/½ page (3¼ x 9½ or 7 x 4); $200/¼ page (3¼ x 4½)

ISSN: 1054-6774

SAN FERNANDO POETRY JOURNAL

Richard Cloke, Editor; Shirley Rodecker, Managing Editor; Lori C. Smith, Pub. Editor

Kent Publications, Inc.

18301 Halsted St.

Northridge, CA 91325

(818) 349-2080

Poetry.

Seeks to fuse diverse elements of contemporaneity, ranging from evocation of scientific and technical advances—with a pronounced interest in poetry of social protest which illuminates the ills of our time, with special emphasis on ecology.

C.J. Roner, Paul Weinman, A.D. Winans, Miriam Cohen, Jack Bernier.
Unsolicited Manuscripts Received/ Published per Year: 7-800/2-500.
Payment: in copies, discounts on subs.
Reporting Time: 2–3 weeks.
Copyright reverts to author.
1978; 4/yr; 500
$10/yr; $3/ea; 20%–30%
100 pp; 5½ x 8½
Ad Rates: $50/page (4½ x 7); $25/½ page (4½ x 3½)
ISSN: 0196-2884

SAN FRANCISCO REVIEW OF BOOKS

Paschal Fowlkes
126 South Park
San Francisco, CA 94107
(415) 543-7372
Fax (415) 243-8514
Reviews, interviews, and profiles of literary works and persons.
Commentary, debates, and essays on everything from baseball to Buddhism, thrillers to post-modernism.
Unsolicited Manuscripts Received/ Published per Year: 100/15
Payment: negotiable.
Copyright held by magazine.
1975; 6/yr; 8,000
$16/yr; $3/ea; 35-50%
48 pp; 8½ x 11
Ad Rates: full page b/w $1100, 4-color $1995
ISSN: 0194-0724
Eastern News

SANDHILLS REVIEW
(formerly **St. Andrews Review**)

Stephen E. Smith, Editor
Sandhills Community College
2200 Airport Rd.
Pinehurst, NC 28374
Publishes fiction, poetry and essays of highest quality from both established writers and promising new authors from all over the U.S. and abroad.
Fred Chappell, Hiroaki Sato, Soichi Furuta, Yukio Mishima, Desmond Egan.
Unsolicited Manuscripts Received/ Published per Year: 800/50.
Payment: 1 copy.
Copyright held by magazine; reverts to author upon publication.
1972; 2/yr; 500
$8/ea; 30%
100 pp; 6 x 9
Ad Rates: $200/page (5 x 7); $100/½ page (2½ x 3½); $50/¼ page (1¼ x 1¾)
ISSN: 1061-3579

SANTA BARBARA REVIEW

Patricia Stockton Leddy
104 La Vereda Lane

Santa Barbara, CA 93108
(805) 969-0861
Essays, poetry, fiction, non-fiction, B/W art.
SBR is a tri-quarterly arts and literary journal which provides a forum for fiction writers, poets and essayists, as well as for graphic artists. **SBR** seeks work for its entertainment and informative value.
Chana Bloch, John Sanford, Tess Gallagher, Stephen Ratcliffe, Marilyn Chandler McEntyre.
Reading Period: year-round.
Payment: 2 copies.
Reporting Time: 2–3 months.
Copyright held by Santa Barbara Review.
1993; 3/yr
$16/yr; $7/ea; 40%
128–160 pp; 6 x 9
Ad Rates: $90/page; $60/½ page
ISSN: 1068-8617
Ingram Periodicals, Ubiquity Dist., Armadillo

SANTA FE LITERARY REVIEW

Colleen Rae
P.O. Box 8018
Santa Fe, NM 87504-8018
(505) 989-7641
Fiction, poetry, art/graphics, essays.
The goal of the **SANTA FE LITERARY REVIEW** is to explore art as it can be rather than as it "should" be, which requires a firm knowledge of what has been.
Richard Goldstein, Steven Counsell, Nedra Westwater, Patricia Hinnebusch, Lisa Greenleaf.
Payment: 5 copies and a 1–year subscription.
Reporting Time: 6 weeks.
Copyright held by Colleen Rae/Haven Hill Press; reverts to author upon publication.
1991; 4/yr; 1,000
$18/yr; $5/ea; 40%
96 pp; 6 x 9
Ad Rates: $100/page (4 x 7)
ISSN: 1055-8446

THE SANTA MONICA REVIEW

Lee Montgomery
1900 Pico Blvd.
Santa Monica, CA 90405
Fiction, poetry, essays.
Guy Davenport, Charles Baxter, Barry Hannah, Peter Handke, Amy Gerstler, Alicia Ostriker.
Unsolicited Manuscripts Received/Published per Year: 2,000/4-6.
Reading Period: year–round.
Payment: copies.
Reporting Time: 1–3 months.
Copyright: first serial rights only.
1988; 2/yr; 1,200

$12/yr; $7/ea
128+ pp; 8 x 5
Ad Rates: vary
ISSN: 0899-9848
Armadillo, DeBoer, Fine Print, Ubiquity

SCARLET

Douglas Oliver / Alice Notley
all mss.—61 rue Lepic
75018, Paris, FRANCE
Inquiries only—Notley/Oliver
898 Union St.
Brooklyn, NY 11215
(718) 789-2846
mss. will not be forwarded.

Poetry, prose, drawings.

SCARLET is a poetry magazine which emphasizes political and spiritual content and is dedicated to the idea that poetry shouldn't be boring.

Amiri Baraka, Denise Riley, Leslie Scalapino.

Unsolicited Manuscripts Received/Published per Year: about 100/about 10.

Payment: 3 copies.

Reporting Time: varies.

Copyright reverts to author.

1990; 4/yr; 500
$14/yr; $2/sample
24 pp; 8½ x 11

SCREENS AND TASTED PARALLELS

Terrel D. Hale
12714 Barbara St.
Silver Spring, MD 20906
(301) 949-6825

Poetry, some reviews.

Dedicated to providing a forum for a variety of alternative poetries and poetics, some prose, mostly poetry.

Arkadii Dragomoschenko, Guido Zlatkes, Johanna Drucker, Maggie O'Sullivan, Saul Yurkievich.

Unsolicited Manuscripts Received/Published per Year: 50/10.

Payment: none.

Reporting Time: 3–5 months.

Copyright reverts back to poets.

1989; 1/yr; 800+
$10/yr; $6/sample
239 pp; 8½ x 11
ISSN: 1042-9786
SPD, Spectacular Diseases (UK)

THE SEATTLE REVIEW

Colleen T. McElroy
Padelford Hall, Box 354330
University of Washington
Seattle, WA 98195-4330
(206) 543-9865

Poetry, fiction, essays, interviews with writers.

THE SEATTLE REVIEW is a journal of poetry and prose published twice yearly. We try to achieve a balance in our pages between the work of nationally-known writers and that of younger writers of promise.

Rita Dove, W.P. Kinsella, Ursula Le Guin, William Stafford, Frances McCue, Jane McCafferty.

Unsolicited Manuscripts Received/Published per Year: 2,000-2,500/8-12 fiction, 80 poems, 2 essays, 1-2 interviews.

Reading Period: Sept.–May.

Payment: varies.

Reporting Time: 3–8 months.

Copyright held by magazine; reverts to author upon publication.

$9/yr, $16/2 yrs; $5/ea

100 pp; 6 x 9

Ad Rates: $160/page (5 x 7); $90/½ page (5 x 4½)

ISSN: 0147-6629

SEEMS

Karl Elder
Lakeland College
Box 359
Sheboygan, WI 53082-0359
(414) 565-3871

Poetry, fiction, essays.

Jeffrey Baker, John Birchler, M.J. Echelberger, Chris Halla, Robert Nagler.

Unsolicited Manuscripts Received/Published per Year: 1,000/25.

Payment: 1 copy.

Reporting Time: 1–3 months.

Copyright held by Karl Elder; reverts to author upon publication.

1971; irreg; 350

$16/4 issues; $4/ea

40 pp; 8½ x 7

ISSN: 0095-1730

SELVATICA

Joseph Richey, Ann Becher
1701 Bluebell Ave.
Boulder, CO 80302

Nonfiction, poetry, investigative articles, politics.

A bilingual (Spanish-English), hemispheric publication devoted to the dissemination of informed opinions and good writing.

Regional and International writers from North, Central, and South Americas.

Payment: 2 copies.

Reporting Time: as soon as we can.

Copyright reverts to author.

1986; 2/yr; 2,000

$6/issue; 40%

96 pp; 10½ x 4

Ad Rates: Write for information

ISSN: 1045-3660

SEMIOTEXT(E)/AUTONOMEDIA

Sylvère Lotringer, Jim Fleming
P.O. Box 568
Brooklyn, NY 11211

(718) 963-2603 (phone/fax)

Fiction, criticism, essays, translation, interview, photographs.

Contemporary radical cultural politics, "movement" literatures. Also sponsors "Foreign Agents," and "Native Agents" small book series promoting contemporary radical politics and culture, philosophy and human sciences, and literature.

Michel Foucault, Roland Barthes, Felix Guattari, Jean Baudrillard, Gilles Deleuze, Kathy Acker, William Burroughs, Harim Bey.

Unsolicited Manuscripts Received/ Published per Year: 350/20.

Payment: none.

Reporting Time: 3 months.

Copyright reverts to author upon publication.

1974; irreg; 8,000

$18/3 issues ind, $36/3 issues inst; $10/ea; 40%

320 pp; 7 x 9

ISSN: 0093-5779

SENECA REVIEW

Deborah Tall

Hobart and William Smith Colleges

Geneva, NY 14456

(315) 781-3364

Poetry, criticism, translation, interviews.

Twice a year the **SENECA REVIEW** publishes poetry and prose about poetry, with a special interest in translation.

Eavan Boland, Rita Dove, Yusef Komunyakaa, Jorie Graham, Rosanna Warren.

Unsolicited Manuscripts Received/ Published per Year: 5,000 poems/70 poems.

Reading Period: Sept. 1–May 1.

Payment: 2 copies.

Reporting Time: 8–12 weeks.

Copyright held by Hobart and William Smith Colleges; reverts to author upon publication.

1970; 2/yr; 1,000

$8/yr, $15/2 yrs; $5/ea; 40%

90 pp; 5½ x 8½

Ad Rates: $75/page (5 x 8)

ISSN: 0037-2145

Small Press Traffic

SENSATIONS MAGAZINE

David Messineo

2 Radio Ave. A5

Secaucus, NJ 07094

Poetry, fiction, photographs, graphics/artwork.

Unsolicited Manuscripts Received/ Published per Year: 200/30.

Reading Period: Jan. and Feb.

Payment: on acceptance, up to $125/poem; $75/story.

Reporting Time: 2 months after deadline.

Copyright held by author.

1987; 1/yr; 2,000 (1995)
$12/sample (send SASE for info)
100 pp; 8½ x 11
Ad Rates: $100/page; $50/½ page; $25/¼ page

SENSITIVE SKIN

Buddy Kold, Christian X. Hunter
P.O. Box 20344
New York, NY 10009
(212) 477-9687

Fiction.

On the edge fiction from new and established writers—makes reading as fun and easy as watching TV!

Darius James, Emily XYZ, Patrick McGrath, John Giorno, Eileen Myles.

Unsolicited Manuscripts Received/ Published per Year: 500/25.
Reading Period: year-round.
Payment: 2 copies.
Reporting Time: 3 months max.
Copyright held by authors.
1993; 2/yr; 1,000
$12/3 issues; $6/ea; 30%
48 pp; 8½ x 11
Ad Rates: $200/page (7 x 9¾); $125/½ page (7 x 4¾); $75/¼ page (3¼ x 4¾)
ISSN: 1073-1865
DeBoer, Ubiquity, Desert Moon

SEQUOIA

Carlos Rodriguez
Storke Publications Building
Stanford, CA 94305
(415) 362-3420

Poetry, fiction only.

We have no set guidelines, nor do we accept simultaneous submissions.

Rita Dove, Seamus Heaney, Susan Howe, Janet Lewis, James Merrill.

Unsolicited Manuscripts Received/ Published per Year: 2,000/80.
Reading Period: Oct.–May.
Payment: in copies.
Reporting Time: 3 months.
Include SASE with ms.
Author retains rights.
1892; 1/yr; 500
$10/yr; $5/ea
80–105 pp; 5½ x 8
Ad Rates: $100/page; $60/½ page
L–S Distributors

THE SEWANEE REVIEW

George Core
University of the South
Sewanee, TN 37375
(615) 598-1245

Poetry, fiction, criticism, essays, reviews.

America's oldest literary quarterly publishes original fiction, poetry, essays on literary and related subjects, book reviews and book notices for well-educated readers who appreciate good American and English literature.

Louis D. Rubin, Jr., George Gar-

rett, Neal Bowerd, Catharine Savage Brosman, Merrill Joan Gerber, Samuel Hynes.
Payment: $10–$12/printed page; 60¢/line for poetry.
Reporting Time: 4 weeks.
Copyright held by author.
1892; 4/yr; 3,200
$18/yr ind, $24/yr inst; $6/ea
192 pp; 6 x 9
Ad Rates: $210/page (4¼ x 7); $132/½ page (4¼ x 3⅜); $96/¼ page
ISSN: 0037-3052

SHENANDOAH

R.T. Smith, Editor
Troubadour Theater
2nd Floor
Washington & Lee University
Lexington, VA 24450
(540) 463-8765
Poetry, fiction, essays, translations, photographs.
Consider work from both new and established writers. Annual prizes in fiction, poetry and the essay.
Seamus Heaney, Northrop Frye, Robert Wrigley, Mary Oliver, Michael Longley, Lynne Sharon Schwartz
Unsolicited Manuscripts Received/ Published per Year: 4,500/less than 1%.
Reading Period: Sept.–May.
Payment: $2.50/line poetry, $25/page fiction.
Reporting Time: 2–6 weeks.
Copyright held by magazine; reverts to author upon publication.
1950; 4/yr; 2,100
$11/yr; $3.50/ea; 50%
130 pp; 6 x 9
Ad Rates: $200/page (4½ x 7)
ISSN: 0037-3583
Armadillo, Fine Print, Ubiquity

SHOOTING STAR REVIEW

Sandra Gould Ford
7123 Race St.
Pittsburgh, PA 15208
(412) 731-7464
Poetry, fiction, essays, reviews, photographs, graphics/artwork.
SHOOTING STAR REVIEW is an award-winning illustrated quarterly that uses the arts to explore the Black experience. Guidelines available with SASE. Sample copy ($3) is sent with next bulk mailing unless 9 x 12 envelope w/$1.21 postage included.
Kristin Hunter, Dennis Brutus, Reginald McKnight, Jerry Ward, Toi Derricote, Doris Jean Austin, Marita Golden.
Unsolicited Manuscripts Received/ Published per Year: 600/60.
Payment: $20/fiction; $10 and up/essays; $4/poems.

Copyright held by magazine; reverts to author upon publication.
1987; 4/yr; 1,500
$12/yr ind, $15/yr inst; $3/ea; 20% consignment, 50% outright purchase
32 pp; 8½ x 11
Ad Rates: $300/page; $150/½ page; $75/¼ page
ISSN: 0892-1407

SHORT FICTION BY WOMEN

Rachel Whalen
Box 1254, Old Chelsea Station
New York, NY 10011

All fiction: short stories, short novels, novel excerpts; 100% original.
Our goals are to encourage woman writers and to give readers an enjoyable, superbly written magazine.
Joan Frank, Edwidge Danticat, Opal Palmer Adisa, Kat Meads.
Unsolicited Manuscripts Received/Published per Year: 3,000/30. SASE for guidelines.
Payment: depends on length and budget.
Reporting Time: 1 month.
Copyright: first serial rights only.
1991; 2/yr; 2,500
$18/yr; $9/ea
160–224 pp; 5½ x 8½

SIBYL-CHILD

Nancy Arbuthnot, Saundra Maley
709 Dahlia St. NW
Washington, DC 20012
(202) 723-5468

Established in 1974, **SIBYL-CHILD** is out of print. Back issues of chapbooks—fiction, poetry, translations—available at $2/ea.
Doris Mozer, David Hall, Ann Slayton, Peter Van Egmond, William Griffiths, Nan Fry.
5½ x 8
ISSN: 0161-715X

SIDEWALKS

Tom Heie
Box 321
Champlin, MN 55316
(612) 421-3512

Poetry, short prose (fiction, memoir, essay), graphics.
A magazine for emerging and established writers of poetry and prose.
Mark Vinz, Robert Cooperman, Kenneth Pobo, Marilyn J. Boe.
Unsolicited Manuscripts Received/Published per Year: 1,000/100.
Payment: copies.
Reporting Time: 1 month after deadline (May 31; Dec. 31).
Copyright: Tom Heie.
1991: 2/yr; 500
$9/yr; $6/ea; 40%

75-80 pp; 8 x 5½
ISSN: 1059-2210

50+ pp; 8½ x 11
Ad Rates: $100/page (8½ x 11); $65/½ page (8½ x 5½); $35/¼ page (4¼ x 2¾)

THE SIGNAL

Joan Silva, David Chorlton
P.O. Box 67
Emmett, ID 83617
(208) 365-5812

Poetry, fiction, criticism, essays, reviews, translation, interviews, photographs, graphics/artwork.

We would like to create a forum for inter-disciplinary work, bridging between literature, art, music; and ecological, socio/political concerns. We encourage submissions in the socio/scientific area; examples would be archeologic, rare travel experiences/philosophic essays on almost anything, but quality of thought and expression should be rigorous and must have literary merit.

Hans Raimund, Natalya Gorbanevskaga, Michele Zackheim, Maurice Kenny, Lloyd Van Brunt, Olga Cabral, Clarissa Pinkda Estes.

Unsolicited Manuscripts Received/Published per Year: 300+/60+.

Payment: in copies.

Copyright held by magazine; reverts to author upon publication.

1987; 2/yr; 500

$10/yr; $6/ea; 40%

SILVERFISH REVIEW

Rodger Moody
P.O. Box 3541
Eugene, OR 97403
(503) 344-5060

Poetry, short short stories, reviews, essays, translations, interviews, photographs.

The only criterion for selection of material is quality. In future issues **SILVERFISH REVIEW** wants to showcase essays on the creative process and on short short stories.

Kevin Bowen, Lauren Mesa, Floyd Skloot, Judith Skillman, Robert Gregory.

Unsolicited Manuscripts Received/Published per Year: 1200/30-40.

Reading Period: year–round.

Payment: 2 copies plus a year subscription, and $5 per page (when funding permits).

Reporting Time: 2–16 weeks.

Copyright held by author.

1979; 2/yr; 1000

$8/2 issues ind, $12/2 issues inst; $50 life subscription (individuals only); $4/ea plus $1.50 postage; 40%

48 pp; 5½ x 8½

Ad Rates: \$100/page (4¼ x 7½); \$50/½ page (4¼ x 4)
ISSN: 0164-1085
Spring Church Book Company Faxon, Ebsco, Boley, IPD

SING HEAVENLY MUSE!

P.O. Box 13320
Minneapolis, MN 55414

Fiction, creative prose, poetry.

A magazine to foster women's writing and the writing of men showing an awareness of women's consciousness, in fiction, creative nonfiction and poetry.

Meridel Le Seuer, Ana Ortiz de Montellano, Chocolate Waters.

Unsolicited Manuscripts Received/Published per Year: 1,000/40.

Payment: an honorarium, depending on funding, plus contributor's copies.

Reporting Time: 2 months first reading, 6–9 months if it goes to second reading. Query for themes and reading period.

Copyright by magazine, rights revert to authors.

1977; 1/yr; 400

\$20/3 issues; \$9/ea

approx. 100 pp; 6 x 10

Olson, Ubiquity, Small Changes

SINISTER WISDOM

Akiba Onada-Sikwoia
P.O. Box 3252
Berkeley, CA 94703

Poetry, fiction, criticism, essays, reviews, interviews, plays, photographs, graphics/artwork by lesbians.

A lesbian/feminist journal of art, literature and politics founded in 1976 by Harriet Desmoines and Catherine Nicholson, passed on in 1981 to Michelle Cliff and Adrienne Rich, in 1983 to Melanie Kaye/Kantrowitz, and in 1986 to Elana Dykwomon, and in 1994 to the current editors. The primary commitment of the magazine is to publish creative work by lesbians from a broad range of racial, ethnic, cultural and class perspectives.

Sapphire, Gloria Anzaldva, Marilyn Frye, Adrienne Rich, Chrystos, Winn Gilmore, Judith Katz.

Unsolicited Manuscripts Received/Published per Year: 300-500/60-90.

Payment: 2 copies.

Reporting Time: 6–9 months.

Copyright held by author.

1976; 3–4/yr; 3,000

\$17/yr ind, \$30/yr inst; \$6/ea; 40%

144 pp; 5½ x 8½

Ad Rates: \$200/page (5⅛ x 8¼); \$100/½ page (5⅛ x 4); \$75/⅓ page (5⅛ x 2⅝); \$50/¼ page (2½ x 4); \$35/2 x 2 or 2⅜ x 2⅜

ISSN: 0196-1853
Bookpeople

SIPAPU

Noel Peatie
23311 County Rd. 88
Winters, CA 95694
(916) 662-3364

Reviews, interviews, conference news.

Newsletter for librarians, editors, and collectors interested in dissent (feminist, Third World. pacifist, etc.) literature, together with small press poetry. Emphasis on peace and environmental concerns; all must have a print emphasis.

Karl Kempton, Loss P. Glazier, Mary Zeppa, John Daniel, Harry Polkinhorn.

Unsolicited Manuscripts Received/ Published per Year: 2/0.

Payment: 5¢/word.

Reporting Time: 5 months.

Copyright held by editor; reverts to author upon publication.

1970; 450

$8/yr; $4/ea

36 pp; 8½ x 11

No ads

ISSN: 0037-5837

Ebsco, Faxon, Popular Subscription Service, Turner

SISTERSONG: Women Across Cultures

Valerie Staats
P.O. Box 7405
Pittsburgh, PA 15213

Essays, letters, fiction, poetry, book reviews, b&w artwork and photography.

A theme journal dedicated to exploring the conditions of contemporary women's lives through letters and art. New authors and works in translation encouraged. Recent and upcoming themes: memory; handwork; friendship; identity; travel; dwellings; grandmother. Send SASE for themes and guidelines.

Lynne Hugo deCourcy, Ana María Rodas, Diane Tong, Margarita Engle.

Unsolicited Manuscripts Received/ Published per Year: 250/60.

Payment: 3 copies.

Reporting Time: about 3 months.

Copyright: reverts to author on publication.

1992; 3/yr; 1,000

$16/yr ind, $28/yr inst; $24/yr overseas; $6/ea

80 pp; 6 x 9

ISSN: 1063-214X

THE SLATE

Rachel Fulkerson, Jessica Morris, Chris Dall

P.O. Box 581189
Minneapolis MN 55458-1189
(612) 871-8532

Fiction, poetry, essays, interviews, plays, short shorts

The Slate is dedicated to reviving a cultural interest in the written word and providing a forum for new expressions. No restrictions regarding subject or content.

Ron Wallace, Stephen Stark, Dan Graves, Ericka Lutz.

Reading Period: year–round.

Payment: 2 copies

Reporting Time: 2 months.

Copyright held by the publisher and reverts back to author 4 months after publication date.

1995; 3/yr; 1,500

1 yr/$15.00; $6/ea; 40%

100–120 pp; 6 x 9

Ad Rates: full page $80; half page $45

ISSN: 1082-0752

SLIPSTREAM

Dan Sicoli, Robert Borgatti, Livio Farallo
Box 2071
Niagara Falls, NY 14301
(716) 282-2616 after 5 p.m. E.S.T.

Poetry, short fiction, graphics.

We publish vital writings (poems & fiction) by many excellent writers whose work is often ignored or overlooked by mainstream or academic publishers.

Charles Bukowski, Denise Duhamel, Gerald Locklin.

Unsolicited Manuscripts Received/Published per Year: 2,000+/100–125.

Reading Period: year–round.

Payment: in copies.

Reporting Time: 2 weeks–2 months.

Copyright reverts to author upon publication.

1981; 1–2/yr; 500

$15.00 includes 2 issues & 2 chapbooks; $5.00 single copy

100 pp; 7 x 8½

No ads

ISSN: 0749-0771

THE SMALL POND MAGAZINE, Inc.

Napoleon St. Cyr
P.O. Box 664
Stratford, CT 06497
(203) 378-4066

Poetry, fiction, essays, reviews, graphics/artwork.

Features contemporary poetry by new and established writers, but also uses short prose pieces of many genres, plus some art work—black and white only.

Marvin Solomon, Fritz Hamilton, Sid Harriet, Rika Lesser, Marilyn Johnston, H.R. Coursen.

Unsolicited Manuscripts Received/ Published per Year: 5,000/75.
Reading Period: year–round.
Payment: 2 copies.
Reporting Time: 10–30 days, longer in summer.
Copyright held by N. St. Cyr. Original mss. which are published become the property of the Beinecke Rare Books & Mss. Lib. at Yale.
1964; 3/yr; 300
$9/yr; $3/ea; random back issue/$2.50; inquire
40 pp; 5½ x 8½
Ad Rates: $40/page (4½ x 7½); $25/½ page (4½ x 3½); $15/¼ page (4½ x 2¼)
ISSN: 0037-721X

SMALL PRESS MAGAZINE

Tom Bodus
121 E. Front St., 4th Floor
Traverse City, MI 49684
(616) 933-0445
Fax (616) 933-0448
Articles about independent publishing, book reviews, excerpts.
SMALL PRESS exists to serve small, independent publishers by printing articles for and about small presses, including reviews and excerpts of small press books and magazines.
Unsolicited Manuscripts Received/ Published per Year: 50/2.
Reading Period: year–round.
Payment: $50-200
Reporting Time: 1-2 months.
Copyright held by magazine.
1983; 6/yr; 7,000
$34/yr; $5.95/ea
90 pp; 8¼ x 11
Ad Rates: upon request
ISSN: 0000-0485
Eastern News, Fine Print

THE SNAIL'S PACE REVIEW

Darby Penney and Ken Denberg
RR#2 Box 403, Darwin Rd.
Cambridge, NY 12816
Poetry and poetry in translation.
THE SNAIL'S PACE REVIEW publishes contemporary poetry and poetry in translation. The editors especially welcome submissions from women, people of color, and members of ethnic and cultural minorities.
Martha Collins, Ai, Fred Chappell, Shirley Kaufman.
Unsolicited Manuscripts Received/ Published per Year: 4,000/75.
Payment: 2 copies.
Reporting Time: 4 months.
Copyright reverts to author upon publication.
1991; 2/yr; 500
$7/yr; $4/ea; 40%
32–36 pp; 5½ x 8½
ISSN: 1054-1632

SNAKE NATION REVIEW

Roberta George, Sharmain van Bloomenstein, Nancy Phillips
110 #2 W. Force St.
Valdosta, GA 31601
(912) 249-8334

Poetry, fiction, essays, photographs, graphics/artwork.

SNAKE NATION REVIEW is a regional quarterly, founded in the fall of 1989. We encourage writing that addresses all areas of life. We look for good writing that encounters change and character; all subjects are acceptable if it meets our one requirement–well written.

Van K. Brock, D. Victor Miller, Judith Otiz Cofer.

Unsolicited Manuscripts Received/Published per Year: 4,000/80.

Payment: Prize money (editors' choice); 2 copies/contribution.

Reporting Time: 6 months.

Copyright: Snake Nation Press.

1989; 2/yr; 1,000

$20/yr ind, $30/yr inst; $6/ea; 40%

100 pp; 6 x 9

Ad Rates: $100/page; $50/½ page; $25/¼ page

ISSN: 1046-5006

SONORA REVIEW

Department of English
University of Arizona
Tucson, AZ 85721
(520) 626-8383

Poetry, fiction, reviews, translation, interviews, criticism, essays.

We're looking for the liveliest new writing we can get our hands on, including experimental and non-conformist work. Most issues are general in nature, though recent special features have profiled "Crossing Borders: Writing from Alternative Traditions" and "Voices from the Southwestern Landscape." We welcome simultaneous submissions.

Alison Baker, Dagober Gilb, Alison Hawthorne Deming, Alyce Miller, William J. Cobb.

Unsolicited Manuscripts Received/Published per Year: 2,000/24.

Payment: small cash payment: copies. Annual contests in fiction, poetry and creative nonfiction. Send SASE for guidelines.

Reporting Time: 2–3 months, longer during summer.

Copyright reverts to author.

1980; 2/yr

$12/yr; $24/2 yrs; $6/ea

120 pp; 6 x 9

SOUNDINGS EAST

Rod Kessler, Claire Keyes
English Dept.
Salem State College

Salem, MA 01970
(508) 741- 6270

Original poetry, fiction, artwork.

SOUNDINGS EAST is a collection of original poetry, short fiction, and art work, published biannually by the students of Salem State College.

Debra Allbery, Robert Cooperman, Antonya Nelson.

Unsolicited Manuscripts Received/ Published per Year: 400/60.

Reading Period: Sept.–Nov., Jan.–April.

Payment: 2 copies.

Reporting Time: 2 to 4 months.

Copyright reverts to author.

1978; 2/yr; 2,000

$6/yr; $3/ea

65 pp; 5½ x 8½

SOUTH CAROLINA REVIEW

Frank Day
English Department
Clemson University
Clemson, SC 29634-1503
(803) 656-3457

Poetry, fiction, criticism, essays, reviews, translation, interviews.

Listed as one of the twenty most outstanding literary magazines in the United States by *The New York Quarterly,* **THE SOUTH CAROLINA REVIEW** is now in its third decade of publication. Our primary goal is to continue to publish fiction, poetry, and criticism of the quality that has earned us several Pushcart nominations, as well as election to *The Best American Short Stories 1982* and *Prize Stories 1982: The O. Henry Awards.*

Stephen Dixon, Rosanne Coggeshall, Joyce Carol Oates, Cleanth Brooks, Leslie Fiedler.

Reading Period: Jan.–May, Sept.–Nov.

Payment: in issues.

Reporting Time: 6–9 months.

Copyright held by magazine.

1968; 1 double-issue per annum; 600

$7/yr ind; $5/ea; 33⅓%

200 pp; 9 x 6

Ad Rates: negotiable

ISSN: 0038-3163

SOUTH DAKOTA REVIEW

Brian Bedard
University of South Dakota
Vermillion, SD 57069
(605) 677-5229

Poetry, fiction, criticism, essays, occasional translation and interviews.

When the material warrants, an emphasis on the American West; writers from the West; Western places or subjects; frequent issues with no geographical emphasis. Periodic special issues on one theme, or one place, or one writer, e.g., Ross MacDonald (Spring 1986), Wallace Stegner (Winter 1985).

Max Evans, Linda Hasselstrom, Bart Paul, Diane Lefer.

Unsolicited Manuscripts Received/Published per Year: 1,000/up to 100.

Reading Period: year–round.

Payment: in copies.

Reporting Time: 2 weeks–2 months, slowest in summer.

1963; 4/yr; 600

$18/yr, $30/2 yrs; $6/ea; 40%

150–190 pp; 6 x 9

ISSN: 0038-3368

THE SOUTHERN CALIFORNIA ANTHOLOGY

James Ragan Editor-in-Chief
Master of Professional Writing Program
University of Southern California
WPH 404
Los Angeles, CA 90089-4034
(213) 740-3252

Poetry, fiction, interviews, graphics/artwork (on cover).

Published through the Master of Professional Writing Program at the University of Southern California, **THE SOUTHERN CALIFORNIA ANTHOLOGY** is a literary journal of fiction, poetry, and interviews. Seventy percent of the pieces are solicited. Volume X (published Dec. 1992) includes works by: Amiri Baraka, Robert Bly, Vance Bourjaily, Donald Hall, John Hollander, David Madden, James Merrill, John Frederick Nims, Joyce Carol Oates, James Ragan, Hubert Selby, Jr., Mark Strand, Henry Taylor, John Updike, Peter Viereck, Richard Yates.

Unsolicited Manuscripts Received/Published per Year: 1,000/10.

Reading Period: Sept. 1 – Jan 1.

Payment: 3 copies.

Copyright held by the University of Southern California, Master of Professional Writing Program; reverts to author upon publication.

1983; 1/yr; 1,000

$9.95/yr; 40%

144 pp; 5½ x 8½

ISBN: 0-9615108-5-4

Blackwell North America, Ballen Booksellers, SPD

SOUTHERN EXPOSURE

Pat Arnow
P.O. Box 531
Durham, NC 27702
(919) 419-8311

Essays, reviews, interviews, photographs, graphics/artwork.

SOUTHERN EXPOSURE is a

winner of the National Magazine Award and is widely respected as the voice of the progressive South. Investigative journalism and oral history are emphasized. Very little fiction and no poetry; mostly nonfiction articles on social issues.
Unsolicited Manuscripts Received/Published per Year: 1,000/1-2.
Payment: up to $200.
Reporting Time: 6–8 weeks.
Copyright held by magazine.
1973; 4/yr; 4,000
$24/yr; $5/ea; 40%
Ad Rates: $400/page; $270/½ page
64 pp; 8½ x 11
ISSN: 0146-809X
Ingram

SOUTHERN HUMANITIES REVIEW

Dan R. Latimer, Virginia M. Kouidis, co-editors
9088 Haley Center
Auburn University, AL 36849
(334) 844-9088

Poetry, fiction, essays, reviews.
THE SOUTHERN HUMANITIES REVIEW publishes fiction, poetry and critical essays on the arts, literature, philosophy, religion, and history. Essays, articles, or stories should, in general, range between 3,500 and 15,000 words. Poems should not exceed two pages in length. No multiple submissions.
Margaret Holley, Robert Morgan, Donald Hall, Peter Green, Yannis Ritsos, Reynolds Price.
Unsolicited Manuscripts Received/Published per Year: 1,500-2,000/40-55.
Payment: copies.
Reporting Time: 1–3 months.
Copyright reverts to author upon publication.
1967; 4/yr; 700
$15/yr; $5/ea
100 pp; 4½ x 7½
Ad Rates: $100/page (4½ x 7½); only with adequate notice.
ISSN: 0038-4186

SOUTHERN INDIANA REVIEW

Martha W. Chapin, Thomas A. Wilhelmus, Matthew Graham, Kathryn Waters
8600 University Blvd.
Evansville, IN 47712
(812) 465-1630
Fax (812) 465-7152

Short stories, poems, essays, photos, drawings, sculpture.
SOUTHERN INDIANA REVIEW is a collection of literary and artistic work from USI alumni and those who have attended our RopeWalk Writer's Retreat.

Liam Rector, Patti Aakhus, Ruzha Cleaveland, Barbara Savadge Horton, Philip Levine.

Unsolicited Manuscripts Received/ Published per year: 167/47.

Reading Period: 12 months.

Payment: 0

Reporting Time: 6–8 weeks.

Copyright held by magazine; reverts to author upon publication.

1994; 1/300

$6.30/yr; 35%

144 pp; 6 x 9

University of Southern Indiana

SOUTHERN POETRY REVIEW

Ken McLaurin
Department of English
Central Piedmont Community College
Charlotte, NC 28204
(704) 342-6702

Poetry, reviews.

Poetry submissions accepted from established and previously unpublished poets. **SPR** is a natural outlet for poets writing in the South, but has no regional bias. Variety in style and content encouraged.

Susan Ludvigson, Linda Pastan, David Keller, Dave Smith, Marge Piercy.

Reading Period: Sept.–May.

Payment: in copies.

Copyright held by magazine; reverts to author upon request.

1958; 2/yr; 1,100

$8/yr; $4.50/ea; 40%

80 pp; 6 x 9

No ads

ISSN: 0038-447X

THE SOUTHERN QUARTERLY: A Journal of the Arts in the South

Stephen Flinn Young
University of Southern Mississippi
Southern Station Box 5078
Hattiesburg, MS 39406-5078
(601) 266-4370
Fax (601) 266-5800

Visit the SoQwwwHome Page
http://www-dept.usm.edu/~soq

Criticism, essays, reviews, interviews, photographs.

A non-profit scholarly journal, **THE SOUTHERN QUARTERLY** includes essays, articles, interviews and reviews on the arts and society—defined broadly—in the southern U.S. General and special issues include research on music, theatre, dance, literature, film, art, architecture, popular and folk arts.

Unsolicited Manuscripts Received/ Published per Year: 30/10.

Payment: 1 year subscription.

Reporting Time: 2–3 months.
Copyright held by University of Southern Mississippi; reverts to author upon publication.
1962; 4/yr; 900
$12/yr ind, $22/2 yrs ind, $30/yr inst; $5/ea; 15%
180 pp; 7 x 10
Ad Rates: $100/page (4½ x 6¾); $75/½ page (4½ x 3⅜)
ISSN: 0038-4496

THE SOUTHERN REVIEW

James Olney, Dave Smith
43 Allen Hall
Louisiana State University
Baton Rouge, LA 70803-5005
(504) 388-5108

Fiction, poetry, criticism, reviews, interviews.

THE SOUTHERN REVIEW publishes poetry, fiction, criticism, essays, reviews and excerpts from novels in progress, with emphasis on contemporary literature in the United States and abroad, and with special interest in Southern history and culture.

Eavan Boland, Ernest J. Gaines, Seamus Heaney, Reynolds Price, Lee Smith, W. D. Snodgrass, Jill McCorkle, Hayden Carruth, A. R. Ammons, M. L. Rosenthal.

Unsolicited Manuscripts Received/Published per Year: 10,000/100.
Reading Period: Sept.–May.
Payment: $12/printed page for prose; $20/printed page for poetry; 2 complimentary copies.
Reporting Time: 2 months.
Copyright held by LSU; reverts to author upon publication.
1935 (original series), 1965 (new series); 4/yrs; 3,100
$20/yr, $36/2yrs, $50/3yrs, ind; $40/yr, $65/2yrs, $90/3yrs, inst. Foreign subscribers: add $4/yr for postage
250 pp; 6¾ x 10
Ad Rates: $250/page (4½ x 7½); $150/½ page (4½ x 3⅝); $100/¼ page (4½ x 1⅔)
ISSN: 0038-4534
DeBoer, Fine Print

SOUTHWEST

Janine Kelley
3490 South Walkup Dr.
Flagstaff, AZ 86001
(602) 774-6159

Fiction, essays, interviews, poetry, film/book reviews.

SOUTHWEST is an international literary magazine celebrating the cultural and artistic diversity of the region publishing writers with a range of light.

Simon Ortiz, James Cervantes, Mary Sojourner, Ruth L.

Schwartz, Ann Walka, Ernesto Carriazo-Osorio.
Unsolicited Manuscripts Received/ Published per Year: 500/17.
Reading Period: Mar. 1 – June 1.
Payment: copies.
Reporting Time: 2–5 weeks.
Copyright reverts to the author upon publication.
1993; 1/yr; 300–500
$5/yr; $5/ea
72 pp; 6 x 9
Ad Rates: $75/4 x 6
ISSN: 1065-0156
McGaugh's Newsstand

THE SOUTHWEST REVIEW

Willard Spiegelman, Editor-in-Chief; Elizabeth Mills, Senior Editor
307 Fondren Library West
Box 374
Southern Methodist University
Dallas, TX 75275
(214) 768-1037
Poetry, fiction, essays, interviews.
THE SOUTHWEST REVIEW is a quarterly that serves the interests of its region but is not bound by them. **SWR** has always striven to present the work of writers and scholars from the surrounding states and to offer analyses of problems and themes that are distinctly southwestern and, at the same time, publishes the works of good writers regardless of their locales.
Thomas Beller, Elizabeth Graver, Joyce Carol Oates, Albert Goldbarth, Wayne Koestenbaum, Rosellen Brown, Reynolds Price, Adrienne Rich.
Unsolicited Manuscripts Received/ Published per Year: 3,600+/60.
Reading Period: Sept. – May 31.
Payment: varies.
Reporting Time: 1 month.
Copyright held by SMU; reverts to author upon publication.
1915; 4/yr; 1,500
$25/yr ind, $30/yr inst; $7/ea; 40%
160 pp; 6 x 9
Ad Rates: $250/page (25 x 42½ picas); $150/½ page (25 x 21 picas)
ISSN: 0038-4712
Fine Print, Total

SOU'WESTER

Fred W. Robbins
Dept. of English
Box 1431
Southern Illinois University
Edwardsville, IL 62026-1438
(618) 692-3190
Poetry, fiction.
Published twice a year, Fall and Spring; **SOU'WESTER** is

somewhat selective and prefers to publish new writers.

Robert Wexelblatt, Jared Carter, Kathleen Thompson, Jeanne Bryner.

Unsolicited Manuscripts Received/ Published per Year: 1,000/45.

Reading Period: no reading in August.

Payment: 2 free copies, 1 yr subscription.

Reporting Time: 3–4 months.

Copyright: first serial rights; released upon request, with acknowledgement.

1960; 3/yr; 300

$10/yr; $5/ea; 40%

84 pp; 6 x 9

Ad Rates: $80/page; $60/½ page; $30/¼ page

ISSN 0098-499X

THE SOW'S EAR POETRY REVIEW

Larry Richman, Managing Editor; Mary Calhoun, Graphics Editor

19535 Pleasant View Dr.

Abingdon, VA 24211-6827

(540) 628-2651

Poetry, reviews, interviews, graphics, photography.

Contemporary poetry exported from and imported into Southern Appalachia. No nostalgia. We publish both established and new poets, with no restrictions on subject matter or style. We use B & W art to complement poetry.

Single poem competition, Sept. and Oct., with $500, $100, and $50 prizes and publication; chapbook competition March and April, $500 prize and publication. Second and third prizes: $100 SASE for guidelines.

Patricia Goedicke, Richard Hague, Lois Marie Harrod, George Ella Lyon, Peter Meinke, Stuart Peterfreund.

Unsolicited Manuscripts Received/ Published per Year: 3,000/150.

Payment: in copies.

Reporting Time: 3–6 months.

Copyright reverts to author.

1988; 4/yr; 500

$10/4 issues; $3.50/ea; 40%

32 pp; 8½ x 11

SPARROW: THE YEARBOOK OF THE SONNET PAMPHLETS

Felix and Selma Stefanile

103 Waldron St.

West Lafayette, IN 47906

(317) 743-1991

Poetry.

A publication devoted to the sonnet, and only sonnets stemming from the great Italian and English tradition, and in contemporary idiom, essays of serious literary nature. Essays are assigned. We pay $3 a sonnet, $6 a page, prose or poetry. The editors also offer a $25 prize each issue for the sonnet judged "best" for the issue. SASE all material.

X.J. Kennedy, Dana Gioia, John Frederick Nims, Annie Finch, Katherine McAlpine, R.S. Gwynn. Query with SASE late in 1991.

Copyright reverts to author on request.

1954; 1/yr; 900

$6/yr; $5/ea for back copies; 35%

102 pp; 8½ x 11

ISSN: 0038-6588

SPD

THE SPIRIT (of Woman in the Moon)

Dr. Sdiane Bogus
P.O. Box 2087
Cupertino, CA 95015
(408) 738-4623
Fax (408) 864-8212

Fillers, cartoons, fiction, nonfiction.

THE SPIRIT features new age stories, essays, poetry and interesting cartoon or fillers of interest to writers, healers, business people, gays, blacks, and women.

Phyllis Wiffe, Robert Fuchs, Linda Morganstein, Judith K. Withers, Phyllis Wheatley.

Unsolicited Manuscripts Received/Published per year: 100+/10+.

Reading Period: Jan.-Dec.

$10 - $100

Reporting Time: 2–6 weeks.

Copyright held by magazine; reverts to author upon publication.

1990; 2–3/yr; 2,000+

$24/yr; $4/ea; 20%

16–24 pp; 8½ x 11

Ad Rates: Cards $75, ½ card $39; ¼ page $125, ½ page $225, full page $375.

ISSN: 1075-3176

Alamo Square/Publishers Only

SPOON RIVER POETRY REVIEW

Lucia Getsi
English Department
Illinois State University 4240
Normal-Bloomington, IL 61790
(309) 438-7906

Poetry, translation, interviews, photographs, reviews.

SRPR wants poetry that is interesting and compelling. Our standards are high—the acceptance rate is about 2%. We publish emerging and established poets, and occasionally feature groups of poets working at the edges and margins of language and American poetics. $500 Editor's Prize entry deadline is May.

Tim Seibles, Roger Mitchell, Dave Smith, Frankie Paino, William Trowbridge, Brigit Kelly.

Unsolicited Manuscripts Received/ Published per Year: 6-7,000/120.

Reading Period: Sept.–May 1.

Payment: one year subscription.

Reporting Time: 8 weeks.

Copyright reverts to author upon publication.

1976; 2/yr; 1000

$12/yr ind, $16/yr inst; $8/ea; 30%

128 pp; 5½ x 8½

Ad Rates: $150/page (5 x 8); $75/½ page

ISSN: 0738-8993

Ebsco, Faxon, Ubiquity, Fine Print

SPRING: The Journal of the E.E. Cummings Society

Norman Friedman, David V. Forrest

33–54 164 St.

Flushing, NY 11358-1442

(718) 353-3631

Essays, poems, photographs, drawings, bibliographies, etc.

We publish material relating to and about E. E. Cummings.

Milton A. Cohen, Richard S. Kennedy, Linda Wagner-Martin.

Unsolicited Manuscripts Received/ Published per Year: 20/10–12.

Reading Period: Oct.–Mar.

Payment: none.

Reporting Time: we publish once a year so far, so there's no hurry.

Copyright held The E. E. Cummings Society.

1992; 1/yr; circulation 3–500

$15/yr; $15/ea

144 pp; 5½ x 8½

STAND MAGAZINE

Jon Silkin, Lorna Tracy, Rodney Pybus

179 Wingrove Road

Newcastle upon Tyne NE4 9DA, UK

Tel/Fax (0191) 273 3280

STAND MAGAZINE is an independent quarterly of new writing. Politically left of centre, **STAND** has shown a strong awareness of social injustices and emphasizes the need for commitment between the writer and his or her community.

Unsolicited Manuscripts Received/ Published per Year: 520–624 stories, 1,000–1,300 poems/10–12 stories, 30–40 poems depending on length.

Payment: £25.00 per thousand words.

Reporting Time: 4–6 weeks.

Copyright reverts to authors, but magazine reserves right of first publication.
1952; 4/yr; 4,500
84 pp; A5 landscape
Ad Rates: £250.00/page; £125.00/½ page; £62.50/¼ page
UK ISSN: 0038-9366

STET MAGAZINE

Cassandra L. Oxley
P.O. Box 75, Cambridge MA 02238
(508) 264-4938 (phone & fax)
Poetry, short fiction, nonfiction, art.
We are a small literary magazine with a national following—we are presently seeking more essays & fiction though we love to present poetry. We hope to publish as a quarterly in '96.
Max Money, William J. Vernon, Estelle Gilson.
Unsolicited Manuscripts Received/Published per Year: 300–500/60–80.
Reading Period: year–round.
Payment: 2 copies.
Reporting Time: 6 weeks–3 months.
Copyright; 1st rights.
1995; 2/yr; 100+
$12/yr; $4/ea
44+ pp; 7 x 8½ or 8½ x 11
ISSN 1060-8028

STILETTO

Michael Annis
P.O. Box 27276
Denver, Colorado 80227-0276
Poetry, short stories, essays, excerpts from fiction, plays, collaborative art & photos, experimental, (but accessible etc.); politics & social works given priority. Bold, uncompromising, often radical.
All genres, street poets to academia. Strong content. Large enough sections to clearly demonstrate the author's ability and vision. If you have a statement to make for posterity, make it here. Guidelines may be found in previous issues. No free samples—these are Cadillacs.
Antler, Wm. Burroughs, Andrei Codrescu, Diane DiPrima, William Heyen, David Ray, Timothy Leary, Nathaniel Tarn, Diane Wakoski, Anne Waldman, Charles Bukowski.
Unsolicited Manuscripts Received/Published per Year: many/12.
Reading Period: year–round.
Payment: 20 contributor copies, 1st Ed.
Copyright reverts to author/artist.
1989; no schedule latest issue 1992
$21.50 Commercial Ed. softcover; prices include postage. 30%
250+ pp; 5 x 11¼

ISSN 1043-9501
Howling Dog Press

STORY

Lois Rosenthal
1507 Dana Ave.
Cincinnati, OH 45207
(513) 531-2222

Short fiction.

STORY is devoted to publishing fine short stories.

Bobbie Ann Mason, Joyce Carol Oates, Madison Smartt Bell, Alice Adams, Tobias Wolff, Charles Baxter, William Vollmann, Susan Power, Abraham Rodriguex,. Jr.

Unsolicited Manuscripts Received/ Published per Year: 15,000/50.

Reading Period: year–round.

Payment: $750.

Reporting Time: 1 month.

Copyright: First North American serial rights.

1989; 4/yr; 35,000

$19/yr; $6.95/ea

128 pp; 6½ x 9¼

ISSN: 1045-0831

Ingram, Eastern News

STORY QUARTERLY

Anne Brashler, Diane Williams
P.O. Box 1416
Northbrook, IL 60065
(708) 564-8891

Fiction and interviews.

STORY QUARTERLY is looking for great fiction.

Unsolicited Manuscripts Received/ Published per Year: 2,500/20.

Reporting Time: 2 months.

Copyright held by magazine; reverts to author upon publication.

1974; 2/yr; 1,500

$12/4 issues; $5/ea; 40%

110 pp; 6 x 9

ISSN: 0361-0144

DeBoer, Ingram

THE STYLUS

Roger Reus
9412 Huron Avenue
Richmond, VA 23294

Fiction, essays

An eclectic literary journal devoted to the writings of John Fante, Charles Bukowski, Edgar A. Poe, Henry Miller, and others. Essays and original fiction.

Joyce Fante, Mark Rich, Don Herron, Peter Cannon, Sam Maio

Unsolicited Manuscripts Received/ Published per Year: 400/10.

Payment: in copies.

Copyright reverts to author upon publication.

1993; 1/yr; 300

$3/copy; $3/ea

38–56 pp; 5½ x 8½

SUB-TERRAIN MAGAZINE

Brian Kaufman, Dennis Bolen, Paul Pitre, Hilary Green, Bryan Wade, Dirk Beck, Ken Gilchrist, Andrea Shearer

P.O. Box 1575, Bentall Centre
Vancouver, B.C. V6G 2P7 CANADA
(604) 876-8710
Fax (604) 879-2667

Fiction, poetry, excerpts of novels, essays, art, photography.

SUB-TERRAIN has garnered substantial kudos for its unusual material, daring art, and contentious commentary. We continue to publish a new front line of writers and artists who might otherwise never get the exposure we strive to offer.

Mark Salerno, Tom Osborne, Steven Heighton, Michael Turner, J. Jill Robinson, Grant Buday, Don Austin, Jean Smith.

Unsolicited Manuscripts Received/ Published per Year: 7–1,000/ 75–100.

Reading Period: Sept.–June.

Payment: in copies; payment for solicited material.

Reporting Time: 2–4 months.

Copyright: 1 time only, reverts to author.

1993; 4/yr; 3,000

$15/yr ind, $20/yr inst; $3.95/ea; 40%

40 pp; 7 x 10

Ad Rates: $300/back cover; $210/page; $120/½ page; $65/¼ page

ISSN: 0840-7533

Canada Magazine Publishers Assoc., US: Desert Moon, Periodicals

SULFUR

Clayton Eshleman

Contributing Editors; Eliot Weinberger, Rachel Blau DuPlessis, Michael Palmer, Pamela Wye.

210 Washtenaw Ave.
Ypsilanti, MI 48197
(313) 483-9787

Poetry, poetics, translations, archival materials, art work and art criticism, book reviews.

Gary Snyder, Anne Waldman, Antonin Artaud, Charoles Bernstein, Mina Loy.

Unsolicited Manuscripts Received/ Published per Year: 2,000/10.

Payment: Average of $40.

Reporting Time: 3–6 weeks.

Copyright held by author.

1981; 2/yr; 800

$14/yr ind, $20/yr inst; $9/ea; $4/resale.

256 pp; 7 x 9

$300/full page (6½ x 8½, vertically placed)

ISSN: 0730-305X

Ubiquity, DeBoer, Specacular Diseases (England)

SUN DOG: The Southeast Review

Michael Trammell, Ron Wiginton
406 Williams Building
Florida State University
Tallahassee, FL 32306
(904) 644-4230

Poetry, fiction, graphic art.

SUN DOG: The Southeast Review reads both fiction and poetry year-round. We are looking for striking images, incidents, and characters rather than particular styles or genres. We also publish the winner and runners-up of the World's Best Short Short Story Contest, as well as the winner and runners-up of the Richard Eberhart Prize in Poetry.

Janet Burroway, David Bottoms, Jesse Lee Kercheval, Leon Stokesbury, Rick Lott, Helen Norris, David Kirby.

Unsolicited Manuscripts Received/ Published per Year: 300–400/ 12-fiction; 20-poems.

Reading Period: year–round.

Payment: 2 copies.

Copyright held by magazine; reverts to author upon publication.

1979; 2/yr; 1,250

$4/ea; 40%

90 pp; 6 x 9

THE SUN MAGAZINE

Sy Safransky
107 N. Roberson St.
Chapel Hill, NC 27516
(919) 942-5282

Essays, poetry, fiction, interviews, photography.

A monthly magazine in its 22nd year of publication, **THE SUN MAGAZINE** celebrates good writing—and the warmth of shared intimacies—in essays, fiction, interviews, and poetry. People write in the magazine of their struggle to understand their lives, often bearing themselves with remarkable candor.

Stephen J. Lyons, Alison Luterman, Poe Ballantine.

Payment: $100–$500/nonfiction; $100–$300/fiction; $25–$75/poetry.

We purchase one-time rights with the option to reprint in any anthology of works from The Sun. All other rights revert to the author.

1974; 12/yr; 30,000

40 pp; 8½ x 11

ISSN: 0744-9666

Armadillo, Bear Family, Daybreak, Desert Moon, Olson, Doormouse, Ingram, Mercury, New Leaf, Serendipity, Small Changes, Stadler, Ubiquity, Wholistic Health.

SWIFT KICK

Robin Kay Willoughby
1711 Amherst St.
Buffalo, NY 14214
(716) 837-7778

Poetry, fiction, plays, translation, photographs, graphics/artwork.

We specialize in unusual formats, genres and styles.

Jerry McGuire, Dennis Maloney, Simon Perchik, Penny Kemp, Maurice Kenny.

Payment: in copies.

Reporting Time: varies.

Copyright held by magazine; reverts to author upon publication.

1980; 4/yr; 200

$20/yr ind, $40/yr inst; $6 + postage/sample (checks payable to editor); 40%

ISSN: 0277-447X

SYCAMORE REVIEW

Rob Davidson, Editor
Department of English
Purdue University
West Lafayette, IN 47907
(317) 494-3783

Fiction, poetry, essays, interviews, translations, drama.

SYCAMORE REVIEW publishes new writers of contemporary fiction and poetry alongside well-known, experienced writers.

Denise Levertev, Philip Dacey, Tom Andrews, Gordon LIsh, Margot Livesey, Ted Kooser, Gregory Orr, Chuck Wachtel, Patricia Henley.

Unsolicited Manuscripts Received/Published per Year: 1,000–1,200/40-45.

Reading Period: Sept.–May.

Payments: 2 copies.

Reporting Time: 4 months or less—SASE must be included for response.

Copyright: Purdue University acquires all rights.

1995; 2/yr; 800–1,000

$10/yr in US; $12/yr foreign; $7/current issue each; $4/back issues each. List available. 1- & 2-yr. subscriptions only.

160 pp; 6 x 9

Ad swaps w/other magazines or small presses. No contest ads.

ISSN: 1043-1497

T

TAKAHE

Bernadette Hall, Isa Moynihan, Cassandra Fusco
P.O. Box 13 335
Christchurch, New Zealand

Short stories and poetry.

Publishes work by both new and established authors and poets. There is a small payment for each item published---currently about NZ$30.00, but subject to change at any time. Quarterly.

Edward Bond, Jonathan Steffen, David Eggleton, Graham Lindsey, Sean Brandon-Brown.

Unsolicited Manuscripts Received/Published per year: 500/120.

Reading Period: any.

Payment: $NZ30.00 but subject to change.

Reporting Time: 3 months.

Copyright held by magazine; reverts to author upon publication.

1989; 4/yr; 320.

$24/yr (Foreign subscriptions - surface mail—$NZ32.00 for 4 issues; $6/ea; 16.6%

64 pp; A4.

Ad Rates: $NZ40.00 for 16cm x 8cm.

ISSN: 0114-4138

Publishers

TALISMAN: A Journal of Contemporary Poetry and Poetics

Edward Foster
Box 1117
Hoboken, NJ 07030
(201) 798-9093

Poetry, essays on poetry and poetics, interviews.

Each issue centers on the poetry and poetics of a major contemporary poet and includes a selection of new work by other important contemporary writers.

Susan Howe, Charles Bernstein, John Yau, Clark Coolidge, Robert Creeley, Rosmarie Waldrop, Ron Padgett, Alice Notley, Leslie Scalapino.
Unsolicited Manuscripts Received/ Published per Year: hundreds/ 20-25.
Reading Period: year-round.
Payments: copies.
Reporting Time: 2 months.
Copyright reverts to author upon publication.
1988; 2/yr; 1,200
$9/yr ind, $13/yr inst; $5/ea; 40%
224 pp; 5½ x 8½
Ad Rates: $100/page; $50/½ page
ISSN: 0898-8684
DeBoer, Anton J. Mikofsky, SPD, IN Book, Spectacular Diseases (UK)

TAMPA REVIEW

Richard B. Mathews, Ed.; Andy Solomon, Fiction Ed.; Kathryn Van Spanckeren & Don Morrill, Poetry Editors; Paul Linnehan, Nonfiction Editor.
The University of Tampa
401 W. Kennedy Blvd.
Tampa, FL 33606-1490
(813) 253-3333, ext. 6266
Poetry, fiction, essays, interviews, photographs, graphics and art.
TAMPA REVIEW is the faculty-edited literary journal of the University of Tampa. It publishes new poetry, fiction, translations, nonfiction and art in a variety of styles and voices. Each issue includes works from other countries, reflecting the international flavor of the city of Tampa and its ties to the international cultural community.
Tom Disch, Eavan Boland, Shang Zhongmin, Dionisio Martínez, Peter Meinke, W. S. Merwin, Elizabeth Jolley, Denise Levertov, Stephen Dunn.
Unsolicited Manuscripts Received/ Published per Year: 1,200–2,000/ 60.
Reading Period: Sept.–Dec.
Payment: $10/page.
Reporting Time: up to 12 weeks after Dec. 31.
Copyright: first North American serial copyright held by Magazine then reverts to author.
2/yr
$10/yr; $5.95/ea
72 pp; 7½ x 10½
ISSN: 0896-064X

TAPROOT: A Journal of Older Writers

Philip W. Quigg, Enid Graf
Fine Arts Center 4290
University at Stony Brook,
Stony Brook, NY 11794-5410
(516) 632-6635

Poetry, fiction, graphics/artwork, reviews.

Publish the works of older writers; interested in "capturing the stories, poems and recountings of events related to and growing from tradition," as well as the realities of our elders' participation in community life. Publication open to members of Taproot Workshops only.

No Unsolicited Manuscripts Received/Published per Year: 15/0.

Payment: 1 copy.

Copyright held by magazine; reverts to author upon publication.

1974; 1/yr; 1,000

$6/ea; 40%

100 pp; 8½ x 11

Ad Rates: $500/page; $300/½ page; $175/¼ page

ISSN: 0887-9257

TAR RIVER POETRY

Peter Makuck
English Department
East Carolina University
Greenville, NC 27834
(919) 757-6041

Poetry, reviews, interviews, essays.

We are looking for poetry that shows skillful use of figurative language. Narrative poems, short image poems, poems in closed and open form are welcome. We are not interested in sentimental, flat statement verse. Though we often publish the work of established poets, we are open to the work of newcomers as well.

1994 *Dictionary for Literary Biography* list us in "Top 10 Magazines for Poetry"

A.R. Ammons, Brendan Galvin, Sharon Bryan, Betty Adcock, Naomi Shihab Nye, Michael Mott, Peter Davison, Leslie Norris, Emily Grosholz.

Unsolicited Manuscripts Received/Published per Year: 4,500/125.

Reading Period: Sept.–April.

Payment: none.

Reporting Time: 5–7 weeks.

Copyright reverts to author.

1965; 2/yr; 1,000

$10/1 yr, $18/2 yrs; $5.50/sample; 40%

62 pp; 6 x 9

THE TEXAS REVIEW

Paul Ruffin
English Department
Sam Houston State University
Huntsville, TX 77341
(409) 294-1429

Poetry, fiction, criticism, essays, reviews.

We are interested in the very best fiction and poetry available; our nonfiction may be literary, historical, or "familiar." We are interested principally in reviews of contemporary poetry and fiction.

Fred Chappell, Richard Eberhart, George Garrett, Donald Justice, William Stafford, Richard Wilbur.

Unsolicited Manuscripts Reveived/ Published per Year: 3,000/150.

Reading Period: Sept.–Apr.

Payment: in contributor's copies plus 1 year subscription to magazine.

Copyright held by magazine; reverts to author upon publication.

1979; 2/yr; 750–1,000

$10/yr (ind and inst); $5/ea; 40%

144 pp; 6 x 9

ISSN: 0885-2685

THEATER MAGAZINE

Erika Munk
Yale School of Drama
222 York St.
New Haven, CT 06520
(203) 432-1568
Fax (203) 432-8336

Playscripts, essays, articles, interviews,performance and book reviews.

The foremost journal on contemporary theater, **THEATER** publishes noted American and International critics, playwrights, and scholars. Each issue features a collection of essays, a new play, reports and reviews.

Harold Bloom, Richard Gilman, Marie-Irene Fornes, Suzan-Lori Parks, Richard Foreman.

Unsolicited Manuscripts Received/ Published per Year: 250/3–5.

Reading Period: academic year, Sept.–May.

Payment: $100 plus issues.

Reporting Time: 4–6 weeks.

Copyright held by Theater Magazine.

1968; 3/yr; 2600/issue

$22/yr ind, $35/yr inst; $8/ea; 25%

120 pp; 7½ x 10

Ad rates: $250/full page (5½ x 8½); $150/½ page (5½ x 4¼); $100/¼ page (2½ x 4¼)

ISSN: 0161-0775

Fine Print, DeBoer, Ubiquity, Inland

THEMA

Virginia Howard
Thema Literary Society
Box 74109
Metairie, LA 70033-4109
(504) 887-1263

Fiction, poetry.

Stories and poems must relate to premise specified for each issue. Upcoming themes: Jogging on Ice, A Visit from the Imp, *I KNOW WHO YOU ARE!*, Too

Proud to Ask, Scrawled in a Library Book and more to be announced.
Kimberly Parke, C. Morgan; Susan Moore Williams, Nora Ruth Roberts.
Unsolicited Manuscripts Received/ Published per Year: 800/75.
Payment: $25 for short story, $10 for poems, $10 for short-shorts and illustrations.
Reporting Time: dependent on deadlines.
Copyright reverts to author.
1988; 3/yr; 300
$16/yr; $8/ea; 40%
200 pp; 5½ x 8½
ISSN: 1041-4851

13th MOON

Judith E. Johnson
English Department
SUNY
Albany, NY 12222

Poetry, fiction, criticism, essays, reviews, translation, interviews, photographs, graphics/artwork, by women.
13th MOON is a feminist literary magazine, placing primary emphasis on the quality of writing. It is specifically interested in work from feminist, lesbian, third-world, and working-class perspectives.
Ursula McGwin, Fanny Howe, Ursule Molinaro.
Unsolicited Manuscripts Received/ Published per Year: 1,000/30.
Reading Period: Sept.—May.
Payment: in copies.
Reporting Time: varies (up to a year).
Copyright held by 13th Moon, Inc.; reverts to author upon publication.
1973; 1/yr; 2,500
$10/ind, $20/inst; $10/ea; 40%
250 pp; 6 x 9
Ad Rates: $200 page, $125/½ page, $75/¼ page

THIS: A Serial Review

Robin Yale Bergstrom
6600 Clough Pike
Cincinnati, Ohio 45244
(513) 231-8020
Fax (513) 231-2818

Poetry, fiction, essays, art, drama, criticism.
We strive to publish new and established artists regardless of bias. We're committed to stretching the literary magazine genre by taking the risks necessary to pull it in directions it has yet to go.
Barry Spacks, James Bertolino, David Shevin, Lynn Lifshin, S.P. Elledge.
Unsolicited Manuscripts Received/ Published per Year: 2,000/130.

Reading Period: 12 months.
Payment: in copies, beginning 1996 cash payment.
Reporting Time: 6–8 weeks.
Copyright held by Pants Dance Productions; reverts to author upon publication.
1994; 3/yr; 500+
$24/yr, $9/ea; 20%
120 pp; 8 x 8
ISSN: 1075-2862
Fine Print

THE THREEPENNY REVIEW

Wendy Lesser
P.O. Box 9131
Berkeley, CA 94709
(510) 849-4545

Poetry, fiction, criticism, essays, reviews, memoirs, graphics/artwork.

THE THREEPENNY REVIEW is a quarterly journal publishing essays on literature, theater, film, television, dance, music, and the visual arts, as well as new poetry, original fiction, and socio-political articles. While based in California, it is aimed at a nationwide audience.

John Berger, Seamus Heaney, Elizabeth Hardwick, Thom Gunn, Amy Tan.
Unsolicited Manuscripts Received/Published per Year: 5,200/20.
Payment: $100–$200.
Reporting Time: 3 weeks–2 months.
Copyright held by magazine; reverts to author upon publication.
1980; 4/yr; 10,000
$16/yr; $6/ea; 30%–50%
40 pp; 11 x 17
Ad Rates: $900/page (10 x 14); $500/½ page (10 x 7½); $360/¼ page (4½ x 7¼)
ISSN: 0275-1410
Ingram, Ubiquity

THUNDER & HONEY

Akbar Imhotep
P.O. Box 11386
Atlanta, GA 30310
(404) 688-3376

Poetry, fiction, interviews, photographs, graphics/artwork.

THUNDER & HONEY is primarily devoted to poetry and fiction. Future issues will have arts-related articles and some interviews.

Charlie Braxton, Nome Poem, R.F. Smith, Askia Toure, Jeanne Towns.
Payment: 25 copies.
Copyright held by magazine; reverts to author upon publication.
1984; 4/yr; 1,500
$3.00/yr; 99¢/ea
4 pp; 8½ x 11
Ad Rates: $210/page (10 x 16); $120/½ page (10 x 8); $60/¼ page (5 x 4)

TIGHTROPE

Ed Rayher
323 Pelham Rd.
Amherst, MA 01002

Poetry, fiction, translation, graphics/artwork. Not reading short fiction until 1994.

We stress excellence and accessibility to unpublished or little published authors. Our format is erratic, but we always emphasize form as well as content.

Steven Ruhl, Linda Burggraf, Gillian Conoley, Lance Liskus.

Unsolicited Manuscripts Received/ Published per Year: 500/25.

Payment: inquire.

Copyright held by magazine; reverts to author upon publication.

1977; 2/yr; 350

$10/yr; $6/ea; 40%

40 pp; size varies; Letterpress

TO: A Journal of Poetry, Prose and the Visual Arts

Seth Frechie, Andrew Mossin
Box 121
Narberth, PA 19072

Biannual.

Contemporary fiction, poetry, and poetics featuring new translation, archival material, essay and review. Each issue features work, in the visual arts with a special emphasis placed on work by contemporary american photographiers.

John Ashbery, Charles Bernstein, Leslie Scalapino, Jack Sturges.

Payment: in copies.

Reporting Time: 6 weeks.

Copyright reverts to author.

1992; 2/yr; 1,000

$15/yr ind, $30/yr inst; $8/ea; 40%

Approx. 140 pp; 7 x 10 page

Ad Rates: $100/page; $50/½ page

SPD, DeBoer

TOMORROW MAGAZINE

Tim W. Brown
P.O. Box 148486
Chicago, IL 60614
(312) 984-6092

Poetry, fiction, essay, B&W Art.

TOMORROW is a magazine that tries not to discriminate against style or subject, although we tend to shy away from academically inclined work.

Hugh Fox, Richard Kostelanetz, Antler, Cheryl Townsend, Paul Weinman.

Unsolicited Manuscripts Received/ Published per Year: 500/75.

Reading Period: year-round.

Payment: in copies.

Reporting Time: 3 weeks to 3 months.

Copyright reverts to the author.

1982; 2/yr; 300

$13/3 issues; $5/ea
32 pp; 8½ x 11
ISSN: 1075-3796

TOOK: Modern Poetry in English Series
Edward Mycue
P.O. Box 640543
San Francisco, CA 94164-0543
Poetry, drama, prose, history, criticism, music, food, art, psychology, self-help, philosophy, film, vinyl/recordings, travel.
Laura Kennelly, Owen Hill, Lawrence Fixel, Martha King, Jules Mann, Betsy Ford, Judy Stedman, Elizabeth Hurst, Agnes McGaha, Helen Sventitsky, Jim Gove, Dan Bellm, William Talcott, Ann Erickson.
Payment: in copies.
Reporting Time: 1 month.
Copyright reverts to the contributors.
1988; occasional; 150
$5/ea
8 to 40 pp; 5½ x 4½
Ad Rates: $50/¼ page

TOP STORIES
Anne Turyn
228 Seventh Ave.
New York, NY 10011
Fiction, graphics/artwork.
TOP STORIES is a prose periodical; a chapbook series which (usually) features the work of one author/artist per issue.
Constance DeJong, Lynne Tillman, Susan Daitch, Tama Janowitz, Richard Prince.
Payment: varies.
Reporting Time: 1 year.
Copyright held by author.
1979; 3/yr; 1,500
$13.50/yr ind, $14.50/yr inst; $3/ea single issue; $6/ea double issue; 40%
5¼ x 8¼
No ads

TOUCHSTONE: Literary Journal
William Laufer
P.O. Box 8308
Spring, TX 77387-8308
Poetry, criticism, essays, reviews, translation, interviews, graphics/artwork, fiction.
We publish fiction, nonfiction, poetry and graphics. We do not care for "Creative Writing Program" fiction. We welcome minority viewpoints, and look for imaginative, experimental trends. We also publish (poetry and fiction) chapbooks, no theme, no reading fee. Send SASE for submission guidelines.
Lyn Lifshin, Rebecca Gonzales, Ramona Weeks, Vassar Miller,

Arthur Smith, Sheila Murphy, Walter McDonald, Annette Sanford.
Reading Period: Jan.–Oct.
Payment: 2 copies (magazine), or 10 copies (chapbooks).
Reporting Time: 6 weeks.
Copyright reverts to author.
1976; 1/yr; 1,000
$5/ea
52–60 pp; 5½ x 8, perfect bound
ISSN: 1715-1697
No ads

TRAFIKA INTERNATIONAL LITERARY REVIEW
Dorsey Dunn, Michael Lee, Jeffrey Young
P.O. Box 250423
New York, NY 10025-1536
Short fiction, poetry.
TRAFIKA is an international review of contemporary poetry and fiction by new and emerging writers throughout the world.
Tor Ulren, Norma Cole, Jarier Marias, Do Phuoe Tien, Luis Leante, Pierre Martory.
Unsolicited Manuscripts Received/Published per Year: 15,000/100
Payment: $15 per page for writers and translators.
Reporting Time: 3 months.
Copyright reverts to author upon publication.
1993; 4/yr; 6,000
$35/yr; $10/yr; $10/issue; 25%
224 pp; 6 x 9
Ad Rates: $500(US)/$300(US) for nonprofit organizations/page (5½ x 8¼)
Fine Print, Ingram, Ubiquity, SPD

TRANSLATION REVIEW
Rainer Schulte
Box 830688
University of Texas at Dallas
Richardson, TX 75083-0688
TRANSLATION REVIEW publishes articles on the art and craft of translation, interviews with well known translators, criticisms of revent translations, profiles of publishers.
Payment: no.
Reporting Time: 3 months.
Copyright held by magazine.
1978; 3/yr; 1,500
$30/yr ind, $125/yr inst; $35/yr Colleges and Univ. Student (US) $20; individual (foreign) $40; library (US) $35; library (foreign) $45.
65 pp; 8½ x 11
Ads Rates: $200/page (7½ x 9) $125/½ page (7½ x 4½ or 3½ x 9); $75/¼ page (2¼ x 3½)
ISSN: 0737-4836

TRIQUARTERLY
Reginald Gibbons
Susan Hahn

Northwestern University
2020 Ridge
Evanston, IL 60208-4302

Fiction, poetry, essays, reviews, translation, interviews, photographs, graphics/artwork.

TRIQUARTERLY is especially dedicated to short fiction, although substantial amounts of poetry are also published regularly in every issue, including long poems. Brief book reviews and occasional essays round out the contents.

Stanley Elkin, Alice Fulton, Linda McCarriston, Sandra McPherson, Jim Powell, Alan Shapiro, Bruce Weigl.

Unsolicited Manuscripts Received/Published per Year: 4,000/100

Reading Period: Oct. 2–Mar. 31

Payment: $20/printed page, prose; $1.50/line, poetry.

Reporting Time: 2–3 months.

Copyright reverts to author upon request.

1964; 3/yr; 5,000

$24/yr ind, $36/yr inst; $5/sample; varies

272 pp; 6 x 9¼

Ad Rates: $250/page (4½ x 7¼); $150/½ page (4½ x 3½)

ISSN: 0041-3097

Ingram, DeBoer, Bookpeople, Fine Print, Ubiquity, Armadillo

TRIVIA: A Journal of Ideas

Erin Rice, Kay Parkhurst
P.O. Box 606
North Amherst, MA 01059
(413) 367-0168

TRIVIA publishes the finest, most "lively and vicious" writing from radical, visionary women. Essays, reviews, translations, interviews, original art and experimental forms that combine rigorous thinking with uncompromising feminist vision. Articles on language and memory, aging, lesbian ethics, feminism's seduction by New Age philosophy.

Nicole Brossard, Michèle Causse, Christina Thürmer-Rohr, Barbara Mor, C. C. Sundance, Lee Maracle, Lou Robinson.

Unsolicited Manuscripts Received/Published per Year: 50–60+/10+.

Reporting Time: 4–6 months.

Copyright reverts to author.

1982; 2/yr; 2,000

$16/3 issues ind; $20/3 issues inst; $5/ea

120 pp; 5½ x 8½

Ad Rates: inquire

ISSN: 0736-928X

Inland, Bookpeople, Small Changes, Fine Print, Spectacular Diseases (UK)

TUCUMCARI LITERARY REVIEW

Troxey Kemper
3108 W. Bellevue Ave.
Los Angeles, CA 90026
(213) 413-0789

Poetry, fiction, essays, nostalgia, memories, vignettes, humor.

TUCUMCARI LITERARY REVIEW is old fashioned and the preference is for types of writing in vogue in the 1930s to 1950s. Most of the poetry is rhyming, in "standard" forms, not disjointed phrases and odd-shaped lines of prose arranged like poetry. The emphasis is on writing that "says something."

Harvey Stanbrough, Marian Ford Park, William J. Middleton, Fontaine Falkoff, Patricia Higginbotham, Daniel Kaderli, Ken MacDonnell, Wilma Elizabeth McDaniel.

Unsolicited Manuscripts Received/ Published per Year: 1,500/400.

Payment: in copies upon publication.

Copyright held by author.

1988; 6/yr; 170

$12/yr ind & inst; $2/ea by mail; 40%

40 pp; 5½ x 8½

Ad Rates: free for readers

TURNSTILE

George Witte, Kit Haines
175 Fifth Avenue, Suite 2348
New York, NY 10010

Fiction, poetry, essays, interviews, photographs, artwork/graphics.

TURNSTILE publishes high-quality fiction, poetry, essays, interviews and artistic works. A passageway for variety and difference, **TURNSTILE** encourages new and emerging writers and artists.

Unsolicited Manuscripts Received/ Published per Year: 1,000+/20.

Payment: in copies.

Reporting Time: 10–12 weeks.

Copyright reverts to author upon publication.

1988; 2/yr; 1,200

$22/4 issues; $6.50/ea; 40–50%

128 pp; 6 x 9

$150/page; $100/½ page

ISSN: 0896-5951

Deboer, Inland, Ingram

TWO GIRLS REVIEW

Lidia Ynkman, Managing Editor
Paige Price, Fiction
Kelly Vie, Poetry
Greg Brokes, Politics
Devin Crowe, Art
341 Adams
Eugene, OR 97402
(503) 484-2446
Fax (503) 344-7955

Fiction, poetry, art, non-fiction, experimental, mixed-genre, all sexualities, border crossing.

Committed to printing underrepresented experimental, culture-crashing work. Treats writing as graphis. We respond to work that torques imagination.

Ysef Komun Yakaa, Kathy Acker, Stephen Dixon, Eurydice, Diana Aleu-Jaber.

Unsolicited Manuscripts Received/ Published per year: 100–200/20–30.

Reading Period: ongoing.

Payment: copies.

Reporting Time: 2–4 months.

Copyright held by author.

1995; 2/yr; 2,500

$6

128 pp; 9 x 12

Ad Rates: 1/8 page/$150; 1/4 page/$200; 1/2 page/$300; full page/$450

Fine Print, Desert Moon, Ubiquity, Book People.

U

UNMUZZLED OX
Michael Andre
105 Hudson St.
New York, NY 10013
(212) 226-7170
Poetry, political.
Library Journal called **OX** "Outrageous and outstanding" perhaps because I published Robert Mapplethorpe; given the current climate I'd settle for "lively." We do publish the dead—a forthcoming issue features baroque librettists; plus W. H. Auden, the late Andy Warhol, John Cage.
Robert Creeley, Dan Berrigan, Allen Ginsberg.
Unsolicited Manuscripts Received/Published per Year: 500/4.
Payment: confidential.
Reporting Time: varies.
Copyright held by Michael Andre.
1971; varies; 15,000
$20/yr; $3/ea; varies
150 pp; 5½ x 8½
Ad Rates: inquire.
ISSN: 0049-5557

URBANUS MAGAZINE
Peter Drizhal, Editor; Geoffrey Manson, Senior Editor
P.O. Box 192561
San Francisco, CA 94119-2561
Fiction, poetry, essays, graphics.
URBANUS is a magazine of contemporary and post-modernist writing; our focus is urban culture and its offsprings.
Yusef Komunyakaa, Louise Rafkin, Clarence Major, Amy Gerstler, Heather McHugh, James Sallis.
Unsolicited Manuscripts Received/Published per Year: 3,000/20.
Reading Period: Dec.–Feb., June–Aug.

Payment: prose: 1¢ per word and copies; Poetry: $5/page and copies.
Reporting Time: 2–10 weeks.
Copyright held by Urbanus Press
1988; 2/yr; 1000
$8/yr; $5/ea; 40%
64 pp; ½ x 8½
Ad rates: $100/page (5 x 8); $50/½ page (5 x 4)
ISSN: 1078-6686
Desert Moon

V

THE VINCENT BROTHERS REVIEW

Kimberly A. Willardson, Roger Willardson, Michelle Whitley-Turner, Valerie Benge
4566 Northern Circle
Riverside, OH 45424-5733

Fiction, nonfiction, poetry, reviews, essays, artwork, photos.

TVBR's purpose is to encourage, promote and support the work of artists, poets, and prose writers through the publication of 3 magazines per year.

Anselm Brocki, Arthur Winfield Knight, and Constance Garcia-Barrio.

Unsolicited Manuscripts Received/Published per Year: 9,000/180.

Payment: $10 minimum for short stories and articles plus 2 copies of issue; 2 copies of issue to all other contributors.

Reporting Time: 2–3 months.

Copyright: all rights revert to artists/authors upon publication.

1988; 3/yr; 400

$12/yr; $6.50/ea

64–80 pp; 5½ x 8

Ad Rates: $75/page (7 x 4); $45/½ page (3¼ x 4); $25/business card (2 x 3½)

ISSN: 1044-615X

THE VINYL ELEPHANT

Matthew Duncan
700 Cotanche #1
Greenville, NC 27858

Poetry, Fiction, B/W Art/Photography.

Literary Journal of Experimental work often edged out due to "extravagances" in subtext matter, "contrivances" in voice or diction, and "inconveniences" of structure or layout.

Guy Beining, Thomas Zimmer-

man, Juliet Cook!, Richard Levesque.
Unsolicited Manuscripts Received/ Published per Year: 1,500/100.
Payment: 1 copy.
Reporting Time: 4–6 weeks.
Copyright reverts to author.
1992; 3/yr; 125
$10/6 issues; $3/ea
44 pp; 8½ x 5½, digest
Ad Rates: $25/page; $15/½ page; $10/¼ page: trade for equal

THE VIRGINIA QUARTERLY REVIEW

Staige D. Blackford
One West Range
Charlottesville, VA 22903
(804) 924-3124
Fax (804) 924-1397

Poetry, fiction, essays, reviews.
One of the oldest and most distinguished literary journals in the country; contains articles and essays covering economics, art, the sciences, politics, and literature. Publishes high-quality fiction and poetry by established and newer authors. 75–100 brief, tightly-written book reviews per issue.
George Garrett, Jay Parini, Joyce Carol Oates, Mary Lee Settle, Ann Beattie, Robert Olin Butler.
Unsolicited Manuscripts Received/ Published per Year: 2,000+/12-16.
Reader Period: year–round.
Payment: $10/page essays & fiction; $1/line for poetry; $50/essay reviews.
Copyright held by magazine/The University of Virginia; reverts to author upon publication.
1925; 4/yr; 4,200
$18/yr ind, $22/yr inst; $5/ea; 50%
188 pp; 5½ x 8
Ad Rates: $150/page (5½ x 8); $75/½ page (5½ x 4 or 2⅜ x 8)
ISSN: 0042-675X

VISIONS–International, The World Journal of Illustrated Poetry

Bradley R. Strahan, Poetry Editor; Shirley Sullivan, Associate Editor
1110 Seaton Lane
Falls Church, VA 22046
(703) 521-0142

Poetry, reviews, translations, graphics/artwork.
We're international in scope and content. We emphasize the interplay between artwork, poem and appearance of the magazine. We look for strong, well-crafted work that has emotional content (without sentimentality). **VISIONS** also publishes issues on special themes (usually once

a year). Many of these, including our specials on Balkan, Scandinavian/ Nordic and Australia/New Zealand poetry, are still in print. We oppose the trend to publish facile word play instead of meaningful poetry. We are always interested in translations, especially from work that has not previously appeared in English and from less translated languages such as: Frisian, Basque, Telegu, Malayan, Gaelic, Macedonian, etc.

Allen Ginsberg, Ted Hughes, Marilyn Hacker, Louis Simpson, Lawrence Ferlingletti.

Unsolicited Manuscripts Received/ Published per Year: 6,000+/250.

Reading Period: year–round.

Payment: in copies or $5–$10 when we get a grant.

Read a sample copy ($3.75) before submitting work.

Reporting Time: 1–3 weeks.

Copyright held by VIAS; reverts to author upon publication.

1979; 3/yr; 750

$15/yr; $4.75/ea; 30%–40%

56 pp; 5½ x 8½

ISSN: 0194-1690

VOICES INTERNATIONAL

Clovita Rice
1115 Gillette Dr.
Little Rock, AR 72207
(501) 225-0166

Poetry, essays, photographs, graphics/artwork.

VOICES INTERNATIONAL focuses on high literary quality poetry, accepting for publication poetry with strong visual imagery and haunting impact. We encourage the beginner and have no preference in subject matter (as long as in good taste) if it presents a fresh approach and special awareness.

Sarah Singer, Eunice de Chazeau, Frederick Zydek.

Unsolicited Manuscripts Received/ Published per Year: 160–180

Reading Period: year–round.

Payment: in copies.

Reporting Time: averages 6 weeks.

Copyright held by magazine.

1966; 4/yr; 325

$10/yr; $2.50/ea

32 pp; 6 x 9

VREMYA I MY (TIME AND WE)

Victor Perelman
409 Highwood Ave.
Leonia, NJ 07605
(201) 592-6155

Russian language literature and commentary. Fiction, essays, poetry, criticism, translation, graphics/artwork, interviews, photographs.

$59/yr ind, $86/yr inst; $19/ea; 40%

W

WASHINGTON REVIEW

Clarissa Wittenberg, Editor; Mary Swift, Managing Editor; James Mahoney, Jeff Richards, Joe Ross, Ross Taylor, Anne Pierce, Editorial Board

P.O. Box 50132

Washington, DC 20091-3066

(202) 638-0515

Poetry, fiction, essays, reviews, plays, interviews, photographs, graphics/artwork.

Bi-monthly tabloid-size journal of arts and literature including poetry, fiction, book and art reviews, essays on the arts, original art work. Emphasis on arts of Washington, D.C. One special issue on single topic each year.

Terence Winch, Doug Lang, Lee Fleming.

Unsolicited Manuscripts Received/Published per Year: 150 fiction, 150 poetry/5-6 fiction, 15-20 poetry.

Payment: \$15–20/review, \$50–100/article if available.

Reporting Time: 2 months.

Copyright held by magazine; reverts to author upon publication.

1975; 6/yr; 1,500

\$15/yr ind, \$25/2 yrs, \$8.50/yr inst; \$2/ea; 40%

Ad Rates: \$250/page (16 x 11¼); \$175/½ page (8 x 11¼); \$135/⅓ page (7⅜ x 8)

ISSN: 0163-903X

WATERWAYS

Barbara Fisher, Richard Alan Spiegel

393 St. Pauls Ave.

Staten Island, NY 10304-2127

(718) 442-7429

Fax (718) 442-4978

Poetry, graphics.

We publish poets of all ages and types provided we like their work and it pertains to our monthly themes. Our page size is small to encourage portability and accessibility.

Joanne Seltzer, Kit Knight, Arthur Winfield Knight, Albert Huffstickler, Ida Fasel.

Unsolicited Manuscripts Received/ Published per Year: 200/20.

Reading Period: year–round.

Payment: 1 copy.

Reporting Time: 1 month.

Copyright held by Ten Penny Players; reverts to author upon publication.

1977; 11/yr; 100–200

$20/yr; $2/ea; 40%–60%

48 pp; 7 x 4¼

ISSN: 0197-4777

WEBSTER REVIEW

Editors
Webster Review
Eng. Dept. SLCC–Meramec
11333 Big Bend Rd.
St. Louis, MO 63122
(314) 432-2657

Poetry, fiction, essays, translation, interviews.

WEBSTER REVIEW emphasizes translations of contemporary fiction, poetry and essays. We look for quality original work in those categories. We are particularly open at this time to nonfiction of a general literary nature.

William Stafford, Jared Carter, Barbara Lefcowitz, Charles Edward Easton, Etelvina Astrada.

Unsolicited Manuscripts Received/ Published per Year: 1,200/50.

Payment: in copies.

Copyright held by magazine; reverts to author upon publication.

1974; 1/yr; 1,100

$5/yr; $2.50/ea; 40%

128 pp; 5½ x 8½

ISSN: 0363-1230

WEST BRANCH

Karl Patten, Robert Taylor
Bucknell Hall
Bucknell University
Lewisburg, PA 17837
(717) 524-1853

Poetry, fiction, reviews.

A twice-yearly magazine of poetry, fiction, and reviews.

Cory Brown, Roger Fanning, Sandra Kohler, Ron Mohring, Jeanne Murry Walker.

Unsolicited Manuscripts Received/ Published per Year: 900+/90.

Reading Period: year–round.

Payment: 2 copies and 1 year subscription.

Reporting Time: 6–8 weeks.

Copyright held by magazine; reverts to author upon publication.

1977; 2/yr; 500
$7/yr, $11/2 yrs; $4/ea
88–106 pp; 5½ x 8½
No ads
ISSN: 0149-6441

WEST HILLS REVIEW

George Wallace, Editor; Walt Whitman Birthplace Association
246 Old Walt Whitman Rd.
Huntington Station, NY 11746
(516) 427-5240

Poetry, essays, photographs, graphics/artwork.

Good lyric poetry. Prose related to Walt Whitman.

John Ciardi, William Stafford, Gay Wilson Allen, David Ignatow, Edmund Pennant.

Payment: none.

Reporting Time: 3 months.

Copyright held by magazine; reverts to author upon publication.

1979; 1/yr; 1000
$6/yr; 50%
32 pp; 5 x 8

WESTERN HUMANITIES REVIEW

David Kranes, Richard Howard, Barry Weller
3500 LNCO/ University of Utah
Salt Lake City, UT 84112
(801) 581-6070

Poetry, fiction, criticism, essays, reviews, nonfiction.

We print fiction, poetry, articles on the humanities (we prefer 2–3M words). Our standard is excellence; we publish work by established writers as well as new writers.

Mary Oliver, Charles Simic, Francine Prose, Sandra McPherson, Philip Levine, Joseph Brodsky, Joyce Carol Oates.

Unsolicited Manuscripts Received/Published per Year: 4,000+/70+.

Reading Period: Oct.–June.

Payment: $50/poem, $150/story-criticism.

Copyright held by magazine.

1947; 4/yr; 1,100
$20/yr ind, $26/yr inst; $6/ea; 40%; 50% to distributors
96 pp; 6 x 9
No ads
ISSN: 0043-3845

WHETSTONE

Barrington Area Arts Council
Sandra Berris, Julie Fleenor, Marsha Portnoy, Jean Tolle
P.O. Box 1266
Barrington, IL 60011
(708) 382-5626

Poetry, short stories, novel excerpts, creative nonfiction.

Prefer to see 3–7 poems or up to 25 pages of fiction or nonfiction. Include SASE.

Bill Roorbach, Eleanore Divine, Alison Baker, John Jacob, Peyton Houston, Edith Pearlman John Dickson.

Unsolicited Manuscripts Received/ Published per Year: 1,000+/15-25.

Reading Period: year–round.

Payment: variable. Work accepted is eligible for annual Whetstone Prizes which are cash awards. 1995 prize—$500.

Reporting Time: 3 months.

Copyright reverts to author.

1983; 1/yr; 700

$7.25/ea postpaid; sample copies, including guidelines for The Whetstone Prize, $3.25 post paid; Trade disc.

100–120 pp; 5⅞ x 9

Will consider ads for 1996 issue.

WHISPERS

Stuart David Schiff
70 Highland Ave.
Binghamton, NY 13905
(607) 729-6020

Fiction, criticism, reviews, graphics/artwork.

WHISPERS is a literary magazine of fantasy and horror. The journal publishes original fiction and art as well as news and reviews.

Stephen King, William Nolan, Ray Bradbury, Harlan Ellison, Ray Russell.

Unsolicited Manuscripts Received/ Published per Year: 300/2.

Payment: varies.

Reporting Time: 1–3 months.

Copyright held by Stuart David Schiff; reverts to author upon publication.

1973; 2/yr; 3,000

No subscriptions; 40%

176 pp; 5½ x 8½

Ad Rates: $90/page (4⅜ x 8); $50/½ page (4¾ x 4½); $30/¼ page (4¾ x 2¼)

WHITE CLOUDS REVUE

Scott Preston
P.O. Box 462
Ketchum, ID 83340

Poetry, one prose piece in 4 issues so far.

WCR is a serially-issued journal specifically interested in delineating and suggesting trends in inter-mountain American West Poetics, divergent from those foisted on hapless readers & writers by the homogenized tyranny of regional MFA syndromes and syndicates.

Charles Potts, Ed Dorn, Rosalie Sorrels, Bruce Embree, Peter Boweb, Brooke Medicine Eagle.

Payment: several copies.

Reporting Time: 2 weeks–2 months.
Copyright reverts to author.
1987; 1½/yr; 200+
$12/4 issues; $3.50/ea; 30%
28–44 pp; 7 x 8½

WHOLE NOTES

Nancy Peters Hastings
P.O. Box 1374
Las Cruces, NM 88004
(505) 382-7446

Poetry.
WHOLE NOTES features work by unknown or beginning writers as well as established poets. We welcome writers whose work is memorable, with fresh images and authentic emotion.
Ted Kooser, Carole Oles, Stuart Friebert.
Unsolicited Manuscripts Received/Published per Year: 800/40.
Reading Period: year–round.
Payment: in copies.
Reporting Time: 3 weeks.
Copyright held by Nancy Peters Hastings.
1984; 2/yr; 400
$6/yr ind & inst; $3/ea; 40%
28 pp; 5½ x 8½
Ad Rates: Contact CLMP for information.

WILD DUCK REVIEW

Casey Walker
419 Spring St. D.
Nevada City, CA 95959
(916) 478-0134

Interviews, articles/essays, poetry and prose, photographs.
Focus on literary arts of Northern California and West, dealing with cultural and ecological issues which, if not met on the local level, threaten the quality and diversity of life.
David Brower, Gary Snyder, Terry Tempest Williams, Senator Tom Hayden, Wendell Berry.
Unsolicited Manuscripts Received/Published per year: 1,000/350.
Reading Period: Continuously
Payment: In copies: 3–10.
Reporting Time: 3–4 months.
Copyright held by Anthology rights to magazine; reprints revert to author.
1994; 6/yr; 10,000
$18/yr; $3/ea
24–28 pp; 11 x 14
Ad Rates: $500/page; $250/½ page; $100/¼ page; $50/⅛ page
ISSN: 1085-8555
Tower Books, Copperfield's Books, Newsbeat

THE WILLIAM AND MARY REVIEW

Forrest Pritchard
P.O. Box 8795
The College of William & Mary

Williamsburg, VA 23187-8795
(804) 221-3290
E-mail: review@mail.wm.edu

Poetry, fiction, criticism, interviews, photographs, graphics/artwork.

THE WILLIAM AND MARY REVIEW is an internationally-distributed literary magazine published by undergraduate students of The College of William and Mary, without faculty supervision or censorship. It is the express purpose of **THE WILLIAM AND MARY REVIEW** to publish the work of established writers as well as that of—and with an emphasis on—new, vital voices.

Amy Clampitt, Julie Agoos, Jay Parini, David Ignatow, Dana Gioia, Robert Hershon, Albert Rios, W. D. Snodgrass, Cornelius Eady.

Unsolicited Manuscripts Received/Published per Year: 300/10.

Reading Period: Sept.–Apr.

Payment: in copies.

Copyright held by College of William and Mary and Editor; reverts to author upon publication.

1962; 1/yr; 3,500

$5.50/yr ind, $8/yr inst; $6/ea; 40%

120 pp; 6 x 9

ISSN: 0043-5600

WILLOW REVIEW

Paulette Roeske
19351 West Washington St.
Grayslake, IL 60030-1198
(708) 223-6601, ext. 2956

Poetry, short fiction, creative nonfiction.

WILLOW REVIEW is a flat-spined annual which publishes poetry, short fiction and creative nonfiction (up to 4,000 words). Its orientation is toward high quality, literary work as opposed to genre fiction and light verse.

Lisel Mueller, Garrett Hongo, Lucien Stryk, Diane Ackerman, David Ray, Gregory Orr, Gloria Naylor.

Unsolicited Manuscripts Received/Published per Year: 1,500/30-35.

Reading Period: year-round, with publication in April.

Payment: Awards of $100, $50, and $25 in both prose and poetry each year for work deemed best of issue; payment in copies.

Reporting Time: 1-2 months.

Copyright reverts to author upon publication.

1969; 1/yr; 1,000

$13/3 yrs; $20/5 issues; $5/ea; 40%

84 pp; 6 x 9

ISSN: 1068-2546

Ad Rates: $125/page (4¼ x 7); $75/½ page (4¼ x 3½); $50/¼ page (2⅛ x 3½)

WILLOW SPRINGS

Nance Van Winckel
MS-1 526 5th St.
Eastern Washington University
Cheney, WA 99004-2431
(509) 623-4349

Poetry, fiction, essays, reviews, translation, interviews.

WILLOW SPRINGS is committed to the imagination and the power of language fully engaged in the act of telling. We publish high quality poetry, fiction, translation, essays, and art.

Russell Edson, Thomas Lux, Alberto Rios, Chase Twichell, Bruce Weigl, Sam Hamill, Kim Addonizio, Donald Revell, Charlie Smith.

Unsolicited Manuscripts Received/ Published per Year: 2,000/80.

Reading Period: Sept. 15–May 15.

Payment: 2 copies on publication, year's subscription.

Reporting Time: 6 weeks.

Copyright reverts to author.

1977; 2/yr; 1,200

$10.50/yr; $4/ea; 40%

128 pp; 6 x 9

Ad Rates: $125/page (4¼ x 7); $75/½ page (4¼ x 3½); $50/¼ page (2⅛ x 3½)

ISSN: 0739-1277

Ingram, DeBoer

WIND

Steven R. Cope, Charlie G. Hughes
P.O. Box 24548
Lexington, KY 40524

Poetry, fiction, essays, reviews of small press publications.

Focus and emphasis are on the writers who have something special to say: nothing cold and lifeless. **WIND** is highly eclectic; any form, subject matter or approach.

Peter Wild, Larry Rubin, T.M. McNally, Richard E. Brown, Carolyn Osborn.

Unsolicited Manuscripts Received/ Published per Year: 4,200/2%

Payment: in copies.

Reporting Time: 2–4 weeks.

Copyright held by author.

1971; 2/yr; 450

$10/yr ind, $12/yr inst, $15/yr foreign; $6.00/ea; $3.50/back issue

100 pp; 5½ x 8¼; perfect bound.

ISSN: 0361-2481

WINDFALL

Ron Ellis
Friends of Poetry
c/o Department of English

University of Wisconsin
Whitewater, WI 53190
(414) 472-1036

Poetry.

We are interested in short, intense, highly-crafted poems in any form. Longer poems occasionally considered. No xerox or dot matrix.

William Stafford, Ralph Mills, Francine Sterle, Sheila Murphy, Joanne Hart.

Unsolicited Manuscripts Received/Published per Year: 400/30.

Payment: contributor's copies.

Reporting Time: 8 weeks.

Copyright held by Friends of Poetry; reverts to author upon publication.

1979; 2/yr; 400

$5/yr; $3/ea

40 pp; 5½ x 8½

ISSN: 0893-3375

THE WINDLESS ORCHARD

Robert Novak
English Department
Indiana University
2101 East Coliseum
Fort Wayne, IN 46805
(219) 483-6845

Poetry, criticism, review, photographs, graphics/artwork.

Our muse is interested only in the beautiful, the sacred, and the erotic. Excited, organic forms, with thinking and feeling done in imagery and epigram.

Ruth Moon Kempher, Elliot Richman, Mike Martone, Michael Emery.

Unsolicited Manuscripts Received/Published per Year: 920/44.

Payment: 2 copies.

Reporting Time: 1 week and up.

Copyright reverts to author.

1970; irregular; 320

$10/yr; $4/ea

52 pp; 5½ x 8

No ads

WINDSOR REVIEW: A Journal of the Arts

Department of English
University of Windsor
Windsor, Ontario, N9B 3P4
CANADA
(519) 253-4232, ext. 2332
Fax (519) 973-7050
E-mail: uwrevu@uwindsor.ca

Poetry, short stories, & original visual art.

Publishes poetry and short fiction. We subscribe to no particular school or "ism."

Walter McDonald, Lyn Lifshin, W.P. (Bill) Kinsella, Deborah Joy Cory.

Unsolicited Manuscripts Received/Published per Year: 10/stories, 52/poems in a volume year (2 issues).

Payment: $50/story; $15/poem.
Reporting Time: 6–8 weeks.
Copyright reverts to author.
1965; 2/yr; 250
Canada: $21.35/yr ind, $32.05/yr inst; USA and others: $19.95/yr ind, $29.95/yr inst. Sample issue: CDN/US $8.
100 pp; 6 x 9
ISSN: 0042-0352

WITNESS

Peter Stine
Oakland Community College
27055 Orchard Lake Rd.
Farmington Hills, MI 48334
(313) 471-7740

Fiction, essays, poetry, interviews, photographs, graphics/artwork.
WITNESS presents nationally known writers, as well as new talent, and highlights the role of the modern writer as witness. The magazine features a diverse selection of writings—fiction, poetry, essays, journalism, interviews—and regularly devotes every other issue to illuminating a single subject of wide concern.
Gordon Lish, Joyce Carol Oates, Robert Coover, Lynn Sharon Schwartz, Madison Smartt Bell.
Unsolicited Manuscripts Received/Published per Year: 1,800/50.
Reading Period: year–round.
Payment: $6/page for prose, $10/page for poetry.
Reporting Time: 2–3 months.
Copyright held by magazine; reverts to author upon publication.
1987; 2/yr
192 pp; 6 x 9
Ad Rates: $100/page (5 x 7); $60/½ page (5 x 3½)
ISSN: 0891-1371
DeBoer, Ingram, Fine Print

WOMAN POET

Elaine Dallman
P.O. Box 60550
Reno, NV 89506
(702) 972-1671

Poetry, criticism, photos, interviews.
The West, the East, and the Midwest.
Marilyn Hacker, Lisel Mueller, Judith Minty, Rosalie Moore.
Unsolicited Manuscripts Received/Published per Year: 150/varies.
$12.95/ea paperback; $19.95/ea hardcover. Resale discount varies.

WOMEN & PERFORMANCE: A JOURNAL OF FEMINIST THEORY

Editorial Board: Judy Burns, Jennifer Fink, Judy Rosenthal, Le-

slie Satin, Jill Lane, Amanda Barrett
721 Broadway, 6th Fl.
New York, NY 10003
(212) 998-1625
Essays, criticism, plays, reviews, interviews, translation.
Hélène Cixous, Marianne Goldberg, Sue-Ellen Case, Jill Dolan, Lila Abu Lugnod, E. Ann Kaplan, Peggy Phelan, Lucy Fischer.
Number of Unsolicited Manuscripts Received/Published per Year: 50/1-2
Reading Period: Sept.–June.
$14/yr ind, $25/yr inst; $7/ea; $9/back issue; 40%

THE WOMEN'S REVIEW OF BOOKS

Linda Gardiner
Wellesley College Center for Research on Women
Wellesley, MA 02181
(617) 283-2087
Reviews, poetry.
In-depth reviews of books by and about women, in all areas, both academic and general-interest; feminist in orientation but not committed to any one brand of feminism or any specific political position.
June Jordan, Diane Wakoski, Jane Marcus, Carolyn Heilbrun, Patricia William, Nancy Mairs.
Unsolicited Manuscripts Received/Published per Year: 60/2.
Payment: varies, $75 minimum.
Reporting Time: 1 month–6 weeks.
Copyright held by magazine; reverts to author upon publication.
1983; 11/yr; 15,000
$20/yr ind, $35/yr inst: $3/ea; 40%
32 pp; 10 x 15
Ad Rates: $1,600/page (10 x 15); $885/½ page (10 x 7½); $460/¼ page (4¾ x 7½)
ISSN: 0738-1433

WOMEN'S WORDS: A JOURNAL OF CAROLINA WRITING

Lisa Granered, Editor; Elaine Selden, Designer
128 E. Hargett St., Suite 10
Raleigh, NC 27601
(919) 829-3711
Poetry, some fiction and essay, graphics.
WOMEN'S WORDS is a journal seeking to promote women writers in North Carolina.
Jaki Shelton-Green, Tara Allan, Laura Bolger.
Payment: none.
Copyright held by the Women's Center, reverts to author upon publication.
1992; 1/yr; 1,000

$11/yr; $11/ea; 40%
100 pp; 8½ x7
ISSN: 1069-4609

WOMEN'S WORK

Andrea Damm
606 Ave. A
Snohomish, WA 98290
(206) 568-5914

Articles, interviews, reviews, biography, fiction & poetry.

Publishes previously unpublished and emerging writers, writers of diverse cultural and economic backgrounds; explores traditional and modern definitions and expressions of "Women's Work."

Carole Bellacera, Sue Pace, Sibyl James.

Unsolicited Manuscripts Received/Published per Year: 250/50–60.

Reading Period: year–round.

Payment: currently in copies and subscription.

Reporting Time: 2–6 months.

Copyright: first serial rights.

1991; 4/yr; 6,000
$12/yr; $4/ea; 40%
32–48 pp; 8½ x 11
Ad Rates: write or call for quote
ISSN: 1058-4870

THE WORCESTER REVIEW

Rodger Martin
6 Chatham St.
Worcester, MA 01609
(508) 797-4770 or (603) 924-7342

Poetry, fiction, criticism, essays, graphics/artwork, photographs.

We look for quality poetry and fiction, and also articles and essays about poetry that have a New England connection.

Stephen Dunn, Walter McDonald, William Stafford, Kathleen Spivack, Stanley Kunitz.

Payment: 2 copies plus honorarium dependant upon grants.

Reporting Time: 4–5 months.

Copyright held by Worcester Review of the Worcester County Poetry Assoc.; reverts to author upon publication.

1973; 1/yr; 1,000
$10/yr; $8/ea; $5 sample; 40%
150 pp; 6 x 9
Ad Rates: $195/page; $100/½ page; $55/¼ page
ISSN: 8756-5277

THE WORLD

Edited by staff of the Poetry Project
c/o St. Mark's Church
131 E. 10th St.
New York, NY 10003
(212) 674-0910

Poetry, fiction.

A magazine of experimental writing.

Lorenzo Thomas, Chris Tysh, Ron Padgett, Juliana Spahn.
Payment: none.
Reporting Time: 3–6 months.
Copyright held by author.
1966; 2/yr; 750
$25 for 2 yrs/4 issue sub; $7/ea
155 pp; 6 x 9
ISSN: 0043-8154
SPD, Fine Print, DeBoer, Inc.

WORLD LETTER

Jon Cone
2726 E. Court St.
Iowa City, IA 52245
(319) 337-6022

Poetry, short prose, translations.
An international literary review. Do not send unsolicited manuscripts. Query first.
Cesar Vallejo, Charles Bukowski, Edouard Roditi, Cid Corman.
Unsolicited Manuscripts Received/Published per Year: 200/1.
Payment: in copies.
Reporting Time: 1 week or as soon as possible.
Copyright reverts to author upon publication.
1991; 1/yr; 200–300
$6/yr; $6/ea; 40%
48 pp; 6½ x 10
ISSN: 1054-8823
Water Row Books, Longhouse Books, Anton Mikofsky, Alyscamp Press

THE WORMWOOD REVIEW

Marvin Malone
P.O. Box 4698
Stockton, CA 95204-0698
(209) 466-8231

Poetry, reviews, translation, graphics/artwork.
Poetry and prose-poems reflecting the temper and depth of the present time. All types and schools from traditional-economic through concrete, dada and extreme avant-garde. Special fondness for prose poems and fables. Each issue has a special section devoted to one poet or topic. One chapbook per year.
Charles Bukowski, Lyn Lifshin, Ronald Koertge, Gerald Locklin, Judson Crews.
Unsolicited Manuscripts Received/Published per Year: 6,000+/350+.
Payment: 3–6 copies of magazine or cash equivalent.
Copyright held by Wormwood Books & Magazines; reverts to author upon request.
1959; 4/yr; 700
$12/yr ind, $12/yr inst; $4/ea;
48 pp; 5½ x 8½
ISSN: 0043-9401

THE WRITERS' BAR-B-Q

Editorial Board: Timothy Osburn, Becky Bradway, Gary Smith,

Marcia Womack, and Myra Epping
924 Bryn Mawr Blvd.
Springfield, IL 62703
(217) 525-6987

Fiction, photographs, graphics/artwork.

THE WRITERS' BAR-B-Q publishes stories and novel excerpts. Our preference is for realistic work that has strong characterization and story. We are looking for excellent, spirited, daring writing from all genres. We encourage work by gays and lesbians, people of color, and other writers who may have trouble fitting into the usual venues. Our idea is to publish good stories, and to have fun doing it. **THE WRITERS' BAR-B-Q** is a potluck of styles, subjects and characters. Almost all stories are fully illustrated.

Lowry Pei, Sharon Sloan Fiffer, Michael C. White, Martha M. Vertreace, Shannon Keith Kelley, Nolan Porterfield, Deborah Insel, Paul Lisicky.

Payment: 3 copies, upon publication.

Copyright held by Sangamon Writers, Inc.; reverts to author upon publication.

1987; 1–2/yr; 1,000.

$10/yr; $5/ea

100 pp; 8½ x 11

Ad Rates: $75/½ page (4½ x 7½); inquire.

DeBoer

WRITER'S FORUM

C. Kenneth Pellow, Editor; Craig Lesley, Bret Lott, Fiction Editors; Victoria McCabe, Poetry Editor; Robert Dassanovsky–Harris, Managing Editor; Paul Scott Malone, Corresponding Editor

University of Colorado at Colorado Springs
P.O. Box 7150
Colorado Springs, CO 80933-7150
(719) 599-4023

Poetry, fiction.

We want the finest in contemporary short story and poetry, with some focus and emphasis on the trans-Mississippi West with its varieties of place and experience.

Gladys Swan, Ron Carlson, Frank Waters, Robert Olen Butler, Yusef Komunyakaa.

Unsolicited Manuscripts Received/Published per Year: 600/35.

Payment: none.

Reporting Time: 3–6 weeks.

Copyright held by UCCS; reverts to author upon publication.

1974; 1/yr; 1,000

Note: Our prices now include cost of postage.
$11.25/yr ind, $9.50/yr inst; $11.25/ea
200 pp; 8½ x 5½

WRITER'S JOURNAL

Valerie Hockert
3585 N. Lexington Ave.
Suite 328
Arden Hills, MN 55112
(612) 486-7818

Essays, poetry, reviews, criticism, interviews, commentaries, writing techniques.

Provides writers and poets with practical advice and guidance, motivation and authorative instruction in the craft of writing. Includes book reviews, software reviews, poetry, advice and references.

Anthony Vasquez, Betty Ulrich, Ester M. Leiper, Cheryl Kempf.

Unsolicited Manuscripts Received/Published per Year: 600/36.
Payment: variable.
Reporting Time: 2–6 weeks.
Copyright held by Minnesota Ink, Inc., reverts to author upon publication.
1980; 6/yr; 49,000
$14/yr; $4/ea; 50%
48 pp; 8 x 10½
Ad Rates: $845/page (6¾ x 8½); $465/½ page (6¾ x 4¼ or 3⅛ x 8½)
ISSN: 0891-9759
Ingram, Armadillo, IPD, Fine Print, ADS

THE WRITING ON THE WALL

Scott Peterson
P.O. Box 8
Orona, ME 04973

Fiction, poetry, essays, photography.

THE WRITING ON THE WALL seeks to combat the negativity of the mass media, promote community, and provide an outlet for issues of the twenty-something generation.

Julie Krikorian Eshbaugh, Stephen Stathis, Lyn Lifshin, Richard Kostelanotz.

Unsolicited Manuscripts Received/Published per year: 250/25.
Reading Period: all.
Payment: 2 copies.
Reporting Time: 3 months.
Copyright held by authors.
1992; 2/yr; 100
$5/yr; $3/ea.
16 pp; 8½ x 11

X

XANADU

Mildred M. Jeffrey, Weslea Sidon, Lois V. Walker, SueKain
Box 773
Huntington, NY 11743
(516) 691-2376

Poetry, essays.

XANADU publishes contemporary poetry and articles on poetry.

Karen Swenson, David Ignatow, Edmund Pennant, William Stafford.

Unsolicited Manuscripts Received/ Published per Year: 500/30.

Reading Period: Sept.–June.

Payment: 1 copy per contributor.

Reporting Time: 3 months.

Copyright reverts to author upon publication.

1975; 1/yr; 300

$5/ea; 20%–40%

64–76 pp; 5½ x 8½

ISSN: 0146-0463

XAVIER REVIEW

Thomas Bonner, Jr., Editor;
Robert E. Skinner, Managing Ediitor
Box 110C, Xavier University
New Orleans, LA 70125
(504) 483-7304
Fax (504) 486-7411

Poetry, fiction, criticism, essays, reviews, translation, interviews.

XAVIER REVIEW is interested in the usual genres of literature and articles in the area of Black literature, Southern literature, religion and literature and Latin American literature (although not exclusively).

Alex Haley, Andrew Salkey, Fred Chappell, John Keller, Gordon Osing, James Baldwin, Andre Dubus, Ernest J. Gaines, Patty Friedmann.

Unsolicited Manuscripts Received/ Published per Year: 300/35.

Payment: none.

Reporting Time: 2 months.
Copyright held by magazine.
1980; 2/yr; 500
$10/year ind, $15/year inst; $5/each; 40%
70-75 pp; 6 x 9
ISSN: 0887-6681

xib

Tolek
P.O. Box 262112,
San Diego, Ca 92126
(619) 298-4927
Poems, drawings, photos, Fiction.
Writing and visual. Gritty, tight, slick, lean, tasty. Visual and writing.
Gerald Locklin, Richard Kostelanetz, Oberc.
Unsolicited Manuscripts Received/Published per Year: 2,000/4%.
Reading Period: year–round.
Payment: 1 copy.
Reporting Time: 2½ weeks.
Copyright: yes—first time author rights.
1990; 2/yr; 500
$10/year; $5/ea; 35%
54 pp; 8½ x 7
Ad Rates: vary, inquire
ISSN: 1058-420x

Y

YARROW

Harry Humes, Editor; Arnold Newman, Associate Editor
English Department
Kutztown University
Kutztown, PA 19530
(215) 683-4353

Poetry, interviews.
A journal of poetry.
William Pitt Root, Gerald Stern, John Engels, Gibbons Ruark, Lola Haskins, Fleda Brown Jackson, Sally Jo Sorenson.
Unsolicited Manuscripts Received/Published per Year: 400–500/50-95.
Reading Period: year–round.
Payment: in copies.
Reporting Time: 1 month.
1981; 2/yr; 350
$5/2 yrs; $1.50/ea
36 pp; 6 x 9

YEFIEF

Ann Racuya-Robbins
P.O. Box 8505
Santa Fe, NM 87504
(505) 753-3648
Fax (505) 753-7049

Poetry, fiction, essays, transactions, drama, interviews, photography, social and literary criticism.
When we all speak what language do we make?
Nicole Brossard, Carla Harryman, Bill Fox, Spencer Selby, Wanda Coleman.
Unsolicited Manuscripts Received/Published per year: 600/60.
Reading Period: all.
Payment: copies.
Reporting Time: 2 months.
Copyright held by magazine; reverts to author upon publication.
1994; 1/yr; 1,000

$7; 40%
176 pp; 7 x 9
Ad Rates: $120/full page (5 x 8); $75/½ page
ISSN: 1074-5629
Fine Print Distributors, Small Press Distribution, Bernhard DeBoer, Inc.

YELLOW SILK: Journal of Erotic Arts

Lily Pond
P.O. Box 6374
Albany, CA 94706
(510) 644-4188

Fiction, poetry, essays, reviews, translations, photography, graphics/artwork, fine arts, science fiction, humor.

YELLOW SILK: Journal of Erotic Arts: Stunning sophisticated stories and poems meet explicit photographs and paintings in what may be the world's only fine literary magazine that is unabashedly erotic.

Marilyn Hacker, Galway Kinnell, Sharon Olds, Mary Oliver, Louise Erdrich.

Payment: 3 copies, 1 year subscription, and varying cash payments.

Reporting Time: approximately 3 months.

Copyright reverts to author after one year following publication; the magazine keeps non-exclusive reprint, electronic, and anthology rights.

1981; 4/yr; 16,000
$30/yr ind, $38/yr inst; $7.50/ea; 40%
60 pp; 8½ x 11
ISSN: 0736-9212
Bookpeople, Inland, Ingram, Ubiquity

YET ANOTHER SMALL MAGAZINE

Candace Catlin Hall
Box 14353
Hartford, CT 06114
(203) 549-6723

Poetry.

YASM publishes short, imagistic poems—special interest in lesser known poets— started broadside inclusion highlighting a single poem.

Lyn Lifshin, Charles Darling, Pat Bridges, Sister Mary Ann Henn, Neil Grill.

Reading Period: Aug. 1–Oct. 31.
Payment: in copies.
Reporting Time: November.
Copyright reverts to author.
1981; 1/yr; 300
$1.98/ea
8–12 pp; 11 x 17
ISSN: 0278-9442

Z

ZEBRA, a journal of literature & opinion
Mario Gortwin
P.O. Box 421584
San Francisco, CA 94142
(415) 753-4600
Poetry, fiction, nonfiction. No romance per se.
Leonard Sanazaro, Phyllis Stowell.
Unsolicited Manuscripts Received/Published per Year: 1,100/200.
Payment: copies.
Reporting Time: 6–8 weeks.
Copyright reverts on publication.
1990; 2/yr; 200
$10/yr; $6/ea; 40%
56–80 pp; 5½ x 8½
Ad Rates: query
ISSN 1052-4967

ZUKUNFT
Prof. Yonia Fain, Joseph Mlotek, Matis Olitzki, Morris Steingart
25 East 21st St.
New York, NY 10010
Poetry, fiction, criticism, essays, reviews.
The **ZUKUNFT** is an independent literary publication. It serves as a vehicle for writers from many countries and is concerned with problems of Jewish life throughout the world. In 1992 the **ZUKUNFT**, the oldest continuously published Yiddish journal in the world, celebrated its centennial. It has served to stimulate literary creativity for generations throughout Yiddish speaking communities.
Unsolicited Manuscripts Received/Published per Year: 60/7.
Reading Period (Yiddish mss.): year–round.
Copyright held by Congress for Jewish Culture; reverts to author upon publication.

1892; 6/yr; 2,500
$25/yr ind; $3/ea; 20%
44 pp; 7½ x 10½
Ad Rates: $100/page; $50/½ page; $25/¼ page

ZUZU'S PETALS QUARTERLY/WEB

T. Dunn, Editor-in-Chief, D. DuCap, Associate Editor
P.O. Box 4476
Allentown, PA 18105-4476
(610) 821-1324
E-mail: zuzu@epix.net
Literary fiction, essays, poetry, articles, book reviews, chapbook reviews.
Our magazine is a celebration of all aspects of the human experience, and is named after Jimmy Stewart's daughter in the film classic "It's A Wonderful Life". *Library Journal* describes it as, "an exciting new little." (November 1993, *LJ*)
Max Greenberg, Gayle Elen Harvey, Mark Soifer, Laura Telford.
Unsolicited Manuscripts Received/Published per Year: approx. 2,000/100.
Reporting Time: 2 weeks–2 months
1991; 4/yr; unlimited
Free on the Internet.
50 pp; 8½ x 11
No ads
ISSN 1060-9571

ZYZZYVA

Howard Junker
41 Sutter St., Suite 1400
San Francisco, CA 94104
(415) 255-1282
E-mail: zyzzyuainc@aol.com
Fiction, essays, plays, poetry, translations, photographs, prints, drawings.
West Coast writers, artists, and publishers.
Rafael Campo, Marilyn Chin, Robert Hass, Ehud Havazalet, Heather McHugh, Leslie Scalapino.
Unsolicited Manuscripts Received/Published per Year: 4,000/40.
Payment: $50–$250.
Reporting Time: prompt.
Copyright held by magazine; reverts to author upon publication.
1985; 4/yr; 4,800
$28/yr ind, $36/yr inst; $9/ea
160 pp; 6 x 9
Ad Rates: $500/page (5 x 7¾); $300/½ page (5 x 3 13/16); $200/¼ page (2 7/16 x 3 13/16)
ISSN: 8756-5633
Ingram

INDEX BY STATE

COLORADO

CONNECTICUT

DISTRICT OF COLUMBIA

FLORIDA

INDEX BY STATE

IOWA

KANSAS

KENTUCKY

LOUISIANA

MAINE

MARYLAND

MASSACHUSETTS

INDEX BY STATE

NORTH CAROLINA

NORTH DAKOTA

OHIO

TEXAS

UTAH

VERMONT

VIRGINIA

WASHINGTON

WEST VIRGINIA